Samurai: A Very Short Introduction

VERY SHORT INTRODUCTIONS are for anyone wanting a stimulating and accessible way into a new subject. They are written by experts, and have been translated into more than 45 different languages.

The series began in 1995, and now covers a wide variety of topics in every discipline. The VSI library currently contains over 550 volumes—a Very Short Introduction to everything from Psychology and Philosophy of Science to American History and Relativity—and continues to grow in every subject area.

Very Short Introductions available now:

Available soon:

HUMAN PHYSIOLOGY
Jamie A. Davies
THE ARCTIC Klaus Dodds and
Jamie Woodwood

HORROR Darryl Jones
DIPLOMATIC HISTORY
Joseph M. Siracusa
BLASPHEMY Yvonne Sherwood

For more information visit our website

www.oup.com/vsi/

Michael Wert

SAMURAI

A Very Short Introduction

OXFORD
UNIVERSITY PRESS

OXFORD
UNIVERSITY PRESS

Oxford University Press is a department of the University of Oxford. It furthers the University's objective of excellence in research, scholarship, and education by publishing worldwide. Oxford is a registered trade mark of Oxford University Press in the UK and certain other countries.

Published in the United States of America by Oxford University Press
198 Madison Avenue, New York, NY 10016, United States of America.

© Oxford University Press 2019, 2021

This book was published in hardcover as *Samurai: A Concise History* (2019).

All rights reserved. No part of this publication may be reproduced, stored in a retrieval system, or transmitted, in any form or by any means, without the prior permission in writing of Oxford University Press, or as expressly permitted by law, by license, or under terms agreed with the appropriate reproduction rights organization. Inquiries concerning reproduction outside the scope of the above should be sent to the Rights Department, Oxford University Press, at the address above.

You must not circulate this work in any other form and you must impose this same condition on any acquirer.

Library of Congress Cataloging-in-Publication Data

Names: Wert, Michael, author.
Title: Samurai : a very short introduction / Michael Wert.
Description: New York, NY : Oxford University Press, [2021] | Series: Very short introductions | Includes bibliographical references and index.
Identifiers: LCCN 2020048484 (print) | LCCN 2020048485 (ebook) | ISBN 9780190685072 (paperback) | ISBN 9780190685089 (ebook) | ISBN 9780190685096 (epub)
Subjects: LCSH: Samurai. | Japan—History, Military.
Classification: LCC DS827.S3 W478 2021 (print) | LCC DS827.S3 (ebook) | DDC 952/.025—dc23
LC record available at https://lccn.loc.gov/2020048484
LC ebook record available at https://lccn.loc.gov/2020048485

1 3 5 7 9 8 6 4 2

Printed in Great Britain by Ashford Colour Press Ltd., Gosport, Hants., on acid-free paper

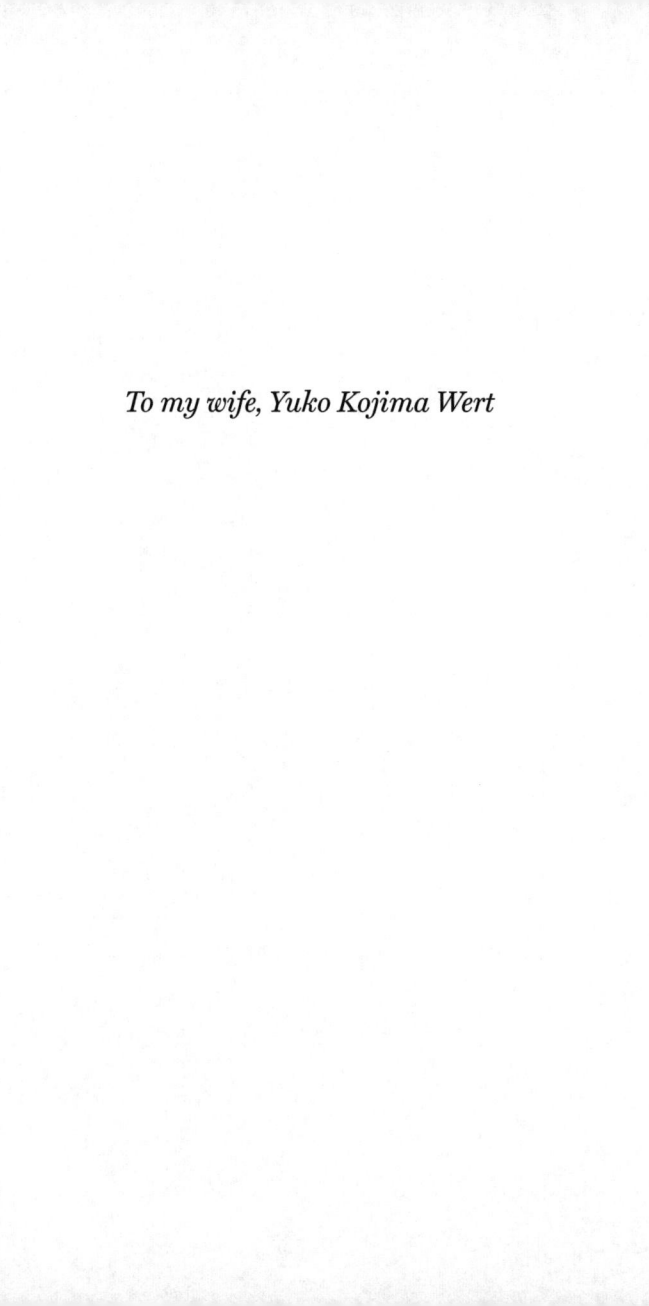

To my wife, Yuko Kojima Wert

Contents

List of Illustrations

Introduction

In the climactic battle scene at the end of the movie *The Last Samurai* (2003), the protagonist, a samurai rebel, leads his army of warriors as they charge to certain death against the newly formed, modern government army. Wearing only their traditional clothing and armed with bows, swords, and spears, they are mowed down by Gatling guns and howitzers as the government's general, himself an ex-samurai, looks on anxiously. This scene has all the familiar tropes in the global fantasy about samurai: tradition versus modernity, hand-to-hand fighting versus guns, and a celebration of honorable death. The event depicted in the film is a historical one, the War of the Southwest in Japan in 1877, when ex-samurai refused to follow a series of laws that stripped all samurai of their privileged status and accompanying symbols; no more wearing swords in public or maintaining topknot hairstyles. A more accurate description of the battle scene flips the cinematic one—the modernized government army took shelter in a castle, the most traditional of defenses, while ex-samurai rebels bombarded them with cannon from outside. As with anything else, the historical depiction is more interesting than the popularized one.

Samurai seem ubiquitous in popular culture; from the novel and television show *Shogun* (1980) to *The Last Samurai* and the successful PlayStation 4 game *Ghost of Tsushima* (2020), audiences never seem to tire of them. They even appear in the most unlikely places; the corporate name of a local coffee shop chain in Milwaukee, Wisconsin, is Giri, which the founder claims "comes from the Samurai code of honor, Bushido, and can be translated to mean 'social obligation.'" It sounds nice, but "obligation" was simply a way to convince samurai to obey their lords no matter the danger or, more likely, the drudgery.

There is no shortage of websites on samurai, and one can hardly throw a rock without hitting some martial art instructor with a distinctive view on the samurai. There are plenty of glossy books that give an overview of some aspect of samurai battles, warfare, castles, and the like, but sifting through what is reliable and what is not can be a chore. On the other hand, scholarly books tend to require too much background information, familiarity with not only Japanese but also Chinese history, religion, and art, disciplinary jargon, and, for some older history books, significant language commitment.

I will describe how samurai changed from, roughly, the eighth to the mid-nineteenth centuries, impart a sense of warrior diversity, and dispel common myths, such as the so-called bushido samurai code, swords as the "soul of the samurai," and supposed fighting prowess. Not all periods of warrior history are covered equally; there are more details of samurai life from the seventeenth through nineteenth centuries (the early modern period) because most depictions of samurai in the West coincide with warriors from that period, and scholars know more about early modern Japan than about the medieval period (ninth through fifteenth centuries). There are so many documents from the eighteenth and nineteenth centuries that one can buy them on internet auction sites for tens of dollars. A recent auction for a collection of hundreds of documents from the eighteenth and nineteenth centuries, belonging to a single family, sold on Yahoo Auction for 73,000 yen, about $660. Some texts from early modern Japan even end up in the trash. After the earthquake, tsunami, and

Fukushima nuclear disaster on March 11, 2011, local historians scrambled to photograph historical documents found in dilapidated storehouses slated for destruction and rebuilding. There were so many documents that local museums and universities did not have room to keep those deemed unimportant, and hence they risked being thrown out. Documents from before the seventeenth century are occasionally discovered but in ever fewer numbers, and they are treated with greater care.

A final word about conventions. In Japanese, the surname precedes the given name. I use the term *warrior* for the ninth through sixteenth centuries and *samurai* for the seventeenth through nineteenth centuries, when they existed as a narrowly defined social status group. *Warlord* and *lord* both refer to *daimyo*, military leaders who held territory and engaged in warfare during the fifteenth and sixteenth centuries, but by the early seventeenth century, they had become decidedly unwarlike governors. In other words, I split warrior history into two imperfect halves, the medieval and early modern periods, with the early seventeenth century as the dividing line. That is when the category of warrior narrowed, fundamentally changing for this group their culture and relationship to the rest of the Japanese population.

Chapter 1
Becoming those who served

Colloquially, even in Japan, the term *samurai* is used as a synonym for "warrior," but this is incorrect. *Samurai* originally had a very narrow meaning, referring to anyone who served a noble, even in a nonmilitary capacity. Gradually it became a title for military servants of warrior families—in fact, a warrior of elite stature in pre-seventeenth-century Japan would have been insulted to be called a "samurai." There were other more common terms for warriors in classical and medieval Japan that reflected their various duties to the state, nobility, and other superiors. Most specialists in Japan and in the West use the generic term *bushi*, which means "warrior."

Warrior is a usefully ambiguous term for referring to a broad group of people, before the seventeenth century, with some military function. This includes anyone expected to provide military service to the state when needed and who received official recognition from a ruling authority to do so, such as the nobility and court in Kyoto or religious institutions. Even the term *warrior* is imprecise because it incorrectly suggests that warfare was this group's sole occupation. Depending on the time period and status, warriors alternatively governed, traded, farmed, painted, wrote, tutored, and engaged in shady activities.

Another caution when using the term *warrior* is the moral value that modern people attach to the concept. The US military uses "warrior" in its various training programs, such as "Warrior Mind Training," a meditation program created for soldiers to help them cope with posttraumatic stress disorder and to prepare them for the rigors of combat. The developer used the image of the samurai to sell the program, "rooting it in the ancient Samurai code of self-discipline." No such code existed. Even phrases used ironically assume the existence of an authentic admirable warrior image—for example, "weekend warrior," suggesting that one is a normal boring person during the week but becomes some other, more primal person on the weekend. In this usage, a warrior is something one *is*, not an occupation one *does*.

But throughout Japanese history, people often despised warriors. Artists and writers portrayed warriors as beasts, no better than dogs, uncouth and murderous. Warriors pillaged, looted, and sometimes murdered their way through villages. They found no love among peasants, who feared warriors because peasants suffered the most from their looting, pillaging, and collateral damage. Ironically, it was only during an age of relative peace, in early modern Japan (1600–1868), that common people began to admire and imitate samurai.

Of course, warriors fought in combat, but in reality they spent most of their time doing something else. That could mean trying to improve their family's position in an elite society dominated by nobility, managing farmers on their estates, or, for the lowliest warriors, even engaging in occasional grift. The limit of samurai activities was determined by the definition of "warrior" as it changed over time. A samurai traveling back in time from the nineteenth century to the ninth might hardly be recognized as belonging to the same category of people.

Warriors of the distant past became a source of entertainment, anxiety, and inspiration for samurai living in later times. One samurai commentator in the early eighteenth century, an era of peace, complained of his contemporaries, "So many men now seem to have the pulse of a woman," nothing like the real warrior men of the previous century, a time of war. In the thirteenth century, a Buddhist nun, Hōjō Masako, invoked the legacy of her late husband Minamoto Yoritomo as a warrior founding father of sorts who fought against a threat from an emperor in Kyoto. And let's not forget the material appeal of the past; samurai of higher status delighted in purchasing a sword or tea bowl once owned by famous warriors.

Warriors used military skills as a means of advancing their careers. Politically, they were outsiders, used as tools by powerful nobles who needed them as muscle to police their lands or to act as a check on other noble families intent on taking land by force. Much of Japan technically belonged to the emperor (*tennō*, literally "heavenly sovereign"), who, according to ancient mythology, was descended from gods, and warriors protected the interests of the emperor's regime based in the ancient capital cities of Nara, Nagaoka, and from 794, Kyoto. They guarded against outbreaks of violence close to the capital, attacked anyone in the provinces far from Kyoto who might threaten the regime, and campaigned against the many "barbaric" tribes located on the outskirts of Japan in the northeast or southwest.

The term *warrior* typically does not include others who lived by violence—namely, mercenaries, bandits, and pirates. But before the seventeenth century, a person's status was not so neatly defined. Some people temporarily connected to a ruling institution could legally participate in warfare, governance, and commerce. For example, though most warrior and royal authorities depicted pirates as violent bandits operating at sea, they sometimes engaged in warfare on behalf of a warrior regime called a shogunate, a religious institution such as a Buddhist temple, or a noble ensconced in the capital, Kyoto. They monopolized sea-based trade, established rules of conduct and expectations from people living along waterways, and wielded authority like a warlord or warrior bureaucracy.

A debate about warrior origins has raged in both the Japanese and English language scholarship on premodern Japan due, in part, to how one defines *samurai*. Were they simply a carryover from ancient soldiers? The earliest evidence for warrior-soldiers predates written history and Japan itself. Terracotta figures (*haniwa*) depicting soldiers, servants, and animals were placed outside tombs that dotted the ancient burial landscape between the third and sixth centuries. The soldiers' arms and armor reflect the influence of contemporary warriors in China and the Korean kingdoms and share a common style that shows the existence of some primitive regime that influenced mostly central and southwest Japan. Hunters and landholders from the eastern provinces? Or professional warriors hired by the Kyoto court? For the sake of argument, it is safe to say that private military specialists emerged as a permanent feature in Japanese history around the ninth century when some of them began wielding authority over others rather than serving as mere soldiers.

Written evidence for warrior history can be traced to the late eighth and early ninth centuries, when the early Japanese state adopted the administrative structure of Tang dynasty China (618–907), the dominant cultural and political power in East Asia. In addition to adapting the various court titles, noble ranks, bureaucratic structures, and culture, the early Japanese sovereigns copied Tang military organization. The court required men to serve in provincial units in times of need. Though a conscript army existed on paper, most showed up only for occasional short-term assignments of up to thirty days or so—for example, to serve in the frontier guard. Most of the year they pursued their own livelihoods. Conscripts were supposed to supply their own weapons and equipment and did not spend much time training. Only officers worked in the military for long periods of time, and some historians have argued that those men were engaged in managerial work rather than intense military training or warfare. Much of the Tang administrative model was abandoned in Japan in the late eighth century and was gradually replaced over the next century and a half with specialist warriors.

In the broadest terms, several different types of warriors existed beginning in the early eighth century. Most warriors did not "own" land, per se, but received a portion of an estate's produce and the rights to collect—and skim—taxes from estates owned by absentee proprietors living in Kyoto. Some enjoyed relative freedom from interference by authorities in Kyoto or their representatives in the provinces. Some possessed land themselves and consigned some of that land to a non warrior noble family in Kyoto in exchange for patronage—that is, for guarantees that others would not stake a claim on a warrior's land. Still other warriors were themselves members of noble families, albeit of a lower rank than most of the powerful nobles who controlled the top bureaucratic positions in Kyoto. Of those, some had established local connections and alliances during a tenure as provincial governor and remained there permanently. They became warrior-lords and relied on minor warrior families while maintaining connections to allies and resources in Kyoto. As the center of rule and the largest city at the time, Kyoto wielded a centripetal force on elite clans throughout Japan. People with aristocratic Kyoto lineage occupied the top social strata in provincial society. Prominent families in the countryside worried about Kyoto-appointed governors sent to monitor them, and politics in Kyoto could threaten local access to wealth.

There was no single model for how these warriors organized themselves. Men might cooperate in bands of warriors connected by kinship, personal loyalty, or common enemies. Others worked together for noble families located in the capital city, provincial officials, or local strongmen. It is no surprise that the ability to fight and organize resources for a military campaign was more efficient among these specialized groups than among conscripts whose livelihoods were interrupted, not enhanced, by warfare. Eventually the state depended on these professionalized warrior groups for police and military functions. Dependency did not mean that warriors took authority away from the state, nor was it the beginning of the end for the royalty, as was once taught; the court and nobility were still in charge.

Most powerful warriors in classical and medieval Japan tended to be those who were themselves nobles and thus had little incentive to challenge the status quo of their community. Although they never achieved the upper echelons of noble ranking, many large, interconnected families that dominated Japan, such as the Taira and the Minamoto, were descended from sons of emperors cast aside because they were no longer in the running for the throne. An emperor bestowed a surname upon these sons who started clans of their own and followed careers common to noble families: serving as functionaries at court, working as important and influential Buddhist clergy, or becoming professional warriors. But not all families within a single surname, such as Minamoto, pursued the same career trajectory.

One might wonder, though, did any warrior try to overthrow the emperor in Kyoto or otherwise carve out a territory of his own, independent from the center? Taira Masakado was the first would-be rebel against the court. He lived in eastern Japan, not far from present-day Tokyo, surrounded by other Taira families who controlled land in the east. Some of them served as the imperial court's representatives. Masakado had once lived in Kyoto under the court's employment, but he was largely a man of the east, a land distant from the center of political and cultural power. What began as a conflict over land among different Taira families and Masakado's own relatives—fighting that the nobility in Kyoto largely ignored—turned into an act of rebellion in 935 when Masakado retaliated against Taira men who were the emperor's representatives. Masakado might not have intended to rebel against the emperor, nor did he have a force large enough to threaten Kyoto directly, but he declared himself the "new emperor" in the east, a career that did not last long—he was killed by a cousin in 940.

Another challenger to imperial and noble authority was Taira Kiyomori. He, too, was descended from an emperor and was raised in Kyoto like other aristocrats. When a succession dispute broke out within the imperial family over who would become the next emperor, Kiyomori led the forces of the victor; the losers, mostly under the control of Minamoto Yoshitomo, were sent into exiled or killed. What began as a clash against forces representing noble patrons turned into a rivalry between Kiyomori and Yoshitomo. Kiyomori beat Yoshitomo and began accumulating aristocratic titles, bureaucratic posts, and provincial landholdings. By the late 1170s, he had become a real threat to imperial power. In Kyoto, he placed allies in important positions not already under his direct control and tried, unsuccessfully, to move the capital to what is now Kobe. There he embarked on massive building projects, including his own headquarters and ports for trade with China. He was the first warrior-noble who attempted to dominate all warriors in Japan. He even put his own grandson, the child emperor Antoku, on the throne. The prince who had been passed up for succession when young Antoku was enthroned asked warriors to overthrow Kiyomori. That challenge started the so-called Gempei War (1180–85), which lasted longer, and was geographically broader, than any previous battle in Japanese history. It even outlasted Kiyomori, who died of natural causes in 1181.

No broadly conceived warrior identity existed before the Gempei War. At the top of warrior society, the most powerful families were themselves part of the aristocracy; the terms *warrior* and *nobility* were not mutually exclusive. For the most part, warriors with noble surnames such as Minamoto and Taira, who resided largely in the countryside, had no incentive to fight against the imperial institution that their ancestors had helped build. Many acted as bridges between Kyoto and the countryside; they feared relatives and neighbors and were hardly in a position to rise up against the imperial institution. At the other end of the social spectrum, the lowly nonaristocratic soldiers and mercenaries often engaged in nonmilitary work. Even midranking warriors shared little in common with their royal betters.

This situation changed to a degree after Minamoto Yoritomo emerged as the victor at the end of the Gempei War. He remained at his headquarters in Kamakura and is credited with creating the first warrior-centered regime, the Kamakura shogunate (1185–1333). Textbooks portray him as the originator of Japan's warrior identity, but that shared identity extended only to the warriors who gathered around him in Kamakura. This beginning of so-called warrior order was not orderly nor did it involve only warriors. But it represented a first step toward a broader notion of warrior culture and identity that would develop over the subsequent centuries.

Chapter 2
Early warrior authority

Minamoto Yoritomo's forces swept from eastern Japan to the west, defeating the Taira armies in 1185. With the help of Kyoto-born nobility and warrior allies, Yoritomo created a warrior regime that lasted until 1333, at which time several prominent warrior clans destroyed the Kamakura regime in the name of the emperor. The shogunate's leading men, first Yoritomo and then a series of regents ruling on behalf of weak titular leaders called shoguns, consolidated their control over Japan at the expense of the nobility. Thus, the typical story about Japan's first warrior regime centers on the institution of the shogunate and how it became the center of a putative "warrior order." It focuses on men who managed estates, created a primitive legal court, and interacted with noblemen as either employers, allies, or foes. In popular culture, these men tend to be in armor on a battlefield constantly engaged in combat. In reality, they spent less time fighting than movies and manga (Japanese graphic novels) would have us believe. The fullness of early warrior history is best captured through its women. All warrior households had military obligations, but those obligations were organized by family units in the broadest sense: large clans comprising women, retainers, and servants who fulfilled menial and complex duties. Military obligation included supplying food, clothing, and labor; it was not simply engaging in combat on the battlefield.

1. Tomoe Gozen is shown dressed in armor—depicted as a combatant rather than as a docile wife. The artist describes her "wielding her halberd like a water wheel."

Moreover, the survival of any warrior family depended on the efficient management of its wealth, smooth relations among allies, and, especially for elite warrior families, connections with nonwarrior aristocrats. Men dominated this process but could not do so without women. In one sense, women were used as objects, through marriage, to solidify an alliance between elite families. But a woman retained any possessions given to her during her marriage, and she continued to live on her parents' estate or in her own residence, often separately from her husband, making her far more independent than her samurai counterparts during later periods. Warrior wives also wielded tremendous influence on their family's position in society. For example, they acted on behalf of either dead or absent husbands; a widow could carry out her clan's military obligations.

Indeed, there might not have been a Kamakura shogunate without women. The Kyoto aristocratic custom of entrusting the future of one's child to female caretakers and their families provided Yoritomo with a stable of warrior and nonwarrior connections vital to his success. Since many of Yoritomo's male relatives were killed, he depended on the women who helped raise him as a child. They supplied him with wealth, male allies in his youth, and information from Kyoto. His mother was born into the Fujiwara clan, the most powerful noble family before the thirteenth century. Her status guaranteed Yoritomo's high position within the Minamoto clan because his father's other consorts were of lower noble blood. And when Kiyomori defeated the Minamoto clan, he spared Yoritomo, it is said, because Kiyomori's stepmother intervened on his behalf. Instead, he exiled Yoritomo to the Izu province in the east, far from Kyoto's center of wealth and power. There Yoritomo grew up under the watch of Hōjō Tokimasa, the twenty-two-year-old head of a minor, obscure family distantly related to the Taira. Like other Kyoto noblemen, Yoritomo was born into a pampered life and must have been shocked by his move to a very rural area as an adolescent.

Elite warrior families like the Minamoto followed the courtier model of marriage and child rearing in which women were at the center. In Kyoto noble culture, nannies and wet nurses came from minor noble families, and the boys placed in their care played and learned alongside these women's own children. Since the boys essentially grew up together, they often became trusted allies as adults despite differences in social status within the noble hierarchy. The noblewomen who knew Yoritomo as a child ensured that he would continue to maintain a decent life in Izu well into adulthood.

For example, one of Yoritomo's wet nurses, the nun Hiki, consistently sent him rice, a form of wealth. She controlled her family after her husband's death, and the heir that she adopted, Hiki Yoshikazu, became one of Yoritomo's closest allies and a top advisor in the shogunate after Yoritomo died. Likewise, her son-in-law, Adachi Morinaga, became a trusted advisor to Yoritomo, and his clan provided much-needed economic support to Yoritomo. Hiki's daughter even served as the wet nurse to Yoritomo's son, the second shogun Minamoto Yoriie. A third wet nurse mediated the connection between Yoritomo and her grandson, Miyoshi Yasunobu, who served Yoritomo in a bureaucratic rather than a military function. Indeed, the only older male relative Yoritomo could count on while in Izu was his maternal uncle, the Buddhist monk Yūhan, who sent a servant to Izu once a month to bring Yoritomo news from Kyoto.

Yoritomo was not destined for greatness even though warriors in later centuries would glorify him. He spent most of his adult life in obscurity. It was not until he reached his early thirties, fully middle-aged for the time period, that he attacked the Taira clan and began to create the Kamakura shogunate, an institution left incomplete during his lifetime. His background, supporters, and the political and economic environment for families in the east contributed to his success in elevating warrior authority, a process that continued long after his death.

Yoritomo gathered allies around him by taking advantage of their economic anxieties. Warrior families did not own land per se but could access land and its resources, human and material, through various managerial and policing duties granted to them by absentee landholders. Warriors did not control the appointment or transferring of those duties, nor could a warrior hope to rise into the upper echelons of nobility that would make him a proprietor. Taira Kiyomori, for example, could not be a landowner and merely appointed himself as protector and governor of lands. He had to imitate noble precedent by copying the Fujiwara family's practice of placing a grandson on the imperial throne.

Adding to economic insecurity were regional threats from neighboring rivals or family members who might take land or titles by force. It might seem counterintuitive, but the greatest threats came from within one's own clan. With no concept of primogeniture (the oldest son inheriting everything), the death of a clan leader might result in immediate infighting among cousins, uncles, and sons from different women who lived separately from their husbands. For lower-ranking warrior aristocrats or clans not based in and around Kyoto, sons were raised by the mother's family, and the wife's family vied for control over wealth and influence.

Thus, when an imperial prince, Mochihito, put out the call for people to oust Kiyomori from his position, those who responded took into consideration intra clan politics, connections to Kyoto nobility, and local rivalries when deciding if, and how, they would act. Yoritomo spent much of his time fighting relatives and clans traditionally allied to the Minamoto in the early stages of the Gempei War. From the beginning, other Minamoto men such as Yorimasa, who was defeated in 1180, and Yoritomo's cousin, Yoshinaka, also mobilized against Kiyomori, rivaling Yoritomo's efforts. Yoritomo gathered around him warriors whose loyalty he secured by promising them titles, access to land, and a pretext to attack local rivals. He provided an alternative to Kyoto-based authority for people living in the east. In fact, once the Taira troops captured and killed Prince Mochihito, the royal court, under Taira influence, declared Yoritomo a rebel. Thus, unlike Kiyomori, whose career was made within the bounds of the imperial government, Yoritomo could confiscate lands from his enemies instead of forfeiting them to the emperor.

The Gempei War did not unfold as one might expect. The initial protagonist, Mochihito, and antagonist, Kiyomori, died in 1180 and 1181, respectively. Mochihito and his Minamoto supporters were cornered and killed, while Kiyomori died of a fever so high, the literary version of the events in the *Tale of Heike* tells us that it was caused by the guardians and flames of hell coming to claim him.

Yoritomo was busy fighting local enemies and rivals, building a headquarters and bureaucracy in Kamakura until 1184, when he marched on Kyoto. In 1185, his half-brother Yoshitsune pursued the Taira as they retreated south from Kyoto. Yoshitsune, not Yoritomo, led the more spectacular battles, including the final one along the coast by the sea of Dan-no-Ura, far southwest from Kyoto and Kamakura. The Minamoto forces destroyed the remnants of the Taira clan, while the Taira noblewomen, one of them still holding onto the child emperor Antoku, Kiyomori's grandson, dived into the seas of Dan-no-Ura and drowned. So tragic was the defeat of Taira warriors, noblewomen, and servants that local legend claims the spirits of the Taira warriors imprinted themselves onto the carapace of small crabs.

The significance of the Gempei War in Japanese warrior history cannot be reduced to a neat list of losers and winners, or of gains and losses. The emperor had no choice but to recognize Yoritomo's emergence as Japan's dominant warrior, making him the "constable" (*shugo*) of all of Japan's provinces. He restored Yoritomo's court rank, eliminating his status as a rebel, and recognized his right to assign warriors as managers to estates

2. A popular legend tells how defeated Taira warriors turned into crabs like this one found in the seas around southwestern Japan. The crabs are said to contain the spirits of the angry, dead warriors, particularly those killed in the pivotal naval battle in the sea along Dan-no-Ura that ended the Gempei War (1180–85).

throughout Japan. But warriors did not control Japan; even Yoritomo coveted noble court rank and recognition from Kyoto. In his portrait he is dressed as an aristocrat, not as a warrior in battle dress. The war engendered a sense of unease for all elites, including Kyoto nobles, members of religious institutions, warriors, Yoritomo and his allies, and prominent local families. Rather than simply "serving" the Kyoto nobility, warriors now encroached on Kyoto's prerogatives of rule, a process that even Yoritomo could not control completely.

Yoritomo's Kamakura

Kamakura, a humble village with ancestral connections to the Minamoto, became a site of power during the 1180s. Called simply

"Ōkura Palace" at the time, it was the location of what is now referred to as the Kamakura shogunate, Japan's first warrior regime. Across Japan, warriors who wanted to benefit from Yoritomo's success declared that they too were his vassals, called "housemen" (*gokenin*), in an attempt to legitimize their local agendas. The shogunate's offices, staffed by minor nobles from Kyoto, monks, and warriors, managed applications for houseman status and tried to adjudicate lawsuits against warriors by other warriors and nonwarriors.

What makes the founding of the shogunate a watershed moment is that it forever changed how one group of warriors related to another. Although this change was limited to those who lived in the city of Kamakura itself, mostly Yoritomo's vassals and those who served the shogunate, it created opportunities for warriors to meet each other on a daily basis. Before the twelfth century, most warriors interacted only with family members, servants, and retainers who may have served them. Other than occasional guard duty in Kyoto or military campaigns, warriors of unrelated clans rarely encountered each other. In other words, the shogunate, especially Yoritomo's palace itself, became a place where warriors developed as a social group—an exclusive one. Most of these warriors were directly connected to Yoritomo. The palace functioned as a space for official meetings and social gatherings. It became a place to strengthen ties among warrior families, arrange marriages, and dole out punishment. The day-to-day business of running a government meshed with social events. For example, Yoritomo had one of his vassals murdered during a board game session (*sugoroku*). Outside the palace, warriors hunted together and engaged in ceremonies that had both pseudo-religious and martial functions—for example, bouts of sumo wrestling or shooting on horseback. These provided opportunities for warriors to strengthen the bonds to each other and to the shogunate, separate from the nonwarrior nobility in Kyoto. Nonetheless, connections to nobility in Kyoto, especially through marriage,

3. Elite warriors in early Japan valued their court-appointed titles more than their status as warriors. The only way a viewer might guess that this is a portrait of a warrior, said to be Yoritomo, is from the short sword on his hip.

remained important to warriors throughout the rest of Japanese history.

Not all of Yoritomo's vassals knew each other, and many falsely claimed to serve him. It was not until 1189, when he ordered his housemen to follow him into war against rebels in the northern city of Hiraizumi, that he could finally distinguish between those who were really housemen and those who were not. Housemen who refused his command were stripped of their titles and coveted privileges. For the most part, warriors were concerned about local issues and only secondarily about relations with the shogunate. Loyalty to the shogunate was sometimes loose and did not extend to the many warriors across Japan who were not Yoritomo's vassals.

Much like Kiyomori before him, Yoritomo placed nobles favorable to him in important bureaucratic posts in Kyoto while building his own independent headquarters. Yoritomo had no grand blueprint for his rule, and he demanded that warriors follow local practices and precedents established by the nobility. Moreover, Yoritomo's victory did not lead to an era of warrior dominance. He and the shogunate reined in warrior aspirations; they did not take over or destroy the Kyoto government. For the remainder of the twelfth century and part of the thirteenth, Kamakura was a junior ruling partner with Kyoto. Much of what defined Kamakura as a semibureaucratic regime developed after 1199, when Yoritomo died in a manner not unheard of among elite warriors—falling from a horse.

Hōjō's Kamakura

As was the custom for noble and elite warrior families alike, Yoritomo's sons were raised by women and the male relatives connected to their mother, the widowed nun Hōjō Masako. She was the closest personal connection between Yoritomo and the shogunate. This put her at the center of a struggle for control over the shogunate that included her brother (Yasutoki), her father (Tokimasa), her son (Yoriie) and his wife's family (the Hiki), and Yoritomo's allies. Although many vassals tried to uphold Yoritomo's legacy through Masako, others challenged that authority—blind loyalty was not the norm. Nearly a dozen people in the Hiki, Hōjō, and Minamoto families died in the succession disputes that followed, and Masako emerged as one of the few sources of continuity in shogunal politics from the late twelfth to the early thirteenth centuries.

Masako, far from being a protective mother supporting her son Yoriie, the second shogun, was closer to her birth family, the Hōjō. According to the late thirteenth-century historical chronicle *Mirror of the East*, Yoriie was an ineffectual leader. Not long after his father's death, Yoriie sent a close vassal of Yoritomo on a false errand in the hope of taking the man's lover while he was gone. The vassal returned to Kamakura having learned about the ruse, and Yoriie planned to preemptively attack the vassal's mansion. Masako occupied the vassal's residence to stop her son's attack and then berated Yoriie in writing. She also made the vassal promise that he would not retaliate at some later date. Even Minamoto men, such as Yoritomo's half-brother Zenjo, sought Masako's protection. She considered Zenjo a potential threat to her family, however, and rejected him; he was eventually hunted down and killed.

Masako's efforts on behalf of her brother, rather than her son Yoriie, pushed Yoriie closer to his in-laws, the Hiki, thus setting the scene for a showdown between the Hiki and Hōjō. The Hiki used him to obtain posts in the shogunate and hold sway over his sons who would inherit the shogun title. For example, the Hiki patriarch, Yoshikazu, envisioned his grandson inheriting the shogun title after Yoriie, thus putting the Hiki in a dominant position in the shogunate. But Hōjō Tokimasa had the same idea, and under his orders, Yoriie's heir was executed, as were some Hiki family members. In 1203, Masako and her father Tokimasa

forced Yoriie to retire after he fell ill. And when Tokimasa heard
that Yoriie was planning to have him assassinated, Yoriie too was
killed, leaving the Hōjō victorious. Naturally, Tokimasa, as the
Hōjō patriarch, had his own ideas about the shogunate's future: he
wanted children from his second wife to control it. But Masako
preferred her brother. In 1205 she had her father arrested and she
controlled the shogunate alongside her brother Yoshitoki.

Tension among warrior families was complicated by warrior
connections to the Kyoto establishment. Once Yoriie fell ill and
died, the last remaining son of Yoritomo was anointed shogun, the
eleven-year-old Sanetomo. But he was less a warrior than an
aristocrat, engaging in activities typically associated with Kyoto
nobility. He studied classical poetry assiduously, learning from one
of the greatest classical poets, Fujiwara no Teika. And he
maintained relatively close ties to Kyoto nobles including the
emperor Go-Toba. Similar to his father, Sanetomo held the title
"shogun" in less esteem than positions awarded to him within the
noble hierarchy. He even surpassed Yoritomo in that realm, having
received a prestigious administrative title, "Minister of the Right,"
a position, largely ceremonial at this time, that oversaw Kyoto's
Council of State. He did not enjoy that title for even a few hours,
however; his nephew, Yoriie's son, murdered him during the
ceremony, blaming his uncle for his father's death. Thus
Yoritomo's line ended with Sanetomo's murder in 1219.

Sanetomo's relationship to the nobility represented a potential
high point between the court and the shogunate. Since he did not
produce an heir, Masako brokered an agreement with Go-Toba in
1218 that would have resulted in an imperial prince becoming the
fourth shogun. This would have been an attractive possibility to
Go-Toba, who could then influence both a new emperor and a new
shogun. Instead, Sanetomo's murder became an opportunity for
Go-Toba to accomplish what Go-Shirakawa had tried to do in the
aftermath of the Gempei War—bring warriors to heel under Kyoto
authority.

The Jōkyū order

Go-Toba's attack against the shogunate, known as the Jōkyū War (1221), named after the reign year, is hardly worth mentioning as a military event. It pitted Go-Toba's hodgepodge of warriors, some Kamakura housemen, and many warriors from the west unaffiliated with the shogunate against the Hōjō and their supporters. Each army had about a thousand soldiers and the fighting lasted less than a month. But it was significant for its role in shifting power away from the emperor and court in favor of the shogunate. The crown prince, an emperor, and three retired emperors were all banished. Here again, Masako seems to have played a decisive role, if the stories of her speech are to be believed, by appealing to the Hōjō fighters' sense of loyalty to her late husband. Loyalty might have motivated some warriors on both sides, but others used the war as a pretext to attack rivals. Moreover, a Go-Toba victory would probably have curtailed warrior authority throughout Japan, not enhanced it. At any rate, it took the Hōjō army only a month to defeat Go-Toba's forces.

Many of the titles, positions, and bureaucratic structures of the Kamakura shogunate were fully developed during the thirteenth century under the Hōjō after their victory. The Hōjō did not conduct themselves with impunity, yet warrior families were eager to maintain stability in the countryside and protect themselves. Even if they did not wholeheartedly support the Hōjō, they were at least willing to cooperate with the shogunate for the time being. The shogunate responded to these anxieties by incorporating a broader range of warriors into the shogunate's rule.

The Hōjō placed more warrior-managers, including at least one woman, on estates throughout Japan, particularly among those of Go-Toba's defeated supporters and in regions where there had been none before the shogunate was established. Rather than follow the myriad pre-Jōkyū customs for tax collection, the shogunate attempted to standardize collection across all estates.

These expansive policies could not have worked under the early shogunate, when Yoritomo and his immediate successors had neither the manpower nor the know-how to challenge Kyoto precedent. In those days, the shogunate followed Kyoto's lead, ruling with Kyoto rather than against it. After the Jōkyū war, however, the shogunate expanded warrior authority and intensified its penetration throughout Japan.

The Hōjō empowered military governors to stop rebellions, to hunt down criminals, to defend the coasts against pirates, and, in distant southern Japan, to try and judge criminals. These military governors could move across estate borders and public land, which local warriors could not do. Nonetheless, appointments to the military governor position were not permanent; governors did not have the power to tax and could not act independently of the shogunate or infringe upon nonwarrior lands.

For example, the Kamakura shogunate's first legal code, the *Laws and Regulations for Judgment* (*Goseibai Shikimoku*), was not enacted until 1232, as a response to the Jōkyū War. Although it is typically described as a set of military laws, it reflects many issues that had been common in the Kyoto bureaucracy. Calling it a *law* overestimates the extent of its impact over the diverse groups of people called *warriors*. The term *law* did not carry with it the meanings it does in the modern world; for example, there were few mechanisms for enforcing rules in the premodern world nor was there a legal culture saturating daily life as there is today. No premodern government could enforce, or even conceive of, the monitoring and categorization of human life and property, from birth to death, as a modern government does. Mostly, the *Laws and Regulations for Judgment* established expectations and consequences laid out for military governors and land stewards— upper and middle management. Many warriors in places far from Kamakura simply ignored the code. Nonetheless, the *Laws and Regulations* marked the first time that a warrior regime in Japan created a model for behavior applicable to warriors across space and time; warrior leaders and intellectuals studied it up to the nineteenth century, long after the Kamakura shogunate had collapsed.

As a *legal* document, in keeping with the practice by the shogunate since its beginning, it emphasized following precedent. "Governors of provinces and estate [nonwarrior] proprietors may exercise their normal jurisdiction without referring to the shogunate authorities." In fact, such proprietors were told that the shogunate would not even entertain requests from temples or shrines that wanted guidance from the shogunate.

The code attempted to restrain newly empowered housemen and administrators after the Jōkyū War. Stewards found skimming tax collections or collecting more tax than was required "shall be deprived of their posts." Even if their deputies committed crimes or otherwise "contravene[d] the laws and precedents," the steward would be held responsible if he knew about it and tried to shield the deputy. Military governors who confiscated property for some offense without making a proper report would "be dealt with criminally."

In the mid-fourteenth century, a trial handbook titled *A Book for Those Unskilled in Legal Matters (Sata Mirensho)* was created that defined simple terms like *plaintiff* and more complicated concepts such as miscellaneous civil cases and criminal cases. Among the civil cases were "money or grain loans with interest; sale of paddy fields, slaves, or semi-free workers; and abduction of servants"; the criminal cases included "rebellion, night attacks, robbery with violence, secret theft, brigandry, piracy, murder, arson, battery, wounding with a sharp weapon, arson, seizing and raping women, creating a panic and stealing people's valuables as they flee, or harvesting another's paddy or dry field."

And what was life like for warriors across Japan? It depended on whom you worked for and your position within that local hierarchy. The shogunate expected its housemen to spend several months during the year performing guard duty in Kyoto, providing service to a provincial governor or perhaps working on an estate in some bureaucratic and police function. Men might be rotated through different positions in order to learn the full range of duties required of shogunal vassals. Warriors who were not directly connected to the shogunate worked in similar capacities locally, serving various functions for a noble family, a Buddhist temple complex, or powerful clans in the countryside with loose or nonexistent ties to Kyoto nobility or the Kamakura shogunate. Some warriors worked directly for the emperor. Since Japan was not in a constant state of war, however, duties tended to be mundane or physical; many warriors worked in agriculture alongside commoners.

Most warriors struggled economically. Estate stewards were typically paid from the taxes they collected, and they often abused their tax collecting power. Economically, clans that had access to land suffered after several generations as the custom of equal inheritance among sons and daughters had whittled away the family estate. Building projects, patronizing Buddhist temples, buying artwork from China, participating in courtly rituals: these were just some of the drains on elite warrior wealth that forced them to borrow money from local merchants, an indebtedness that was never resolved. Nor could their traditional sources of income—namely, produce from land—maintain pace with a growing commercial economy. These problems did not occur suddenly, but they were exacerbated by the Mongol invasions.

The Mongol incursion

In 1215, Kublai Khan, the grandson of Chinggis Khan and leader of the Mongols, achieved what his grandfather could not: the conquest of China. From Beijing, Kublai embarked on several decades of invasions with mixed success. He subjugated Korea, for example, but despite repeated attempts, failed to conquer Java, the Vietnamese kingdoms of Dai Viet and Champa, and Japan. Warrior history was never completely separate from events elsewhere in Asia, and although the Mongols never made gains in Japan, their invasions exposed weaknesses in the "warrior order."

In the standard account of the invasions, the Mongol-led forces, which included many Chinese and Koreans, attacked the southern island of Kyushu twice. In 1274 and again in 1281 the Japanese warriors met a vastly superior force in terms of troop size, organization, and technology, including the use of explosives. Military historians blamed the so-called traditional form of Japanese combat—announcing one's lineage and engaging in one-on-one combat—for the Japanese losses. The first invasion lasted only a day before a great storm blew the Mongols back into the sea. The Japanese prepared defenses along Hakata Bay, including a wall, and held the Mongols off for several months before another storm came along to save the day. The storms became known as the *divine wind (kamikaze)*, a term that became popular only in the wartime propaganda of the 1930s and 1940s. During the end of World War II, the Japanese military hoped that a "divine wind" of suicide pilots would prevent a new invasion of another superior, foreign horde—the Americans.

Recent scholarship suggests that the storms might have been a myth. Instead, religious institutions had pushed the divine intervention story in order to accrue rewards for doing their part to defeat the Mongols. Some historians claim that the storms alone could not have defeated the Mongols. So why did the Mongols retreat? Perhaps the Japanese were not outmatched and defeated the Mongols through combative effectiveness. Or the Mongols did indeed overwhelm the Japanese and only wanted to test Japanese military strength, not commit to a full-scale invasion. Kublai was still fighting the Chinese throughout the 1270s and had embarked on invasions elsewhere during the 1280s; he had neither the means nor the inclination to fully invade Japan.

Defending Kyushu and preparing for a third invasion that never came enhanced Hōjō presence in southern and central Japan. The number of military governors in those areas increased, and they were often members of the Hōjō family or its branches. The shogunate recruited men from estates that had been free from any shogunate intervention before the Mongol invasions. Once the shogunate reached into estates not owned by its own vassals, they never again left them alone. Hōjō jurisdiction over major temples and shrines, previously limited to eastern Japan, now extended to those in western Japan as well.

The Mongol invasions did not create new problems for warrior rule; rather, they exacerbated old ones. Many warriors who mobilized their men to defend Kyushu hoped to receive rewards for their efforts. With no national tax or much economic support from the shogunate itself, the burden fell upon those warriors to collect more tax from the lands around them. The Hōjō themselves had few newly acquired lands to hand out, and those who received some rewards were typically warriors in Kyushu. The Hōjō ordered Kyushu families to limit inheritance to male offspring, taking economic prerogatives away from daughters, a practice that, over time, extended to warriors throughout Japan. Gradually, inheritance fell to the oldest son, subordinating even the other male offspring.

The Hōjō also issued a series of prohibitions against warriors selling their land or giving it to nonrelatives. These culminated in a "virtuous edict" that forced anyone who had received land from a warrior family, either as collateral on debts or as commodities sold under the guise of gift giving, to return it to the original warrior families. These debt cancelations were "virtuous" because land was not a commodity to be bought and sold but an inherent part of a warrior clan's heritage. As with other premodern edicts, these were often unclear. Many times, even the beneficiary's claims were unenforceable, and some shrine priests believed the edict applied to them too. Execution and enforcement of the prohibitions were frequently impossible.

Kamakura in decline

Rank-and-file Kamakura vassals and the shogunate suffered from internal disputes during the latter half of the thirteenth century. Two of the Hōjō family's most powerful vassals, Taira Yoritsuna and Adachi Yasumori, began fighting each other after the death of the powerful shogunal regent, Hōjō Tokimune (1284). In 1285, Yoritsuna tried to hunt down Yasumori, which led to a series of murders, purges, and suicides among their supporters and underlings until Yoritsuna himself was killed in 1293. Such violent political intrigues rippled throughout Kyoto, where nobles split into groups of those who resented Hōjō involvement in court politics and those who supported the shogunate. Warrior branch families began breaking off from the main clan by answering the call to defend Kyushu on their own and not simply under the orders of the clan leader. Gradually, warrior clans allied less with their geographically distant kin and more with neighboring warriors.

Adding to the tensions at the top of society, at the bottom there were growing numbers of bandits, pirates, mercenaries, and marauders simply referred to as "evil bands" (*akutō*). Neither the Kamakura shogunate and its vassals nor the court in Kyoto maintained a monopoly over violence in Japan. In the latter half of the thirteenth century these bands of men grew from perhaps a few dozen at most to several hundred. Their numbers peaked during the early fourteenth century, as did their complexity; some even built forts, joined forces with local warriors, or worked for local temples. Many diverse groups of people armed themselves in order to attack the ever-monetizing, commercializing economy of the thirteenth century and to defend themselves against threats from the top of society as well as the bottom.

The legacy of the first warrior regime

Toward the end of the samurai era, in the mid-nineteenth century, warrior pundits linked their existence to Yoritomo's legacy. For them, Yoritomo was a founding father of warrior rule. In general, however, such lavish praise for Yoritomo occurred only late in premodern warrior history. During his lifetime, Yoritomo was not universally well regarded. Yoritomo killed his cousin (Yoshinaka) and his half-brother (Yoshitsune). When Yoritomo wanted to meet the Chinese monk Chin'na Kei, who rebuilt the Todaiji Temple in Kamakura after it burned down in 1180, the monk, repulsed by Yoritomo's violent ways, rebuffed him. When Yoritomo sent him gifts, Chin'na refused to receive them except for a horse saddle and a suit of armor. He donated the saddle to the temple and had the armor melted down and refashioned into nails. Political machinations within the shogunal leadership throughout the late twelfth and thirteenth centuries were violent. Kinsmen remained murder targets; none of Yoritomo's direct descendants died peaceful deaths, and his line did not endure.

The story of Japan's first warrior regime was one of gradual change. Its existence began with the events in Kyoto among the nobility and the emperors. Bureaucratic models, and often the bureaucrats themselves; measures of wealth; patronage of religious institutions; literary conventions; and even marriage politics originated in Kyoto. Whether claiming to be a Minamoto "man," invading noble or temple lands, or using their Kamakura-appointed position to rob locals, warriors had to contend with institutions and customs not of their own creation.

On the other hand, the Kyoto elite could never contain warrior authority. The emperor "bestowed" the title of shogun but that never implied control. Neither Yoritomo nor the Hōjō had to ask to be shogun; they demanded it. At least several Kyoto sovereigns tried to take back warrior power, first with Go-Shirakawa who played Yoritomo against his half-brother Yoshitsune, and again with Go-Toba whose fight against the Hōjō was short-lived. A third emperor, Go-Daigo, succeeded in challenging the shogunate in 1333, but even then the court was unable to check warrior aspirations. Nobles in Kyoto and prominent warriors in Kamakura never completely split into separate realms. After Sanetomo's death in 1219, shoguns came from the Kyoto nobility, not from warrior families.

Legal documents from the Kamakura shogunate speak to the importance of family, broadly defined, which included not only blood relatives but also warrior retainers, nonwarrior servants, nannies and wet nurses, and branch lines distant both geographically and temporally, all of whom could be one's greatest allies or most dangerous enemies. This is true not only of those at the top of warrior society but also among marginal clans, whose desire to persevere and expand could either be threatened or strengthened through military, religious, and noble networks around Japan.

Weak though it might have been, the Kamakura shogunate established a model for subsequent warrior regimes. In 1862, a warrior bureaucrat, complaining about meddling by the Kyoto nobility and their supporters, noted that warriors had been in charge of Japan's politics since the Kamakura shogunate. His boss, Japan's last shogun, eventually surrendered to the emperor in 1868, and a year later a newly formed modern government announced, "Now the evil of misrule by the warriors since the Kamakura period has been overcome and imperial government has been restored."

Chapter 3
War and culture

The sixteenth-century Jesuit Luis Frois described the pirate lord Noshima Murakami as being "so powerful that on these coasts as well as the coastal regions of other kingdoms, all pay him annual tribute out of fear that he will destroy them." His ships continually "flew across the sea." Noshima, like other sixteenth-century warlords, no longer depended on patronage from Kyoto aristocrats to secure wealth, power, and influence. During early warrior history, the centers of power in Kyoto and Kamakura loomed large in the lives of many warriors across Japan, but from the fourteenth to the sixteenth centuries, there was a gradual shift to regional networks, culminating in a century of war in which the "bottom overtook the top" (*gekokujo*).

Warfare was endemic during the three centuries after the fall of the Kamakura shogunate and the Hōjō family in 1331, which affected the relationship between aristocrats and warriors and the nature of warrior wealth and power. Yet, counterintuitively, at the most violent moments in history, warrior support and participation in the art world was also at its height. The sixteenth-century conqueror Oda Nobunaga burned down Buddhist temples and slaughtered thousands of lay supporters, but he also studied Noh theater—performing parts of the play *Atsumori* before embarking on the Battle of Okehazama.

The Kyoto problem

The first crack in Hōjō power since the Jōkyū War (1221) coincided with the rise of yet another emperor, Go-Daigo, who plotted against the Hōjō as Go-Toba did in 1221. Go-Daigo became emperor as a stopgap between the death of the previous emperor, his half-brother, and the ascension of the next one. Unlike those other emperors, however, he was an adult, not an easily controlled child, and he was surrounded by advisors who could support his political aspirations. Not only did he refuse to step down as emperor, which he, the shogunate, and the nobility had agreed would be the case, but he even installed his own son as the next emperor in order to maintain control of Kyoto. He gathered a wide range of supporters, claimed suzerainty over all warriors, and, in 1331, issued a call to arms against the shogunate. The Hōjō quickly put an end to this, exiled him, and purged many of his supporters. Still, not everyone abandoned Go-Daigo's cause. His general, Kusunoki Masashige, kept organizing sympathetic warriors not connected to the shogunate. Go-Daigo promised them titles and wealth just as Yoritomo had done more than a century earlier. Annoyed but confident, the Hōjō sent another army led by Ashikaga Takauji, the newly ascended twenty-eight-year-old head of the Ashikaga clan, longtime powerful Hōjō allies. Instead of fighting Go-Daigo's army, he attacked the shogunate's headquarters in Kyoto. Another Hōjō ally, the Nitta clan, similarly rebelled against the Hōjō in the east. For the first time since the late twelfth century, an emperor finally succeeded in ruling without having to share power with a warrior regime.

But Go-Daigo could not celebrate for long. For three years, from 1333 to 1336, he took control of the shogunate's prerogatives, becoming the sole authority to guarantee warrior appointments and land claims. Meanwhile, however, Takauji's influence grew and Go-Daigo failed to restrain him. Takauji gathered warriors loyal to him as he fought his way to Kamakura to put down a Hōjō resurgence there, and then he fought more enemies on his return trip to Kyoto. Meanwhile, Kyoto erupted in violence. An anonymous author posted complaints about the political situation in Kyoto by the Nijō riverbed: "Things common in the capital these days are night attacks, robbers, counterfeit edicts, criminals, fast horses [to indicate trouble in some place], random fighting, severed heads…"

Like Taira Kiyomori centuries before, Takauji placed his own candidate on the throne in Kyoto, and he began building what would become known as the Muromachi shogunate (1336–1573), named after the district in Kyoto that became the center of his regime. Go-Daigo established his own court just fifty miles south of Kyoto in Yoshino, where he died peacefully. Heirs from both sides fought each other until 1392, when the Yoshino line was crushed, but not forgotten—at the end of World War II, one man claimed to be descended from the southern court and demanded that he replace the northern imposter Hirohito.

The new Ashikaga shogunate depended upon regional warrior families to govern. On the southwest island of Kyushu, where the Mongols tried to invade, military governors essentially ruled as they saw fit. Likewise in the east, around Kamakura, the Ashikaga had to delegate authority to warriors who declared loyalty to them. Though they were never completely independent of shogunal authority, these governors nonetheless gradually assumed rights that their Kamakura predecessors never had: levying taxes, judging and enforcing laws without consulting the shogunate, and collecting fees from local plaintiffs to carry out sentences. With greater revenue, military governors built armies larger than those of the governors of the Kamakura period. Still, not all land in Japan was under the jurisdiction of a military governor. Local strongmen, those not subsumed under the shogunate's bureaucratic purview, also controlled territory. Since many military governors lived in Kyoto and left their provinces to be managed by underlings, strongmen either sought an official title from the shogunate or simply forced the governor to recognize their dominance in the region. The shift to local concerns happened gradually throughout the fifteenth century. For men like the pirate Noshima, regional networks, concerns, and sources of wealth mattered more than ties to the political center in Kyoto. This is the origin of those who would become known as the "great names" (daimyo), the warlords of the sixteenth century.

Tools of warfare

Long before movies depicted samurai wielding lightsaber-sharp swords or charging into battle on mighty horses, warriors themselves enjoyed fantastical descriptions of warrior combat. Warriors and nonwarriors alike read, listened to, and watched performances of "war tales," a genre of writing that had existed since at least the thirteenth century. Historians have cautioned against accepting these tales as accurate portrayals of historical events, but even history textbooks tend to include these problematic literary descriptions of early samurai warfare. The most persistent myth is the belief that warriors announced their family lineages before engaging in battle. It has a wonderful cinematic appeal but is not backed up by historical evidence, and military historians no longer accept it as established practice. A contemporary account of the Mongol invasions describes Japanese warriors who actually tried this, only to be laughed at by the Mongol troops. But these warriors might have simply imitated the heroics described in war tales, in the same way that Japanese Mafioso (*yakuza*) imitate the clothing style featured in Japanese gangster movies.

Nevertheless, warfare was not only about combative effectiveness. Warriors might ignore orders or even target an ally if they felt offended. Warriors painted and decorated their armor not to intimidate but to be noticed as crowds gathered to watch battles unfold. In these battles, killing a lowly rank-and-file soldier did not earn as many accolades as defeating an elite or well-known warrior. In the skirmish tactics of pre-fifteenth-century warfare, some verbal exchanges might have occurred, but that was certainly not the norm.

Early warfare involved armies that were small in comparison to the large-scale warfare of the Warring States era (1477–1590). Samurai vassals might have up to a few dozen men they could bring into battle, but many had only a handful. They could draw on local men as temporary retainers, and, by joining forces with other vassals who served an aristocratic warrior such as Yoritomo, an army could be as small as a few hundred or as many as a few thousand. The first major war, the Gempei War, might have involved several thousand to an unlikely forty thousand troops, depending on the historical source. Given the Gempei War's broad geographical range and the presence of defenses that changed the landscape, like trenches, it is likely that nonwarriors participated as well.

Kamakura-period combat was conducted among warriors on horseback accompanied by men on foot who either fought each other or attempted to unseat mounted warriors. This might seem like an unlikely technique if one imagines the size and speed of modern horses charging through enemy armies. Even Japanese tourists are fascinated by heart-racing demonstrations of mounted shooting (*yabusame*) at shrines around Japan. The archers stand tall above the crowd, galloping at full speed without holding the reins, as they shoot at a series of wooden plank targets. But the premodern reality is a bit less dramatic. Medieval horses in Japan were about the size of a pony, and with an armored man on top, they were hardly fast or durable.

Nonetheless, throughout much of premodern Japanese history, the bow and arrow, not the sword, was the primary weapon of choice for elite warriors. Mounted archery was so common that the phrase "the way of the horse and bow" (*kyūba no michi*) referred to military arts in general. On the early, skirmish-style battlefield, shooting it out against other mounted warriors or picking off footmen were common methods of conducting warfare. Reward petitions and battlefield reports indicate which kinds of weapons were the deadliest. Arrows accounted for most injuries and fatalities up to the fourteenth century. One shot alone usually did not kill warriors, especially wealthier men who could afford decent armor. Not only did the armor itself stop many arrows, but a blanket-like cloth that billowed behind a warrior's armor as he rode away from the enemy could make targeting him difficult by partly obscuring his outline, and it also stopped some of an arrow's momentum. However, with only primitive battlefield medicine, even a stray shot or an unfortunately lodged arrow withdrawn in the wrong way resulted in a slow, sometimes painful death as a warrior bled out.

Swords are another source of fascination for modern audiences, supposedly representing the soul of the samurai and so sharp that they could cut with just a touch. But the sword was merely a sidearm until the fourteenth century, and even then it was used only to gain advantage over an enemy during close-range combat, to finish off a downed opponent, or to decapitate him for later reward. The prototypical sword seen in popular culture was a later invention. Before the Mongol invasions, swords were heavy and had long blades used to attack a horse's leg like a large cleaver. Momentum and weight gave these early swords brute bludgeoning force, making sharpness less important. Extant battle reports and archaeological finds show crushed skulls to be the typical sword fatalities during the medieval period, not subtly delivered cuts to vital arteries.

Besides the iconic sword and bow, weapons included pikes (also referred to as spears), halberds, crossbows, shields, battle axes, large mallets, long rake-like weapons known as "bear claws," and even rocks. Crossbows were common in Chinese armies, and one might expect to find them in Japan. They existed, but perhaps because of their limitations such as slow rate of fire and limited trajectory, they never became popular. Mention of a large crossbow, possibly mounted on a turret, called a "great bow" (*ōyumi*) appears in ancient texts, but no artifacts or even illustrations exist.

The traditional story of how guns came to Japan begins with a Portuguese ship blown by storms onto a small island called Tanegashima. In 1543, so the story goes, the lord of the island realized the importance of the ship's guns and ordered local craftsmen to reverse-engineer them, thus starting a domestic gun-making industry just as the demand for guns spiked during a time of national war. Military historians in Japan have noted that primitive harquebuses, early matchlock guns with ball ammunition loaded from the front, entered Japan as early as the mid-fifteenth century from Okinawa, Southeast Asia, and China. The Europeans did not introduce arms to Japan, but they brought large quantities and probably better-quality weapons during the latter half of the sixteenth century. Guns could make the difference in battle, although they did not change the essential nature or tactics of warfare in Japan.

The biggest myth told about guns in Japan is that the samurai eventually abandoned them in favor of the sword because the sword was more honorable and represented the soul of the samurai. This is simply not true. First, people continued to use guns in the few, small-scale battles and uprisings during the otherwise peaceful era that followed the Warring States period. Lords gave them as gifts, and commoners and warriors alike used guns in hunting and for recreation. From the seventeenth to the early nineteenth centuries, cannons positioned at Japan's largest port, Nagasaki, were equivalent to those used in Europe. And samurai used guns against Chinese accused of smuggling in the southern port of Nagasaki. Thus, warriors never "gave up" guns; they still used them. But the opportunities to use them dwindled after the Warring States period.

The archetypical samurai armor has a long history, but like weapons, it changed over time. Armor from the Kamakura period (1180–1333) consisted of pieces of lacquered wood woven together, with some metal reinforcement on the chest. It covered most of the body except for the face but did not protect the extremities well. This type of full armor was expensive, and most foot soldiers wore nothing more than basic armor that covered the torso. Chain mail, like the European version but made with smaller chains, was used from the fourteenth century onward and was combined with an older style of armor made of metal plates. Helmets varied depending on the status of the warrior. They were made from a range of materials that included iron, steel, metal plates riveted together, and hardened leather for common soldiers. Armor changed to reflect shifts in battle tactics, especially during the fifteenth and sixteenth centuries, when war was conducted at a much larger scale with better organized units of men attacking with pikes, volleys of arrows, and guns. Immaculately preserved armor can be found in museums throughout North America and Europe, but most of these pieces date to the seventeenth through nineteenth centuries when there was little warfare, and armor was either worn in warrior processions or simply displayed in the home, seeing no combat at all. There are occasional echoes of European influence in Japanese armor, such as helmets shaped like those worn by European counterparts, but those are rare.

Japanese warriors did not use European-style, single-handed shields. Japanese shields were typically as tall as a man and were made of wood. They often included a stand so that a line of men could move and place them side by side to create a movable wall. Often these were impromptu defenses of opportunity: wooden doors, portions of walls, or tatami woven flooring ripped from buildings during battle.

And what of castles? There are two issues that might disappoint. First, castles as Westerners imagine them, with moats and walls surrounding a central keep, were a relatively late development in Japanese history, dating to the sixteenth century at the earliest. Some castles supposedly have earlier origins, but those were rebuilt several times after the Warring States era. During earlier times, such as the Gempei War, some fortifications existed, but nothing grand or permanent. Warriors who served the Kamakura shogunate might have had a large compound with walls and several buildings at most. Since many warriors worked as managers, police, and governors, there was little need to build large structures. Even Yoritomo's Kamakura palace, which housed many of the shogunate's offices, no longer exists.

Only in the sixteenth century did the Japanese build castles designed to keep an enemy out and to confound him should he penetrate the outer defenses. Despite the stylistic difference with European castles, they shared many features: moats, sturdily built narrow gates to keep enemies from flooding in, and small windows that allowed warriors to shoot arrows or pour boiling liquid onto intruding forces. The biggest difference between European and Japanese castles was the walls. Although their construction changed to accommodate the introduction of guns into Japan, these walls nonetheless did not suffer from punishing, artillery-led sieges as did their European counterparts. The greatest threat to the integrity of Japanese walls was earthquakes. To provide some protection from them, the walls were not built vertically straight using stones stuck together with mortar. Instead, Japanese walls had a slight curve, and builders cut and stacked stones to fit perfectly, filling gaps with smaller stones, without the need for mortar.

Although there are many castles throughout Japan today, only a dozen of them have keeps older than a hundred years. Keeps rarely served a military function; they were used mostly to project authority across the landscape. Fires throughout the Tokugawa period (1600–1868) destroyed many keeps and other wooden structures such as watchtowers or guard posts. Since keeps look

4. A full set of armor from the eighteenth century imitates the style of the twelfth to thirteenth centuries, illustrating how warriors of later periods idealized their medieval forerunners. Many museum armor pieces are in excellent condition because they were not used in combat but displayed in warriors' homes.

5. Himeji Castle, a UNESCO World Heritage site, is one of the largest and oldest castles in Japan. Originally constructed in the fourteenth century, it was partially built and rebuilt after the warlord Toyotomi Hideyoshi took it over in the late sixteenth century. Like many Japanese castles, it was used by the Japanese military during World War II.

impressive, they have been added to castles that never originally featured one. Local politicians have realized that castles are big tourist attractions and symbols of civic pride. Most of the castles in Japan are post–World War II fabrications that accompanied the postwar economic boom. Some of the reconstructions are inaccurately built or use too much concrete, giving castles a shiny but inauthentic look.

The most "authentic" castle is probably Himeji Castle, a UNESCO World Heritage site. Himeji survived the fate suffered by other castles that were either torn down after the Meiji Restoration (1868) and sold for scrap, destroyed by natural disasters, or bombed by the United States during World War II. However, even Himeji has undergone repairs and has been criticized by some as being much whiter than it would have been before the twentieth century. Nonetheless, Himeji is considered the archetypal Japanese castle, and many castle reconstructions have been modeled after Himeji regardless of the historical differences.

The warrior in combat

For much of Japanese history, compensation was the key to obtaining service from warriors. Yoritomo's success hinged on his ability to reward allies, the Hōjō lost support when they could not deliver enough rewards to those who fought the Mongols, and Emperor Go-Daigo was able to buy samurai away from the last enemy general who tried to fight him in 1333. So how did warriors prove their service? By submitting reports and petitions for rewards, and collecting evidence—namely, heads.

Taking heads had its origins in police duties. Early warrior violence primarily involved chasing down criminals and decapitating them to prove that the execution had been carried out. Heads would be collected, tagged, and publicly exhibited around Kyoto. During larger battles, headhunting functioned as a way for warriors to record their achievements and thus receive payment for their service. Heads would be cleaned and displayed on a board for a general to examine. Well-known enemies earned them the highest rewards, but differentiating middle- and lower-ranking warriors could be trickier; prisoners helped identify heads. Heads from common soldiers were typically ignored.

The downside of beheading an enemy during battle is obvious; a warrior could be killed while taking a head. Some generals solved this problem by issuing "cut and toss" orders, which tended to rely on eyewitness accounts of the beheading, thus skipping the collection side of the process. Warriors also gamed the system by scouring the battlefield for wounded men who were not yet dead, beheading noncombatants, forging or switching nameplates, and looking for abandoned heads, activities that were deemed unseemly and worthy of ridicule.

No notions of honor, rooted in maintaining a reputation, trumped the desire to emerge victorious. There were no written codes of conduct, no tactics deemed unacceptable. These included arson, which killed indiscriminately, and ambushes and night attacks, when the enemy was caught unaware. Trickery, particularly clever trickery, could earn a warrior praise, such as the following from a sixteenth-century military chronicle titled *The Military Mirror of Kai*:

> During the Battle of Toishikuzure there was an enemy separated from his comrades and armed with a long spear. When Imai chased after him, the enemy, a warrior of the warlord Uesugi Kenshin, changed the position of his spear and was going to strike Imai from his horse. Because the enemy was walking he could move about freely, but Imai was on a horse and could not. Imai, famed warrior that he was, tricked his opponent by calling out to him as if he were an ally. As the enemy lowered his spear to greet him, Imai's men moved in to attack. Imai is a martial expert even though he was not adept with a sword and did not know much about martial arts.

There are few details about how warriors trained together in groups during the Kamakura period. But we know that training was a social activity that helped develop some degree of group identity. During the Kamakura period, men used hunting as an opportunity to learn group coordination. Warrior managers on estates had portions of land reserved for hunting or falconry, which helped warriors learn how to survey terrain. Ceremonial shooting from horseback began among warriors in Kyoto in the eleventh century at the latest, but the tactic is often associated with Kamakura, where Yoritomo held shooting events at large shrines. Dog shooting was another activity that was recreational, social, and useful for military preparedness. Professional dog handlers kept and released dogs into an enclosed area while warriors shot at them from horseback with blunted arrows.

6. An early fourteenth-century hand scroll scene depicts the Battle at Rokuhara, when the Minamoto clan attacked Taira Kiyomori's base at Rokuhara palace. The Minamoto lost both the battle and the Heiji Rebellion (1160). Here, two Taira men descend on a Minamoto warrior, pulling him back to decapitate him.

Training and ritual often occurred in Buddhist and Shinto spaces, and thus, warfare and religion intertwined. Buddhist temples and Shinto shrines wielded political, military, and economic power. They possessed land, collected taxes, lent money (with interest rates as high as 300 percent), and provided protection for a variety of merchant guilds, including alcohol (sake) and weapon production. The notion that there were white-scarfed "warrior monks" armed with glaives (*naginata*) derives mostly from art history, literature, and popular culture. However, monks whose previous career included military experience continued to fight on behalf of temples. Major temples could rely on lay supporters, sometimes retired warriors, who acted as an institution's "muscle." They helped collect loans or protected the temples from bandits, pirates, and warriors who intruded on their estates.

Religious institutions confronted their enemies with supernatural weapons; prayers and chanting were more akin to spell-casting than prostrations for good luck. Clerics expected to be rewarded for calling upon the gods and Buddhas for the "divine winds" that they claimed destroyed the invading Mongol forces. Warriors had Sanskrit words inscribed on their weapons and armor to protect them from harm. The invocations and imagery of esoteric Buddhism mattered more than Zen meditation to a warrior heading into combat. They read about, or learned from other warriors and monks, spells such as this one that told the chanter how to escape from an attack by fire: "To escape from an enemy who attacks you with fire, face the direction of water, or at the sky, and chant 'praise to the god of rain and water' seven times. Then incant '*on, su'u ruinō ten sowaka*' and pour water down a bow from its top."

Warriors also paid homage to divine beings associated with war. This included the Buddhist god-like Marishiten, who carried an assortment of weapons in her six hands while riding atop a wild boar, and Hachiman, another Buddhist god of war. Deities appeared in dreams and could portend positive results in war. Some warrior hegemons promoted their rule as divinely ordained or were promoted as gods by their followers after death.

An era of war

The fifteenth and sixteenth centuries saw an interesting mix of warfare and high culture. During the latter half of the fifteenth century, the most influential warrior clans, including the Ashikaga, suffered from internal succession disputes that became violent. Even after those conflicts burned through Kyoto over the course of a decade, the rest of Japan experienced a new kind of warfare fundamentally different from anything it had experienced before. Battles were no longer conducted under the logic of chasing down enemies in the name of punishing rebels (Gempei War) or uppity emperors (Jōkyū War); warriors fought to expand and defend territory.

Like previous wars, the Ōnin War (1467–77) originated from the structural tensions at the political top. Three warrior clans, the Hosokawa, Hatakeyama, and Shiba, served as military governors but also rotated among themselves a newly created position during the Muromachi shogunate known as a "deputy shogun." After the death of the third shogun, Yoshimitsu (died 1408), the subsequent shoguns no longer had the ability or influence to control the shogunate on their own. Nor was there a single family like the Hōjō, connected to the shogun via marriage, powerful enough to dominate. Therefore, the deputy shogun and his family cooperated with the other clans to maintain stability in the shogunate. It was an efficient system when the clans were internally cohesive and interacted well. Their rivalry ensured that no single clan dominated. But when the clans were not strong or when tensions arose among the deputy shogun families, the shogunate weakened. Disputes that broke out within these families were tied to issues of who would control the shogunate at any given moment. Moreover, military governors, in what was a temporary post with little authority during the Kamakura era, gradually began to function as semi autonomous lords.

It was easy to dismiss the Ashikaga clan entirely after the death of its last, great leader, the third shogun, Yoshimitsu. Even after he retired he still controlled the shogunate through his son, the fourth shogun. Warriors, nobles, and even the Ming Chinese respected Yoshimitsu, but they despised his son. The fifth shogun died young, and the sixth shogun, Yoshinori, who showed some real ability to rule, was deemed too tyrannical by many of the important military families, and for good reason: cooks who underperformed, gardeners who broke a tree branch on a plum tree, fifty-nine members of the nobility, and even some warriors were killed, purged, or fled for their lives from his wrath. The military governor Akamatsu Mitsuhide brutally assassinated Yoshinori after learning that Yoshinori might take land from him and give it to someone else. Mitsuhide held a party in his villa on the outskirts of Kyoto and invited Yoshinori and other prominent warriors to partake in a favorite warrior pastime, viewing Noh theater. Horses suddenly rushed through the gardens, creating a distraction and allowing the assassins to break in and decapitate Yoshinori. A courtier at the time wrote that Yoshinori "died like a dog."

His son, the seventh shogun, died in childhood, so the shogun's position passed to another son, the much-maligned Yoshimasa. Although Yoshimasa represented the height of warrior involvement in noble culture—he was an accomplished poet—he was an indecisive shogun who had just enough influence in the shogunate to destroy it. Wanting to retire and having failed to produce an heir, he asked his brother Yoshimi to take over the shogun position. He planned to formally adopt his brother, a common solution for warriors who needed to secure an heir when no biological son was forthcoming. Yoshimi, quite rightly, was suspicious; what if Yoshimasa's wife suddenly gave birth to a son? And besides, Yoshimi, like other noble sons no longer in line to become head of the family, was happily ensconced in an unrelated career—in his case, as a Buddhist abbot. Unfortunately for everyone involved, after Yoshimi accepted his brother's offer,

Yoshimasa's wife gave birth to a son. The various supporters of Yoshimi and his newborn nephew battled it out in Kyoto, exacerbating an already volatile situation that grew into the Ōnin War.

The fighting of the Ōnin War signaled a shift toward a new kind of combat. Although some of the fighting occurred in the countryside, most of it took place inside the city of Kyoto itself. It represented neither the earlier logic of hunting criminals and rebels nor the engagement of participants in open field combat. Defensive blocks of men armed with pikes proved better suited to urban warfare than mounted warriors. Fighting occurred haphazardly in yards, gardens, and streets by those who were not warriors as such, but commoners recruited to fill the ranks of otherwise small armies. The purpose was simply to defeat an enemy and, in many cases, to exact revenge. In previous wars, when an elite opponent was not decapitated, he would be allowed to retire in exile. But during the Ōnin War, violence was so intense that some warriors made cups from an enemy's lacquered skull. The war was so devastating that when a reporter asked the seventeenth head of the Hosokawa family, Hosokawa Morisada, father of Prime Minister Hosokawa Morihiro (1993–94), about his family's legacy, Morisada replied, "Yes, our family used to have many excellent treasures but they burned up during the War." The reporter thought that "the War" referred to World War II, but Morisada clarified, "Oh, by 'the War' I mean the Ōnin War."

The shogunate itself never fully recovered, and warriors who remained in the countryside began to assert themselves against their neighbors, rivals, and absentee superiors. With Kyoto destroyed, many of its residents flooded out of the city to the growing number of castle towns being erected around Japan. Military governors who focused their energies on regional bases continued to maintain power locally, but others with little or no connection to prominent warrior families fought to obtain and secure territory. Contemporaries invoked Chinese history to describe the era as a time of "warring states," referring to the conflicts in antiquity immediately before the founding of imperial China. Skill in warfare alone was not enough; warlords needed to monopolize trade, encourage commerce, increase income, and attract noble-born literate men from Kyoto to establish laws that helped them pacify the realm. No potential alliance was overlooked as they gathered warriors, mercenaries, and noncombatant supporters to serve them.

It is no wonder that a Jesuit missionary writing to his brethren in Europe referred to these warlords as "kings." Domains were neither states nor kingdoms, but a warlord wielded authority in his realm with little regard for the shogunate, a far cry from the pre-Ōnin War military governors.

"The bottom overthrowing the top" was a phrase used at the time to describe the phenomenon of relatively unknown aspirants taking control of a domain or carving out a slice of land on their own. Even warlords with an impressive lineage were not guaranteed victory. The Ōuchi family, which had once supported the Ashikaga during the conflict between the Northern and Southern Courts, was one such prominent clan that fell into obscurity. They dominated southern Japan and ruled their coastal domain from a castle town called Yamaguchi. There they accrued wealth from trade with nearby Korea and China and, eventually, European traders who began arriving in Japan during the sixteenth century. At one point, Yamaguchi became so economically dynamic that it rivaled Kyoto itself, and the Ōuchi even planned to move the emperor permanently to Yamaguchi. Eventually, however, the Ōuchi were overthrown by one of their vassal clans, the Mōri, and Yamaguchi collapsed, never to regain its former glory.

The shogunate remained a potential source of legitimacy for warlords like Oda Nobunaga (1534–82). Nobunaga was the first of three warlords to conquer large swaths of territory and pacify the country. Nobunaga's rise to power illustrates how a warlord took

7. Portraits of warriors usually show them clean-shaven and without much facial expression. This Shibata clan warrior appears mischievous in this iconoclastic sixteenth-century portrait that signifies a time when the upheaval of warfare allowed people to overturn aesthetic norms.

advantage of upheaval. His family, the Oda, were only minor warrior vassals serving the Shiba, a branch of the Ashikaga clan. The Shiba rotated the deputy shogun position with the Hosokawa and the Hatekeyama, and like them, the Shiba were weakened from internal family disputes of the sort that characterized the Ōnin War and were unable to control warriors in their provincial lands. The Oda, who carried out mundane functions in the province on behalf of the absentee Shiba, overthrew the Shiba and took over the province.

Nobunaga inherited titles and land from his father, but he had to spend many years securing control over the Oda clan. As was true throughout warrior history, family members were targets— Nobunaga killed his brother. He also negotiated with local influential men in the province, a necessary strategy because the province, Owari, was centrally located, close to Kyoto, and agriculturally productive. A combination of political alliances, strategic and tactical skills, and Nobunaga's ability to incorporate the men of his defeated enemies drove his success. Eventually he attracted support from the shogun Ashikaga Yoshiaki. The two men needed each other. Yoshiaki required Nobunaga's military might, and Nobunaga wanted the legitimizing approval of the shogun regardless of how weak the shogunate might have become. But Nobunaga never accepted titles from the shogun. Doing so would have made him the shogun's subordinate and complicated Nobunaga's ambitions. As with the Hōjō and Go-Toba in 1221, and Ashikaga Takauji and Go-Shirakawa during the 1330s, Nobunaga was forced to defend himself against an older institution of rule, using force to do so.

Nobunaga probably did not set out to destroy the political relevance of the shogun and his regime, but relations between the two men waned. Yoshiaki sought help from Nobunaga's rivals, including the powerful warlord Takeda Shingen who, like Nobunaga, had successfully conquered large swaths of territory. Nobunaga, in turn, sent Yoshiaki a list of complaints about the shogun's behavior. Eventually the shogun declared war on Nobunaga in 1573, and despite Nobunaga's offers of peace, he lost patience with Yoshiaki, who fled Kyoto, never to return. Nobunaga defeated Yoshiaki's coalition and ordered the beheading of the shogun's top three warlords—he then had their heads lacquered and painted in gold dust to show to the troops.

Nobunaga eliminated his final enemy, institutional Buddhism, over the course of the next several years, killing tens of thousands of adherents of the True Pure Land faith, including commoner men and women. In so doing, he forever eliminated Buddhism as an institution of rule. For more than five hundred years, major temples had enjoyed patronage from the Kyoto aristocracy and warrior elites. After Nobunaga's campaign, temples no longer maintained armies or possessed the wealth they once did. In 1582, the court, which had supported him since his victory over the shogun, offered him the title of shogun. But before he could accept, one of his own generals, Akechi Mitsuhide, attacked him, cornering him and his son in a temple. Wounded and clearly defeated, both Nobunaga and his heir committed suicide after ordering that their bodies be burned. Nobunaga's career ended as it had started, in the constant "bottom overthrowing the top" that defined the times.

Nobunaga had conquered about a third of Japan, established policies to encourage trade, and amassed a sizable army, but, as with any warlord, the issue arose as to who would inherit that legacy. His remaining son, Nobutaka, was far from Kyoto when news arrived that his father and older brother had been killed. He blamed his cousin for the betrayal, as kinsmen were the usual suspects in prominent warrior families. He was forced aside, leaving one of Nobunaga's generals, Hideyoshi, to avenge Nobunaga and take control of his forces.

Nobunaga exemplified one type of Warring States story, a vassal family usurping their patrons. Hideyoshi represented another type, an individual of obscure, lowly origins who rose through the ranks. He and his early biographers cultivated this image; he told foreigners that a ray of sunlight had entered his mother's womb, indicating divine birth. In other words, he used both sides of the classic hero story—the everyman of humble beginnings and also divine birth that would lead to heavenly ordained greatness. At any rate, he built on Nobunaga's gains and secured alliance, obedience, and dominance from warlords across Japan. He accomplished this by fielding the largest army in the world at the time, as many as two hundred thousand men, much larger than any contemporaneous European army. He personally owned 12 percent of Japan, including some of the largest cities, such as Kyoto, and the major ports that handled lucrative trade from China, Korea, and European merchants.

We should not attribute Hideyoshi's successes to his abilities alone; the warlords themselves were willing to acquiesce to his policies so that they could block threats from within their domains. After all, only a few decades before Hideyoshi's unification, the vassal family Mōri had overthrown their lords, the Ōuchi. The final decades of the late sixteenth century and early years of the seventeenth are a story of preventing the types of upheaval that many of these warlords themselves took advantage of. For example, warriors were removed from villages to keep them from building local power bases independent of the warlord's authority. Hideyoshi tried to disarm villagers knowing that local people posed a significant threat to his conquest over Japan. They sometimes created egalitarian leagues of farmers, merchants, mercenaries, militant monks, and other "nonwarriors" who nonetheless armed themselves and fought collectively. *Warrior* was still an ambiguous term. Often there was no clear distinction between who counted as a warrior and who did not. People of all statuses joined together to form leagues that protected their members against warlords with large armies. An attack on one member of a league prompted a response from them all, something like a premodern Japanese North Atlantic Treaty

Organization. Geographic proximity or even a shared religious affiliation was enough to justify collective defense.

Hideyoshi solidified his conquest in 1590, but his vision extended beyond Japan to China, and he started what became the largest war in premodern world history, the Imjin War (1592–98). Not long after Hideyoshi had unified Japan, he sent messengers to European representatives in Asia: the Spanish governor of the Philippines and the Portuguese stationed in their colony of Goa, now a state in India. They responded with a mix of confusion and minimal acknowledgment of this man whom they had never heard of before, but Hideyoshi took their response as recognition of his greatness. Such was the extent of Hideyoshi's confidence. He asked the Korean king to allow him access to the peninsula to make way for his armies that would conquer China. The Koreans demurred, and in 1592 Hideyoshi ordered warlords, mostly from the south, to lead their samurai to Korea.

Many have speculated about why Hideyoshi invaded Korea. Some have argued that he wanted to keep the warlords and their samurai busy to prevent a revolt. Although this is not a consensus view, it has one element of truth—namely, that Hideyoshi liked to move warlords around to keep them occupied and their resources strapped. Others believe that he wanted to rid himself of Christian warlords. Nearly a quarter of a million Japanese had converted to Christianity since Catholic missionaries had arrived in the latter half of the sixteenth century. Most conversions occurred in the southwest, on the island of Kyushu, where missionaries first landed as they traveled north along maritime routes from South and Southeast Asia (earning them the name, in Japan, of "southern barbarians"). Many warlords sent to Korea were among the converts.

Initially the Imjin War went well for the Japanese. Nearly 158,000 men, at least twice as many as in any European army, invaded from the south and made it to the northern capital in a few weeks.

For the Korean kingdom of Choson, it was the perfect storm: the Koreans' military organization was not good, the peninsula had been at relative peace for centuries, and now they were facing battle-seasoned Japanese. The Korean king called upon his patron, the Ming Chinese emperor, who sent a small force. Initially, the emperor had not felt threatened by the Japanese— until the first army he dispatched was wiped out. Eventually he sent an army of approximately one hundred thousand. Chinese support and the Korean naval successes under Admiral Yi Sunsin, who cut off Korea-based troops from Japan, forced the Japanese to retreat. For several years Hideyoshi engaged in peace talks with the Ming, during which time some Japanese soldiers gave up arms and blended into local Korean communities or defected to the Ming army. Finally, shortly before dying of illness, Hideyoshi gave the order to retreat completely; the warlords were all too happy to comply.

The war devastated Korea, which took centuries to recover. In the modern period, the Imjin War became the first historical source of tension between Korea and Japan. Attempts to rectify this tension have failed. In Kyoto, for instance, there is a national historical site called "Ear Mound," which is a bit misleading; twenty thousand Korean noses were buried there. Warriors had brought them back to Japan, instead of decapitated heads, for reward. During the 1990s, there was a campaign by South Koreans and Kyoto city officials to remove the mound and send its contents to South Korea for proper burial. But Japan's central government denied the request because it was designated a national cultural asset.

Until recently, Chinese scholars have downplayed the war's impact on Ming China. After all, Japanese warriors never made it to China. But the Ming emperor committed enough resources to the "Korean campaign," as it was known in China, that it drained Ming coffers. This made it more difficult for the Chinese ruler to

8. **During the invasions of Korea, Japanese warriors collected the ears and noses of enemy troops and civilians as trophies. Previously known as Hanazuka (Nose Mound), Mimizuka (Ear Mound) symbolizes the Japanese invasions of the Korean peninsula in both the premodern and the modern periods and is dedicated to the souls of the maimed individuals.**

put down rebellions from within China and fight enemies to the north.

Japanese warlords brought back with them Korean slaves, especially artisans and intellectuals. Among them were potters who were forced to establish Korean ceramic workshops in Japan. In fact, Hideyoshi's invasion was also called the "pottery war." Why did daimyo want intellectuals and potters? What was the connection between warfare and culture?

Warrior "values"

From the beginning, elite warriors depended upon connections to Kyoto that required some degree of cultural literacy. A significant number of shoguns during the Kamakura era came from Kyoto noble families with no military identity as such. Warrior regimes in Kamakura and then in Kyoto, as well as small local governments, drew talent from middling noble families. Thus it should be no surprise that elite, literate warriors participated in and patronized art in its many forms—from art collecting and poetry writing to the funding of Buddhist temples, statues, and religious artwork. The city of Kamakura even had its own Zen Buddhist temple system that mirrored the one in Kyoto.

For warriors with court rank ambitions, writing was essential for interacting with elite nobility and clergy. But we should not think of poetry in the modern sense of the term—as a leisure activity, a pastime with no function beyond observations about contemporary society. Poetry in premodern Japan could be used to comment on current events, but more important, poetry demonstrated one's knowledge of classical Chinese and Japanese literature. Good writing, in content and in form—handwriting mattered—was a means for noblemen in Kyoto to climb the career ladder. The monk Jien exchanged poetry with Yoritomo, which led to a mutually beneficial relationship; Jien needed to secure rights for his estate and Yoritomo wanted information from him. People also wrote poetry together as a social activity, linking one poem to another; an elite warrior could expose himself to public humiliation if he failed to write adequately.

As warriors took up permanent residence in Kyoto during the Muromachi period, they deferred to courtier sensibilities. They intensified the adoption of aristocratic culture into their own families, using Chinese learning when creating their own clan rules, and forming a parallel set of warrior etiquette that mimicked aristocratic traditions. In other words, nascent warrior culture and identity had its roots in noble culture.

One text that imparts what it meant to be a proper warrior is a letter purportedly written during the early fifteenth century by a military governor, Imagawa Ryōshun, to his son. It emphasizes the importance of nonmilitary learning, respect for the clan over the individual, and the way to manage a clan and its properties. The text was not written in a historical vacuum; some themes had appeared in earlier warrior texts for elites. Buddhist notions of the respect for life and Confucian ideas about proper behavior when interacting with others punctuate Imagawa's letter, as they did many early East Asian writings. The Imagawa "house code" includes these precepts:

- As you do not understand the arts of peace, your skill in the arts of war will not, in the end, achieve victory.

- You like to roam about, hawking and cormorant-fishing, relishing the purposeless taking of life.

- To build your own dwelling, you razed the pagoda and other buildings of the memorial temple of our ancestors.

- You permit yourself to forget the kindness that our lord and father showed us; thus you destroy the principles of loyalty and filial piety.

- You disregard other people's viewpoints; you bully them and rely on force.

- You excel at drinking bouts, amusements, and gambling, but you forget the business of our clan.

- Expertise in the military arts and warfare are the way of the warrior. What first makes him distinguished is the capacity for management.

- It appears clearly from the Four Books [of Confucianism], the Five Classics [of China], and military texts that he who can only defend his territory but has no learning cannot govern well.

These precepts did not necessarily apply to lower-ranking warriors but to elite men like Imagawa. Only the upper echelons of the warrior community had access to an education that allowed them to read the Chinese classics (in fact, familiarity with Chinese philosophy can help the modern student of samurai history understand warrior ideals). During the fifteenth and sixteenth centuries, military governors and warlords used Imagawa's letter in their own clans and adopted it to create similar teachings. The Imagawa letter reached the peak of its popularity during the Tokugawa period (1600–1868), an age of peace when warrior education focused on management and civil learning, not military skill.

Warrior thought is also reflected in the teachings of Hōjō Sōun, a fifteenth-century warrior loyal to the Imagawa clan during the Warring States era. He was not directly related to the Hōjō clan of the Kamakura period (1185–1333) but consciously adopted the surname in order to inherit their powerful legacy—warriors idealized the past. His teachings spread throughout all warrior ranks in the lands he controlled, including such aphorisms as these:

- Rise early in the morning. If you wake up late your servants will be negligent and they will be of no use to you. Your public and private affairs will go into disarray. Your lord will forsake you. Think carefully about this.

- Do not think that you should have fine swords and clothes like others have. Just be sure they do not appear slovenly; that's enough. You'll be ridiculed if you borrow what you don't have or spend too much effort on such things.

- In seeking good friends, find those who are good at writing and learning in general. Bad friends to exclude are those who play *go*, *shogi* [a form of chess], the flute or the *shakuhachi* [an end-blown bamboo flute]. It is not a shame to be ignorant of those pursuits. These are simply ways to pass the idle time. The good and bad of a man is determined by the friends he keeps. [Then, quoting the *Analects* of Confucius,] "When three men walk together, among them, I have teachers. I choose to follow what is good about the good man, and learn to better myself from the bad man."

- Of course you should know the ways of culture [*bun*] and war [*bu*], along with the military arts [literally, "bow and horse"]; there is no need to write more about this. From antiquity it has been the rule that civil culture is on the left and military learning is on the right; one must practice both.

Sōun also has much to say about how to serve one's lord: always show respect to one's seniors, follow orders to the letter and without delay, and maintain one's residence. Like the Imagawa letter, Sōun's writing deems civil arts to be just as important as the martial arts.

Warriors in Kyoto culture

During the Muromachi period, warriors also began entering the Kyoto artistic realm not of their own making: the world of art collecting, connoisseurship, and performance. The intertwining of politics and art intensified with the Ashikaga presence in Kyoto. Even the relatively uninitiated, like Oda Nobunaga, could not resist the social and political gains to be made by engaging the nobility and wealthy commoners through art.

What we might today think of as "traditional" Japanese culture, such as Noh theater or the tea ceremony, expanded during an era of war and benefited from warrior patronage. These activities became new fields of knowledge as artists themselves created new types of networks by interacting with the nobility and warrior patrons. Theater had long existed in Japan, but we know few details about it until it became an artistic field of knowledge, written about and codified as "Noh," during the fourteenth and fifteenth centuries. That is, there were no texts that attempted to define theatrical standards, training, or aesthetics. It was only when Zeami, regarded as the creator of Noh, received patronage from the third Ashikaga shogun, Yoshimitsu, that he had connections to intellectuals who provided him with the education and vocabulary to elevate theater from entertainment to high art.

Noh played to its newfound audience; many performances featured warrior heroes, drawing from the classic *Tale of Heike*.

Art had a practical function; warriors gained access to social networks among nonwarriors through cultural activities. Only after spending time in Kyoto, with nobles, did Nobunaga start practicing *kemari* (often referred to as kickball but closer to hacky sack). Nobles and even Kamakura shoguns hired kemari teachers to improve their game, and other elite warriors wanted to become involved. Likewise, art collecting allowed warriors to mingle with the wealthy and to form alliances with other warriors through gift-giving or by bestowing rewards on subordinates.

The tea ceremony was among the iconic aristocratic pastimes that moved into the warrior sphere and eventually came to represent it. The tea ceremony combined two activities: collecting and connoisseurship with physical practice. Tea gatherings began as social events where rare objects could be displayed, perhaps as a part of other day-long events such as poetry writing or even gaming. But gradually it became an intimate affair when a few men of varying social classes gathered in a small, unassuming room where attention centered on the host, who would prepare the tea for his guests. Here too, Nobunaga is often regarded as the first prominent warrior who engaged in this practice, keeping two well-known tea experts on his payroll, including Sen no Rikyū, the first tea master to write extensively about tea aesthetics and whose teachings are followed even today.

Hideyoshi, like other warriors, took his cultural cues from Nobunaga. He continued to employ Rikyū, relying on him almost as a collaborator. Rikyū helped Hideyoshi set up tea gatherings, display tea-related objects, and learn the aesthetics of tea as defined and redefined by Rikyū. Hideyoshi even held a large open-air tea event, inviting anyone, regardless of status, to attend. But the constantly changing world of tea clashed with warrior desire to impose order; those who did not attend the event were forbidden to participate in future communal tea gatherings. One can imagine the tension between a hegemon with designs on conquering China and his tea master who was regarded as a cultural icon.

As an indication of his importance, Rikyū oversaw the installation of a statue of himself over the gate of an important Zen temple. This was regarded as an insult to Hideyoshi, who might pass under Rikyū's feet. In 1591 Hideyoshi ordered Rikyū to kill himself. After writing a death poem and piercing his abdomen with a short sword, he was shown the mercy of decapitation by a warrior in attendance. Whatever reasons Hideyoshi might have had for executing Rikyū, the tea master nonetheless represented a challenge to Hideyoshi's authority in the world beyond politics and war—people obeyed Hideyoshi but they listened to Rikyū.

Chapter 4
Warriors in an age of peace

The samurai loom large in the scholarship of the Tokugawa period (1600–1868), also known as the Edo period or simply "early modern Japan." Despite being known as a time when commoners wrote and produced knowledge more than ever before, when commoner urban popular culture eclipsed the Kyoto-centric highbrow culture, samurai remained central to macro historical analysis. For some types of history, especially diplomatic and political histories, this makes sense; samurai rule achieved its peak during the Tokugawa period. Nobunaga eliminated institutional religion as a political, economic, and military force even though religion, broadly conceived, helped legitimize and promote political action. And until the very end of the Tokugawa period, the nobility and emperors in Kyoto no longer had the authority they once did. They depended on the shogun's largess and sent ambassadors to the Tokugawa shogunate headquartered in the city of Edo (modern Tokyo). No emperor even considered challenging the warrior regime during the Tokugawa period.

Scholars of economic, institutional, intellectual, religious, and cultural history all address the role samurai played in either constraining or fostering changes in early modern society. One could even argue that the real age of the samurai began in the Tokugawa period. Some historians have depicted this as a dark time, when a putatively rigid status system kept commoners in their place, denying them access to the decision-making processes at the top and condemning them to physical toil at the bottom. Others see this as a relatively bright era when health and standard of living were generally good compared to European countries at the time. Likewise, popular culture, literature, art, and theater are viewed as either sites of resistance against or vehicles for escape from the pressures of warrior rule. In comparative East Asian history, Japan is considered either similar to China and Korea because they all underwent bureaucratization at roughly the same time, or as fundamentally different because Japan was ruled by warriors, unlike its neighbors.

Tokugawa Ieyasu represented the last generation of warlords who experienced a life of war; after the early 1600s they were simply "lords." The Matsudaira clan, Ieyasu's birth family, gave him as a child hostage to the Imagawa clan in exchange for help fighting against the Oda; hostages and marriage were the two methods for securing alliances among warlords. But he was kidnapped en route and handed over to the Oda, with whom he lived for several years. He returned to the Imagawa during a hostage exchange involving one of the Oda sons. This might sound like a rough childhood, but he was scarcely mistreated; he received an education under the Imagawa, led armies on their behalf, and married an Imagawa woman.

Ieyasu lived with the Imagawa until they were defeated by the Oda, after which he returned to his homeland and took control of the Matsudaira. He became Nobunaga's ally and, eventually, his vassal. Nobunaga trusted Ieyasu, and for good reason. When Ieyasu was forced to decide between maintaining his alliance with Nobunaga or killing his own wife and son under Nobunaga's orders (they were suspected of secretly colluding with enemies), Ieyasu chose the latter. During the Warring States era, loyalty could not trump ambition.

When Hideyoshi took over Nobunaga's armies, Ieyasu joined forces with him until Hideyoshi died. Ieyasu had agreed to help Hideyoshi's son, Hideyori, rule. But he eventually fought against the warlords who supported Hideyori and emerged victorious at the decisive Battle of Sekigahara in 1600. Ieyasu then extracted the title of shogun from the emperor in 1603 and turned on Hideyori, who was holed up at Osaka Castle. Ieyasu finally defeated Hideyori and his few allies by attacking Osaka castle, from 1614 to 1615, a siege that ended with Hideyori's death. Richard Cocks, head of the British East India trading company in Japan, recorded in his diary, "They say the taking of this fortress hath cost above 100,000 men's lives on the one part and other, and that on the Prince Hideyori's part no dead man of account is found with his head on, but all cut off.... Neither can the body of Hideyori be found; so that many think he is secretly escaped. But I cannot believe it (June 19, 1615)." His suspicions were correct; Hideyori was captured by the Tokugawa and beheaded along with his eight-year-old son. Ieyasu destroyed the Toyotomi clan shrine, thus ending any possibility of a counterrebellion based on the same strategy that the Minamoto had used against Taira Kiyomori in the late twelfth century. Ieyasu himself died of natural causes in 1616, shortly after the siege, at age seventy-five.

Tokugawa Ieyasu created the last warrior regime in Japan, and his successors ruled as shoguns with few real challenges from the court and lords until the nineteenth century. The shogunate established obligations due from the lords, and expectations from samurai, outlined in a 1615 document titled *Codes for Warrior Households*. Some of the articles in the code continued to emphasize themes found in older warrior precepts, such as studying the civil arts along with military arts, living frugally in accordance with one's station in the military hierarchy, and avoiding frivolous activities like drinking and gambling. For commoners, the shogunate issued constantly changing and sometimes contradictory edicts that defined a variety of crimes. It also had the last word on foreign policy but depended on the lords to conduct international relations on its behalf. Japan's political authority was centered in the city of Edo, but Japan was not centralized. There was neither a national army nor a national tax. Lords ensconced in their domains maintained separate currencies, legal codes, and courts.

Many features associated with the last samurai regime had their roots in the sixteenth century. The main difference between the Tokugawa period and its predecessors was the degree to which those features became more strictly defined during the seventeenth century. During the Warring States period, anyone could be considered a daimyo if he was powerful enough, but from the early seventeenth century onward, a man had to be officially classified as one. The image of the samurai as a relatively strictly defined group distinct from other types of people in Japanese society can be attributed to the Tokugawa period. In earlier times, "warrior" was a plastic concept; some men were born and raised as warriors or served as military vassals or retainers, but others might have been part-time warriors, pursuing other occupations when not at war. In the Tokugawa period, only the lords (daimyo) or shogunate could confer that status.

Hideyoshi initiated a process of pacifying Japan later inherited by the early Tokugawa shoguns and largely complete by the late seventeenth century. He issued an edict known as the *sword hunt* that forbade farmers from owning weapons of any kind and ordered them to hand over weapons to local warrior authorities to be melted down for use in a great Buddha statue. But, as in any premodern society, regulations enacted by the sovereign were never completely and uniformly enforced. Some commoner elites, such as village officials or commoners with warrior roots, still held weapons in secret. Villagers used muskets for hunting, but they were locked up in village headmen's offices and given only to those with written permission from a local authority.

Perhaps Hideyoshi's farthest-reaching act was a countrywide land survey used to determine taxes based on agricultural output. It doubled as a primitive registry. Villages, their residents, and the number of people in a resident's house, including servants, were classified as commoners rather than warriors, thus separating warriors from commoners spatially and economically. But it was only under the Tokugawa shogunate that warriors became distinct from commoners culturally and politically. In general, warriors could no longer live in the countryside except in a few domains where a portion of the samurai population engaged in farming as part of their military obligation. Instead, the shogunate's laws forced samurai to move into castle towns that served as domain capitals, leading to massive urbanization. Edo became the largest city in the early modern world. Merchant activity flowed from the villages into local cities as the Tokugawa population grew. Commoners in the countryside were no doubt glad to see the samurai population leave their villages, but samurai officials made regular forays into the countryside to assess production there.

The shogunate also controlled a third space: the borders between Japan and European countries. Catholic missionaries traveled mostly throughout southern Japan, where nearly a quarter of a million Japanese, some of them warriors, converted to Catholicism. Although these conversions might have been true acts of faith, the reality is that where missionaries traveled, merchants followed. In the sixteenth century, merchant activity increased the wealth for warlords in the south and helped them gather European weapons and ammunition. Of the three warrior hegemons, Oda Nobunaga had nominally accepted Catholicism in Japan, probably as a way to antagonize and weaken his Buddhist institutional rivals. But Hideyoshi and Ieyasu suspected foreigners, their overly zealous and exclusive religious beliefs, and the potentially troublesome southern warlords who hosted them.

Ieyasu's prohibition against Christianity in 1612 was directed primarily at the top. Although the edict outlawed Christianity in general, its implementation targeted lords and samurai converts. This changed in 1637 when rebels in the southwestern region of Shimabara used Catholic imagery—namely, crosses and crucifixes—on their flags during the rebellion. Across Japan, the shogunate required people to join local Buddhist temples to prove that they were not Christian, and authorities forced converts to publicly renounce their faith. The shogun also banned visitors from foreign countries, except from Japan's neighbors, and, oddly, the Dutch—they promised never to bring Catholic-related objects or texts into Japan. Overseas Japanese could not return to Japan, nor could Japanese travel abroad. The shogunate shut down oceangoing ship construction, and all foreign ships had to arrive in Nagasaki, far to the south, far away from Edo. More than just imposing a Catholic ban, the shogunate also wanted to monopolize any foreign contacts, taking away profitable European connections that mostly southern warlords had once developed.

The lords (daimyo)

The first issue facing the early Tokugawa shoguns was how to prevent challenges from the warlords themselves. The shogunate removed many warlords from their bases of power and put them into unfamiliar territory. During the first fifty years of the Tokugawa period, there were at least 281 instances of lords being relocated. A little more than 200 daimyo were completely stripped of land and title, and roughly 170 samurai were promoted to the rank of daimyo. The shogunate awarded another 200 or so lords with more land. It executed particularly threatening enemies, dissolved their domains, and redistributed their land to Tokugawa allies.

The Tokugawa clan existed as a first among equals and maintained a tenuous dominance throughout the Tokugawa period. It controlled sixty thousand warriors and nearly a quarter of the land in Japan, including the area around the major cities of Edo, Kyoto, Osaka, and the sole official international port in

Nagasaki. These lands supplied the shogunate with the resources it needed for mundane operations, including paying its samurai and providing support to the court and emperor in Kyoto. Those same lands funded the shogunate's national responsibilities. When extremist samurai assassinated some Europeans in the nineteenth century, the shogunate had to pay the indemnities to the families. The Tokugawa had their own samurai loyal to them. Most of them served as bureaucrats within the shogunate. The Tokugawa shoguns could not reach into another lord's domain and withdraw men or resources. The samurai in the 250 to 300 domains that existed throughout the Tokugawa period were loyal to their local lord's clan. Although the shogunate could force a daimyo to supply samurai labor for infrastructure projects, such as building dams or bridges, the shogunate could not bypass the lord. It was the lord's responsibility to fulfill the order. If the shogunate needed more samurai to deal with a rebellion or defend against foreign invasion, it would call upon the most loyal daimyo to mobilize their own samurai. The nineteenth century tested the limits of the shogunate's prerogative. Sometimes lords close to the Tokugawa clan answered the call to mobilize against rebels, but when the Tokugawa clan most needed help, some lords demurred, to disastrous effect.

Daimyo staffed all of the top advisory positions in the shogunate, creating a group that, on the one hand, had their destinies tied to the fate of the shogunate. But as lords, they enjoyed relative autonomy in their own independent domains. Theoretically, no lord could have more than one castle, and even repairs to a castle had to be approved by the shogunate to prevent turning a castle "repair" into an expansion. Even Ieyasu's closest allies were not exempt from this rule. One vassal lord who fought with Ieyasu during the Battle of Sekigahara was punished for expanding his castle: the shogunate confiscated 90 percent of his land and sentenced him to home confinement.

With some exceptions, the shogun relied upon the daimyo to interpret the rules as they saw fit, to enforce them as needed, and to mediate relations with Japan's neighbors. Thus, relations with the Koreans to the east, the Ryukyu Kingdom to the south, and the Ezo lands to the north were all managed by daimyo who lived closest to those countries. The lord of Tsushima Island, located between Japan and Korea, acted as a diplomat between the two countries and monopolized Korean–Japanese trade. The shogunate bestowed the rank of daimyo upon the northernmost clan in Japan, the Matsumae, solely because of their role as a go-between for the Tokugawa and the aborigines in Ezo.

But lords had no jurisdiction across domain borders. When a samurai from one domain committed a crime in another domain, only the Tokugawa regime could order the arrest. The shogunate also wanted to prevent neighboring domains from sending troops into one another's territory, which could be the first step in building a regional army used to overthrow the shogunate. This edict had its drawbacks. When the shogunate needed help putting down an insurrection in the south, an event known as the Shimabara Rebellion (1637–38), lords close to the conflict refused to help, fearing that doing so would break the shogunate's rules. Subsequently, the shogunate allowed troops from any domain to cross a border to protect the coasts from invasion or quell insurrection if a domain needed assistance.

To prevent rebellion, the shogunate also wanted to eliminate the age-old practice of using marriage to form strategic alliances. Article eight in the *Codes for Military Houses* explains, "Marriage is the union symbolizing the harmony *of yin* and *yang*, and it cannot be entered into lightly. The Chinese *I-Ching Book of Changes*, says 'Marriage is not to be contracted to create disturbance. Let the longing of male and female for each other be satisfied....To form a factional alliance through marriage is the root of treason.'" Thus, all daimyo marriages had to be approved by the Tokugawa regime.

Early in the Tokugawa period the shoguns enforced rules strictly. To maintain stability in the realm, clans were expected to practice primogeniture; a lord's oldest son, regardless of competency, would become the next daimyo. If a lord did not declare an heir before he died, and if the shogun did not approve the heir himself, then the family lineage could be dissolved and the domain confiscated. Samurai from those domains became "masterless samurai" (*rōnin*) and had to travel to find employment, often ending up in Edo. Complaints from some lords, and the rising problem of masterless samurai causing trouble in Edo, led to the loosening of strict rules beginning in the latter half of the seventeenth century. Thus, while primogeniture was still the norm, lords might delay announcing a son's birth, lie about the birth order of several sons in order to choose a suitable heir, or even postpone announcing the death of a daimyo until the clan's advisors could choose an appropriate successor.

Under a policy of "alternate attendance" (*sankin kōtai*), the shogunate required lords to travel between their home domains and Edo every other year. This practice began as a military expectation, not a requirement. After all, since at least the eleventh century warriors had spent time away from home performing guard duty or some other military service in Kyoto or Kamakura. During the early 1600s, going to Edo to serve the shogun and have an audience with Tokugawa Ieyasu was part of being a close ally. But by the 1640s the practice of alternating time in Edo and the home domain became institutionalized and expected of all lords.

Alternate attendance was rooted in a pre-Tokugawa custom of hostage exchange. Daimyo wives and children lived in Edo permanently to discourage daimyo rebellion. Wives and children were relatively free within the city, but wives were generally forbidden from leaving at all except for pilgrimages to religious sites in the Edo hinterland. In fact, inspectors working at checkpoints along the five official highways that connected Edo to the rest of Japan always monitored samurai women closely. A samurai woman heading away from Edo could indicate the beginning of a rebellion as lords sent their women to safety. For the same reason, travelers heading toward Edo were checked by the inspectors for any guns. Heirs could travel to their domain homeland, but their visits could never overlap with their fathers' presence in the domain—again, to prevent rebellion. Lords expected their teenage heirs to visit the places they would one day rule. But what could attract them to a life in some small, countryside domain? After all, they grew up in the political, commercial, and entertainment capital of Japan. One clan advisor even scolded an heir who, repeatedly citing illness, a common excuse for shirking duties, had refused to visit his domain for many years: "Most daimyo heirs of your status have already made the trip to the domain.... This may lead to rumors that your illness is grave or that there is some discord between you and the lord. People may also be wondering whether you have postponed making the trip to Tosa because you lack the ability to govern."

In addition to keeping a tight leash on the lords' close family, the alternate attendance system drained the lords economically. Even though there was no national tax on the daimyo, the shogunate had ways of extracting economic support from the lords. Daimyo provided funds, labor, and materials to repair the immense Tokugawa castle in Edo and other Tokugawa castles located in other cities, including Kyoto. Lords had to maintain walled compounds in Edo, with a mansion for the family, quarters for full-time servants and guards, barracks for samurai who lived in Edo, stables, training areas, and even gardens. When lords moved back and forth from Edo biennially, they brought with them a retinue of samurai appropriate to the size of the domain as well as a large support staff. Smaller domains might bring only several hundred samurai; larger domains sent several thousand. Edo compounds and the alternate attendance system together composed 50 to 75 percent of a domain's annual budget.

The shogunate coordinated travel so that neighboring lords did not serve in Edo at the same time, perhaps to prevent possible Edo-based collusion between neighbors or to ensure that a lord was always in a particular region in case of uprisings or foreign attack. For the most distant lords, the trip could last several months, and the clan was supposed to pay for food and lodging in the expensive, officially approved inns along the highways. And weather did not always cooperate. Travel back and forth from Edo every other year was a long, burdensome, and costly process. The daimyo were happy to see alternate attendance abandoned when the shogunate weakened and collapsed during the mid-nineteenth century.

Nonetheless, even the strictest laws could be skirted or bent because all of the shogunate's prominent counselors were themselves daimyo and thus sympathized with daimyo burdens. A lord who was busy reforming his domain's finances or otherwise dealing with complex internal political issues could beg off alternate attendance by claiming "illness," the go-to excuse for any samurai bureaucrat desperately seeking a method to protest or skip some duty. A lord required to contribute to a large infrastructure project, such as construction of dams, would also receive a temporary release from alternate attendance. Early in the Tokugawa period, the shogunate expected daimyo to repair Edo Castle, but, in a surprising reversal, the castle went unrepaired while the shogunate sometimes lent money to daimyo to repair their own castles. The shogunate strictly monitored the daimyo in the seventeenth century, but eventually, these inspections became a ritualized affair with few consequences. As long as the lord maintained the appearance of following the shogunate's laws without fail, there were acknowledged workarounds to the daimyo obligations.

Geographically, the most threatening warlords were located far from Edo. A little less than a dozen of the roughly one hundred or so of these "outer" (*tozama*) domains represented some of the largest landholdings in Japan other than those of the Tokugawa clan itself. Many of the outer lords were classified as such because they were not Ieyasu's vassals before 1600. Others received outer daimyo status and were placed far to the south to hem in potentially threatening daimyo. Politically, these *tozama* lords had no access to the decision-making process in the shogunate, but economically they influenced the region around them, especially lords based in the southwest. Some were so powerful, such as the Shimazu clan in the Satsuma domain, that even Tokugawa Ieyasu could not relocate them in the early seventeenth century as he had done to weaker daimyo. Despite the Tokugawa clan's preeminence, it still had to negotiate power with warlords such as the Shimazu in order to solidify its national authority. The oldest and largest outer clans had once been the Tokugawa clan's peers, not subordinates; their claim to power was independent of the Tokugawa. Although the Tokugawa period might have been an era of relative peace, it was not void of tension. Once a year in the Satsuma domain, the samurai dressed in full armor and meditated upon their ancestors' defeat at the Battle of Sekigahara. Warrior mothers in the Chōshū domain told their boys to sleep with their feet facing Edo, an insult to the Tokugawa. For Tokugawa-period samurai, support of, or conflict with, the Tokugawa clan became part of their identity.

The "vassal" (*fudai*) lords served Tokugawa Ieyasu before 1600. Almost half of all lords were vassal daimyo, numbering from just over 100 to a peak of about 130 in the mid-nineteenth century. Some of the most senior vassal lords began as samurai vassals to Ieyasu, men not considered daimyo during the sixteenth century. As the Tokugawa clan and the shogunate expanded, so too did the number of vassal daimyo. Although none of their domains were as large as the largest outer domains, they staffed all of the important offices within the shogunate. Theoretically, the shogunate expected them to serve in times of need; their destiny was tied to that of the shogunate. But they were also potential rivals. Ieyasu confiscated lands from several powerful vassal lords over minor pretexts and even eliminated some clan lines entirely. By the end of the Tokugawa period, however, the title of *vassal* was merely symbolic. It granted a lord the privilege to hold positions in the shogunate but it otherwise guaranteed no special treatment. Many of these daimyo refused to help the shogunate when it attacked rivals in the mid-1860s.

A smaller group of "related" (*shimpan*) lords, never more than around twenty, had kinship ties to the Tokugawa clan itself. The most trusted decision-makers typically came from these families, who were supposed to be the most loyal to the Tokugawa and the shogunate. Their domains were located close enough to Edo to protect it, but not too close—allies and relatives could still be a threat, even in a peaceful era. Some had no landholdings at all. One clan, the Mito, was exempt from alternate attendance and instead resided permanently in Edo. Of these *shimpan* lords, the so-called three houses, the three major branches of the Tokugawa clan, used the Tokugawa surname and supplied heirs to the shogun when one was not otherwise forthcoming.

The samurai life cycle

With some exceptions, birth was the only entrance into the warrior status group. Samurai girls learned how to care for a future husband and his family, while boys learned what it meant to serve the domain, its lord, and his household. Samurai children, even those of modest means, grew up in a household staffed with commoner servants. Families felt pressure to keep up appearances even if they could not afford it. Family planning through abortion or infanticide was a common option for samurai and commoners alike. Health problems compounded a family's financial challenges. Children of both statuses were susceptible to the same diseases, such as smallpox, which could be fatal. Some samurai children, especially those of elite families, faced at least one danger that most commoners did not—lead poisoning. A samurai woman's makeup contained lead that could pass to infants during breastfeeding. In general, commoners also maintained a more diverse diet while samurai suffered from a thiamine deficiency, called beriberi, because they ate too much polished rice and few other grains and little meat. Ironically, commoners who worked in the fields were usually more physically fit as well.

If a samurai boy survived childhood, he passed through several phases marked by changes in clothing and hairstyle until he became an adult, officially, sometime between twelve and sixteen years of age. As with everything else in early modern Japan, there was no uniform approach to samurai education. In general, a boy began his studies around seven years of age outside the home, with tutors and mentors acting as his primary source of early education. Friendships formed at this age were important; childhood peers became colleagues during their adult working life. Mentors and older boys might court a younger boy romantically, even securing permission from the father to establish a relationship. This could blossom into a close platonic friendship in adulthood—though sometimes these affairs became violent.

In the eighteenth century, daimyo started to build domain schools where young samurai studied classical Chinese texts including Confucius's *Analects*, or Japanese military tales such as the *Tale of Heike*, which recounted the war between the Taira and Minamoto families. In addition to basic reading and writing skills, boys learned ethics and what it meant to be a warrior. Not all samurai education was created equal; inequality within the warrior status group began at a young age. In the seventeenth century, boys born into higher-ranking samurai families typically received more education than those at the bottom, but in general, education and literacy rates rose over time.

Not surprisingly, samurai teenagers studied martial arts, either through private training halls (*dōjō*), at a domain school, or a mixture of both. Even martial arts became a source for discrimination among samurai. Only wealthy, higher-ranking samurai might learn how to ride a horse, which was considered a martial art, or study how to shoot from horseback (*yabusame*).

Swordsmanship, however, could be studied by warriors of all stripes. A typical practice session might include engaging in predetermined attack and defense drills (*kata*) with wooden swords and repetition of basic techniques. But lords and high-ranking samurai dominated certain styles, such as Yagyū Shinkage-ryū, the first institutionalized style of swordsmanship. It was named after the Yagyū family, whose headmen taught swordsmanship to the Tokugawa shoguns and received daimyo status for doing so. Like the relationship between artists and shoguns during the Muromachi period (1336–1573), the Yagyū masters met other intellectuals through their connection to the Tokugawa shoguns, and that interaction influenced how swordsmanship was institutionalized and taught. In some domains, samurai students who studied an elite style like Yagyū Shinkage-ryū received a stipend for their equipment and training. They even demonstrated their skills in front of their local lord as part of annual events. Lower-ranking samurai also studied swordsmanship but were limited to lesser-known, newer, or even local styles. Those students often did not receive stipends or permission to perform before their lord. Since these styles did not have as close a connection to warrior officialdom, however, their practitioners could be more creative in how they developed their art—low-ranking samurai engaged in freestyle fencing, the forerunner to the modern sport of kendo.

The shogunate expected samurai to be prepared to mobilize in case of insurrection or invasion, but most samurai had little interest in military training. They rarely practiced beyond their teenage years and, as adults, only attended the occasional mandatory training sessions—Tokugawa samurai had become "sword-wearing bureaucrats." Primarily, samurai used martial arts as a way to connect to their warrior heritage or to interact with men like themselves. They were less concerned about practical application in combat. In many domains, military preparedness was no longer a fact of life. During the latter half of the Tokugawa period, lords no longer required the lowest-ranking samurai to own rifles or carry bows. In fact, martial skills needed to apprehend criminals were considered the lowliest of arts, because samurai rarely conducted physical police-type work. Outcasts and other marginalized commoners hunted down and arrested criminals, guarded prisoners, and tortured and executed offenders.

In adulthood, a Tokugawa samurai's life revolved around his family and the domain. Honor, as far as there was such a notion, was defined by one's conduct and loyalty to the lord's family. Gone were the days of serving a powerful warlord who might have commanded respect by his prowess on the battlefield or his political acuity. The Tokugawa custom of primogeniture did not always guarantee an able or charismatic lord. Thus, samurai worked to uphold the domain's reputation rather than to act out of love for a daimyo. They idealized the legacy passed down from Warring States–era predecessors and honored fictitious ties to famous clans such as the Minamoto or Kyoto nobles like the Fujiwara. A samurai's career trajectory was determined, in order of importance, by the rank of the family, seniority, and talent.

The oldest son typically inherited his father's position. This included a job that might be as menial as guarding one of the gates to the local domain castle for several months out of the year or as important as becoming one of the lord's closest advisors. The situation was worse for younger brothers, who were not guaranteed consistent work by the domain. Since the oldest brother inherited the family property as well, the younger brothers were at his mercy. If they were lucky, they could marry into an heirless warrior family or be adopted by a childless samurai. Otherwise, they had to find some temporary employment or abandon their samurai status. Samurai who tired of searching for menial domain jobs, especially second and third sons, left the samurai life to become scholars, writers, priests, and teachers.

Older scholarship about Tokugawa samurai exaggerated the lack of social mobility within the samurai status. There is a certain intuitive appeal to this argument; warriors before the Tokugawa period could rise through the ranks based on their exploits in war, but in an age of peace, few opportunities existed for a samurai to showcase his talents. Recent scholarship tends to correct past assumptions about samurai inertia. A samurai born into a high-ranking family might begin his career with simple work. As he grew older and demonstrated talent, the domain advisors would give him more responsibility. Low-ranking samurai faced more difficulties rising through those social ranks, but even then, especially when domains faced fiscal or political crises, some could be promoted based on talent alone.

Most rank-and-file samurai were not busy with official duties. Samurai who lived in Edo during their tenure on alternate attendance worked for a few hours every day, and then, with permission from their lord, left the domain compound to go on pilgrimages to Edo-area temples and shrines, essentially a form of sightseeing. Merchants sets up stalls to sell their wares, while street performers and fortune tellers flocked to take advantage of tourists, transforming some temple properties into permanent fairgrounds. Even today, Asakusa Shrine in Tokyo attracts tourists as it did throughout the Tokugawa period. Aside from gambling, drinking, and, if they could afford it, visits to the pleasure quarters like Yoshiwara, samurai studied literature, poetry, music, martial arts, and philosophy alongside commoners or samurai from other domains.

Many samurai supplemented their meager hereditary income with small-scale work. Called *by-employments*, these included micro farming, weaving, pottery-making, trade, and handicraft production (like toys and umbrellas). But not all samurai used their time so nobly. Some of the lowest-ranking samurai gambled, begged, and borrowed their way through life. Katsu Kokichi, a nineteenth-century samurai, recounts his life as a ne'er-do-well in an autobiography written as a warning to his son, the statesman Katsu Kaishū. Kokichi was born the second son of the Otani, an undistinguished samurai family connected to the Tokugawa clan. His father was not a warrior but the third son of a wealthy, blind moneylender who was adopted into the Otani family. He then married into the Katsu family and became its heir. Despite his newly acquired samurai status, Kokichi could not find any steady employment and lived on a meager hereditary stipend, as many lowly samurai did. He eked out a living by renting out a small plot of land, buying and selling swords, begging, stealing, and engaging in other shady activities, some of which landed him in trouble. Like many samurai, he spent much of his life in debt. One samurai writer complained about poor warriors: "They head for guard duty wearing outfits that they have conned the pawnbroker into temporarily restoring to them. Once they have come back from guard duty, they return the outfits directly to the pawnbroker. Their servants mock them for this."

A family history written during the 1930s details similar hardships for a samurai clan from the Mito domain. Despite living hand to mouth, samurai families were under pressure to maintain standards of appearance. As the samurai proverb tells it, "A hungry samurai keeps a toothpick in his mouth even if he has nothing to eat." They had to maintain a certain number of retainers commensurate with the family's rank. In theory, these retainers would join the master of the house during military campaigns, but with war unlikely, this practice became a meaningless custom. Thus, samurai hired commoner men on a temporary basis to accompany them during ceremonial events.

The commoner–samurai gray zone

Did commoners ever dream of becoming samurai? Wealthy rural commoners often used their position and wealth to accrue warrior privileges, such as the right to carry swords or use their surname in official documents. But for the most part, they did not want the drudgery of a low-ranking warrior job. Still, some commoners during the seventeenth century petitioned to receive samurai status. Kian was one such commoner who dreamed of becoming a warrior. His grandmother, the daughter of a samurai, raised him, so he grew up listening to her stories about warriors. As the fourth son of the family, he could not hope to carry on his family's trade, which would pass to his oldest brother. So, in 1655, at age sixteen, he began researching his family's history in order to secure warrior status. He asked neighbors to share documents they had, and he visited the local Buddhist temple to look for old gravestones and records. He eventually abandoned his quest and became the heir to another commoner family, but he still used his research to coauthor a history of the region.

It was rare, but possible, for a commoner to achieve warrior status. An elite commoner could marry into a low-ranking warrior family and become its heir, as Katsu Kokichi's father did. Domain officials granted warrior status to well-known fencing teachers of commoner status in order to employ them as official sword teachers. Wealthy merchants who lent daimyo large sums of money acquired samurai status and worked as economic advisors to the domain. A poor samurai could "sell" his status by officially adopting a commoner as an adult. Often these examples of status crossing were only superficial, used to show off to other commoners, and carried no obligations or offers of actual warrior employment. In any case, a commoner wealthy enough to buy samurai privileges would not desire the lowly, unprofitable work of a samurai.

Complicating the divide between commoners and warriors were those who occupied a gray zone. In many domains, a group of people known by various titles such as "rural samurai" or "landed samurai" lived in the villages and claimed, falsely or otherwise, to have warrior ancestry. They could carry swords or use a surname in an official capacity and represented domain interests in the countryside. In parts of the Kanto region outside of Edo, when wandering gangs of young men caused disorder in the nineteenth century, the shogunate asked landed samurai to establish and train local militias. Daimyo bestowed landed samurai status on rural entrepreneurs for their contributions to the domain, such as bringing new lands into production, which added to the domain's tax base. In Edo, too, entire families known as the "thousand men of the same mind" (*sennin dōshin*), who originally worked as guards during the Warring States period, served as minor officials on the outskirts of Edo. These families interacted socially, often intermarried, and maintained a strong communal identity. Some even trained together in their own style of swordsmanship, Tennen Rishin-ryū, in order to express pride in their warrior ancestry. Shogunate officials sometimes acknowledged them as "warriors"; after all, sennin dōshin worked for the shogunate. At other times, the shogunate revoked their privileges, considering them mere commoners, much to their chagrin.

Despite such warrior–commoner gray zones, samurai writers claimed that no commoner could ever become a true samurai. The most widely read military text of the Tokugawa period, *The Military Mirror of Kai*, stated, "Even if a townsman imitates a samurai his heart is still that of a merchant. In the heat of battle he would worry about losing his property. He lacks the essence of bushido and would not be of any use." In this case, the term *bushido* does not refer to an institutionalized "code" of behavior for the samurai, as no such code existed. It simply indicated the fundamental difference between samurai and commoners: a samurai was born into his status and performed whatever duties were expected of him, even if that work overlapped with commoner occupations. Other than paying taxes and providing corvée labor, a commoner had no such intimate ties to the warrior regime. For more than 260 years, the warrior regime kept nonsamurai out of its decision-making process while also attempting to limit, often unsuccessfully, what commoners could do in their daily lives. It is no wonder that most people, even some samurai, were glad to see warrior authority collapse.

Chapter 5
Inventing the samurai

It might seem that an invisible wall separates samurai and nonsamurai, and, thus, we think of their inherent differences: samurai could wear two swords and use surnames whereas commoners could not; samurai resided in the castle towns while peasants lived far away in the countryside. Commoner–warrior relations were often antagonistic. Commoners had to pay taxes to the warrior regime, and warriors, in theory, could cut down a commoner if he insulted a samurai, a practice referred to as a "disrespect killing" (*burei uchi*). As generalizations, these might be true sometimes. Records indicate that in one domain a disrespect killing occurred about once every four years. But rather than trace the differences and antagonisms between samurai and commoners, we should consider their similarities. If the age of the samurai began during the Tokugawa period, then so too did the modern idealized image of Japanese warriors.

In establishing the samurai as a distinct social group, the shoguns unwittingly created an idealized image of the samurai that was available for consumption by commoners as well. The samurai might have numbered no more than 8 percent of the national population, but the invention of samurai identity during the Tokugawa era penetrated commoner culture. Commoners imitated, celebrated, parodied, and criticized samurai. When swordsmanship became a social activity to help create bonds among samurai men, wealthy commoner men wanted to participate. Manuals that taught samurai men how to conduct themselves in a romantic relationship with their juniors became popular among wealthy merchants, too. Even kabuki theater, the exemplar of urban culture, associated with red-light districts, commoners, and gaudy presentation, existed in Edo City, initially, as theater performed mostly in daimyo compounds for a warrior audience.

The collapse of the last samurai regime is often explained in terms of domestic political upheavals, economic woe, and foreign pressure. But at least some of the decline can be explained by the recognition among samurai and commoners that an irreconcilable gap existed between samurai ideals and samurai reality, a gap that had been widening throughout the Tokugawa period.

Even the most mundane features of samurai life became a source of fascination for commoners. The most widely read text in Tokugawa Japan was the "warrior roster" (*bukan*). Published several times a year, it listed details of all the daimyo in Japan and most of the prominent samurai working in the shogunate. It included family crests, clan lineage, addresses, gifts received from and given to the shogun, the distance from a lord's compound to Edo Castle, and the positions samurai held in the Tokugawa regime. Samurai needed to know who their colleagues and superiors were within the Tokugawa bureaucracy, especially because jobs constantly changed. But the quantity of rosters published suggests that commoners purchased them even more than samurai. Commoners in big cities like Edo, Osaka, or Kyoto, where the rosters were sold, needed these details to serve their samurai customers. Identifying a samurai crest during a daimyo procession or knowing where to deliver products was part of doing business. But possessing and updating the rosters for free at a bookstore several times a year by having new pages pasted in was much like the excitement of obtaining the latest baseball roster in the modern world. In other words, commoners enjoyed access to information about warriors that had been unavailable to them before the seventeenth century.

The simple act of publishing information about samurai and daimyo differentiated Tokugawa-era warriors from their predecessors. This process had roots in an earlier era when warrior identity was defined through texts. Elite, literate warriors in the fifteenth and sixteenth centuries learned warrior culture through etiquette manuals (*kojitsu*) that described appropriate behavior such as how to dress during ceremonies or to conduct oneself during an archery competition. Warrior customs and rituals dated back to the Kamakura period but applied mostly to the housemen who lived in or frequented Kamakura city itself. Writings about warrior culture in general increased during the Muromachi period, when warriors and nobility interacted with greater frequency and royal culture influenced warrior thought. Etiquette manuals from that time continued to be popular during the Tokugawa period, but the rosters did more than simply trace the contours of elite warrior culture. They defined exactly what made warriors important. Moreover, they created a degree of occupational uniformity that had not existed much before the seventeenth century.

Newly installed lords and elite warriors took seriously the pressure to define themselves. Many unemployed samurai (*rōnin*), who had been left adrift in the aftermath of the Warring States period, found work as teachers and advisors to daimyo in Edo and castle towns throughout Japan. These masterless samurai helped families plan and participate in warrior ceremonies that increasingly became part of warrior social life, especially in Edo. Minor lords had to create genealogies in order to foster clan identity where previously there had been none. Wandering samurai also published military histories and military science books, such as the early Tokugawa-era text *Military Mirror of Kai*, whose author, Obata Kagenori, became a sought-after teacher of military science.

Warrior ideals

Commoners were exposed to warrior values through popular culture. In Edo, kabuki began as theater for largely warrior audiences, and as such, plays celebrated warrior heroes and values. After kabuki opened to the masses, the Edo dandy replaced the warrior as the archetypal hero, but even he was depicted as embodying warrior traits such as bravery, martial prowess, and loyalty.

The most frequently performed kabuki play was called *The Treasury of Loyal Retainers*, also known as the *Akō Incident* or the *47 Rōnin*. It appeared first as a puppet play based on a historical event that occurred in the early eighteenth century when a daimyo named Asano attacked a senior shogunate samurai, Kira, during a ceremony within the shogun's castle. It is unclear why Asano assaulted Kira, but it is commonly believed that Kira insulted Asano for not knowing proper etiquette. Kira, a master of ceremony for nearly forty years, was in charge of ensuring that all attendees knew their roles, including the much younger, small-domain-holding Asano.

Since drawing a sword in the shogun's castle was forbidden, shogunate police immediately arrested Asano, "executed" him by *seppuku* (ritual suicide by disembowelment and decapitation performed by a trusted colleague, if one was lucky), and dissolved his Akō domain, forcing his retainers to become masterless samurai (rōnin). After nearly two years of planning to avenge their lord's death, forty-six of the forty-seven rōnin attacked and killed Kira. Some contemporaries argued that the rōnin hoped to avoid harsh punishment because their actions reflected loyalty to their lord. Instead, they were sentenced to seppuku. Earlier warrior regimes had no single form of capital punishment, nor did pre-Tokugawa-era samurai disembowel themselves often. But Tokugawa-era samurai idealized seppuku as warrior machismo of a bygone time, going as far as writing manuals standardizing the ritual. The Tokugawa shogunate established seppuku as capital punishment.

Although the incident itself passed with little comment when it first occurred, audiences loved the dramatized versions. The attack and mass ritualized suicide made for dramatic scenes. Moreover, these were lowly samurai acting in unison against authorities and sacrificing themselves as a group, a theme that might have appealed to urban commoners who often interacted with low-ranking warriors.

On the one hand, the historical event and its subsequent popularity represented a crisis for Tokugawa samurai because it exposed the tension between warrior ideals and warrior reality. Samurai, as men of action, were supposed to display loyalty to their lord's clan and domain. They celebrated past warrior heroes and their bravado. On the other hand, samurai were no longer supposed to be violent. The shogunate attempted to prevent war at the top, among daimyo, through rules for daimyo activity such as expanding castles, pursuing warrior crimes across borders, and the like. It also forbade samurai from engaging in fights and punishing offenders with execution. Samurai writers promoted Confucian learning and self-cultivation, not violence, as admirable traits. In other words, how could a samurai think of himself as a warrior in a world with no warfare and without being violent? That tension was never fully resolved during the Tokugawa period, and samurai pundits did not agree on any one image of the ideal samurai.

Some samurai writers praised the forty-seven rōnin because they acted out of a personal sense of loyalty to their lord. Others argued that the rōnin had acted improperly because it was not Kira who killed their lord; the shogunate executed Asano for his criminal offense—the shogunate's law trumped personal notions of action, honor, and loyalty. One writer criticized them for waiting more than a year to carry out an attack when they should have killed

Kira immediately after Asano's execution. Hayashi Hōkō, head of the Confucian academy in Edo, synthesized the two views, citing classic Chinese texts to explain the heart of being a warrior.

> First I will view their vendetta from the perspective of the hearts of the forty-six men. It was imperative that they "not share the same sky with their master's enemy" and that they "sleep on reeds, using their sword as a pillow" [both quotations from the Chinese *Record of Rites*]. To hang onto life by enduring shame and humiliation is not the way of the samurai. We must also consider the vendetta from the perspective of the law. Anyone who sees the law as his enemy must be put to death....These two perspectives are hardly identical, but they might complement each other in operation, without contradiction. Above, there must be humane rulers and wise ministers who govern by clarifying law and promulgating decrees. Below, there must be loyal retainers and righteous samurai who readily vent their anger in the determined pursuit of their cause.

The eighteenth-century book *In the Shadow of Leaves* (*Hagakure*) contains the most extreme reaction to the bind between the violent legacy of warriors and their pacification. Tokugawa warriors would, in theory, be executed for fighting each other regardless of the reason. So what should a samurai do if he is insulted by another samurai, especially a lower-ranking one? He could be executed and his family punished if he attacked the offender. But if he ignored the slight, he risked losing face in front of his warrior peers. The answer, according to Yamamoto, the book's author, was to choose death. Yamamoto had his own opinion of the forty-seven rōnin—they should have killed Kira immediately without worrying about their fate. Dishonor was worse than the death of an individual samurai because his death is singular while dishonor can spread to his family and, more importantly, could affect the reputation of his lord's clan. The *Hagakure*'s opening line, "The way of the samurai is in death," and his criticism of local samurai and the shogunate made it quite controversial. It circulated privately among samurai in the Nabeshima domain and was generally unknown until its resurrection as propaganda during the height of war and fascism during the 1930s.

Within the Tokugawa world, violence was no longer appropriate samurai behavior. Though cultivating the self by studying the Chinese classics like *The Analects* was part of warrior learning before the seventeenth century, Tokugawa samurai values relied on later Chinese interpretations of those ancient texts, a school of thought called Neo-Confucianism. Neo-Confucianism informed Tokugawa samurai attitudes toward lord, family, and society. "Cultured" learning (*bun*) should still be tempered with training in martial learning (*bu*), argued warrior leaders, but there were no longer opportunities to display one's martial prowess other than within the confines of martial arts practice. Martial arts had become nothing more than the physical manifestation of *bun*-focused cultivation.

These values did not square with the reality of most samurai who, like Katsu Kokichi, worried about basic survival. And if they had at least some pretension of wealth, they were more interested in pursuing extracurricular activities. The putative golden age of samurai identity always existed in an idealized past. As one samurai commentator complained in 1818, "In past ages, it was common for warriors to mock those who pursue elegance as 'courtiers.' Now, though, it is the better warriors who behave like courtiers; the majority have become like women."

Samurai writers connected this "spiritual" impoverishment to economic decline, and they often blamed urbanization for the stain of commoner fashions on warrior lifestyle. One intellectual chastised warriors in Edo for spending money "as if living in an inn." By being forced to move back into the countryside, samurai would be allowed to return to a self-sufficient lifestyle, live a simpler life, and relearn the "purer" warrior values reminiscent of an earlier age. Others noted that urban commoners would follow samurai to the countryside and focus on farming rather than working for the large samurai populations in castle towns.

Beginning in the eighteenth century, the shogunate enacted a series of reforms to address the twin problems of samurai economic distress and declining samurai identity. Matsudaira Sadanobu, the grandson of the eighth Tokugawa shogun, a senior advisor in the shogunate and the architect of late eighteenth-century reforms, envisioned a Confucian-styled society based on order, with the morally superior gentlemen warriors firmly at the top. The reform included edicts that tried to censor publications, curtail merchant activity, and eliminate heterodox teachings. But he was particularly interested in cutting shogunate expenses and demanded that samurai practice frugality and focus on developing their *bun* and *bu*. He too idealized the rural origins of the samurai and took his own samurai retainers on hikes in the countryside.

Despite the warrior authorities' attempts to reinvigorate samurai identity and behavior, samurai themselves poked fun at the image. A well-known satirical response to Sadanobu's reform went, "*Bun bu, bun bu,* I can't sleep at night!" Many of these writers, who came from low-ranking samurai families, abandoned dead-end careers for intellectual pursuits. One such man was Hiraga Gennai, a teacher, writer, and inventor who lampooned the stuffy samurai image in an essay titled "On Farting" (1771) about a performer who excelled at farting as a musical talent. Gennai used a country bumpkin samurai named "Crankshaw Stonington, Esquire," as the straight man to critique warrior values. Crankshaw admonished the fartist and the crowd, telling them that the shogunate allowed street performances in order to teach the public about fealty and loyalty; he cited the forty-seven rōnin incident depicted in the *Treasury of Loyalty Retainers* as an example. "Flatulence," he added, "is, after all, a personal matter and should not be aired in public. Any proper samurai would be mortified to the point of suicide if he were inadvertently to let, uh, fly in polite company." Gennai's critique illustrates how commoners appropriated culture in their own ways, even as the shogunate tried to promote warrior values via popular culture. He also mocked the notion of samurai honor—even a harmless fart could push a samurai to commit suicide rather than risk public shame.

Samurai parody frequently appeared in popular literature as well. The Tokugawa period's most famous novel, *Shank's Mare*, written by the son of a minor warrior, recounts the adventures of two men, Kita and Yaji, who drink, play, and bumble their way from Kyoto to Edo. In a roadside bar the two encounter a drunk samurai, a few young women (one of them named Shime), and a buffoon:

> "Oh, you horrid man," cried the girls. "Look at his face. Look what strange eyes he makes. How bright and glaring they are!"

> "You are insulting," cried the samurai, in a sudden burst of anger. "Look at your own faces instead of mine…" He stood up, but the waitresses caught hold of him. "There, There," they said. "There's nothing for you to get angry about."

> "Don't be rude, Shime," said the buffoon. "I'll tell you what we'll do. We're getting rather bored, so to liven things up, let's be as jolly as if we were in a steam bath."

> "A steam bath is an empty bath," said the samurai. "He takes me for an idiot. I've a good mind to beat him for his rudeness." Apparently the samurai was an angry drunk.

The samurai summoned the girls and the buffoon to entertain him for the evening, but in the end, he tried to reinforce the notion that nonsamurai should know their proper place when interacting with a samurai, twice accusing them of rudeness. But rather than cower from him, they continued to tease him, knowing that his drunkenness and futile attempts to lord his status over them only made him seem powerless.

9. The artist Hokusai, best known for his "Great Wave" woodblock print, pokes fun at the warrior sense of duty. Here three retainers wait close by, unwavering, as their master smells up the outhouse.

Writers and artists understood that bodily functions were the same across class divides, and they used bathroom humor to critique any group, especially samurai, that put on airs. The artist Hokusai, famous for his "Great Wave" woodblock print, published a book of prints containing a scene titled "Privy," which depicts samurai retainers standing dutifully by while their superior relieves himself. The three retainers believe in the samurai ideals all too much, sacrificing their own comfort in the name of duty.

Commoners and warrior identity

Unlike their pre-Tokugawa counterparts, commoners helped create warrior culture. They purchased warrior rosters, studied swordsmanship, hired warrior tutors, and bought military-related books. They celebrated samurai ideals in popular culture, both in rural areas and in the cities. Villagers in the countryside organized kabuki plays that featured battle scenes with large casts that incorporated members of local youth associations. Quite simply, war plays broke the monotony of everyday life. Some commoners even studied martial arts not only for self-defense and as a way to rub elbows with samurai but also to use the techniques in rural theater and village festivals.

To a certain extent, samurai writers promoted commoner participation in warrior culture. Commoners either read or listened to public recitations of a fourteenth-century war tale called *The Chronicle of Great Peace* (*Taiheiki*). The *Taiheiki* recounted the conflict between the northern and southern courts in that era. The authors glorified Emperor Go-Daigo's general Kusunoki Masashige and celebrated values such as loyalty and self-sacrifice. As an educational text, it taught young commoners how to read Chinese characters (*kanji*) and imparted moral lessons. The *Taiheiki* was so well known that authors used it as a historical setting to comment on politically sensitive events—the forty-seven rōnin incident, for example—rather than risk arrest for writing about taboo topics.

Other pre–Tokugawa period warrior texts circulated among commoners and samurai. Books like *A Woman's Imagawa* and *A Commoner's Imagawa* copied themes found in the fifteenth-century "Imagawa Letter," a widely read letter of advice to warriors, and emphasized the importance of cultured learning (*bun*). Of course, not all peasants could read, but some village headmen lectured to villagers about morals using the same military writings popular among samurai.

The shogunate alternatively forbade and encouraged the most martial of samurai activities, namely, swordsmanship and archery. Consider the following 1805 edict from the shogunate that circulated throughout the nineteenth century in many domains surrounding Edo:

> We have heard that in this region there are unemployed samurai wandering about. Peasants are learning martial arts and gathering together for practice which might cause them to ignore their agricultural work. They forget their status and become uppity. They should be told to stop and martial art instructors should not introduce their arts to the villagers.

The edict introduces several issues facing warrior authorities during the nineteenth century. It begins by illustrating samurai unemployment. *Rōnin* who were desperate to make a living ignored shogunal decrees that prohibited them from making warrior culture available to commoners. By providing samurai culture to commoners in the form of martial arts instruction or tutoring, they unintentionally recognized its universal appeal and applicability to anyone who could afford it. Wealth, not birth, could buy at least some warrior fantasy. Commoners had eclipsed warriors as an economic force even though warriors controlled the land. Sadanobu's reforms and the ones that followed it failed to solve the decline of samurai identity and economic woe. The edict also demonstrates that the regime could not prevent commoners from appropriating warrior culture in their own way. Whether commoners were emulating or parodying them, samurai did not control how they were perceived or how they were portrayed.

As economic and social disorder spread throughout the greater Edo region during the mid-nineteenth century, the shogunate began to rely on commoners to provide self-defense. Its Kantō Regulatory Patrol, created to deal with rising criminality in the Edo hinterland, depended on rural elites for information about local criminals. Villages joined together to form defense leagues. They were organized by larger, wealthier villages that hosted criminal holding centers. The village headmen received privileges typically reserved for samurai—the right to wear swords and use surnames in official documents. League members practiced swordsmanship for its practical use and to strengthen internal social cohesion.

The increasing presence of Westerners in the seas around Japan exposed many structural weaknesses of warrior rule. Officials in Edo were so worried that the imperial Ise Shrine was vulnerable to Westerners that after an 1855 inspection, they asked the Shinto priests to survey temple bells that could be melted down to be used for cannons and rifles and to start training commoners in martial arts, especially gunnery, as a first step toward local defense against invasion. This effort culminated in 1863 when the shrine formed a peasant militia. Peasant militias became more common in the mid-nineteenth century as foreign and domestic threats were too much for the shogunate to contain with warriors alone. Warrior reality, it seems, could not match the heroic feats enacted on stage, in books, and in the fencing academies.

Collapse and "restoration"

There were many problems that led to the Meiji Restoration (1868), a conflict between samurai led by *tozama* daimyo who fought in the name of the teenage Meiji emperor and the Tokugawa shogunate and its allies. Although it was not as large a war as the US Civil War, it nonetheless has the status of being the mythic "origin" of modern Japan. In the decades before the Restoration, several interconnected problems squeezed the samurai regime and warriors in general: the threat from Western countries, strife within the shogunate itself, and the changing relationship between samurai and nonsamurai. These pressures originated in the early seventeenth century at the latest and arose from policies enacted by the warrior regime to maintain samurai hegemony.

By the early nineteenth century, leaders in the shogunate worried about how to address the growing presence of Westerners on the edges of Japan. In 1825, as more European ships tested Japan's waters, coastal daimyo were ordered to fire on those ships to drive them away, an effort that was largely unsuccessful. The shogunate eventually abandoned that order, but it illustrates the shogunate's inability to adequately prepare for foreign threats. More American whaling ships in the Pacific and increasing trade in China led to a rising number of shipwrecked sailors in Japan. The British, French, Dutch, and Russians had been trying to expand commercial access and diplomatic relations throughout Asia, and the shogunate did not want to fall prey, as the Chinese had done during the Opium Wars (1839–42), to a series of conflicts over Britain's opium trafficking in China. To some warriors, the Europeans were nothing more than opportunistic merchants, an occupation that samurai deemed selfish and lowly. But these warriors believed that if they could contain foreign merchant activity to Nagasaki, they could avoid diplomatic entanglements. Unlike in Europe, trade among East Asian countries at the time did not presuppose any diplomatic relations between governments. During the latter half of the eighteenth century, after repeated attempts by Russians to open relations to Japan, the shogunate allowed them to conduct minor trade in Nagasaki, hoping that this would mollify them. It did not, and a Russian captain landed on Tsushima Island in 1861 and demanded that the daimyo there lease him land. Unable to scare the Russians off, the shogunate had to ask the British for help.

Western pressure culminated with the arrival of US admiral Matthew Perry in Edo Bay in 1853. The shogunate had heard from the Dutch and the Ryukyu kingdom that Perry was on his way, but the appearance of his "black ships" so close to Edo instead of Nagasaki caused a panic within the shogunate's leadership. Many samurai were benignly curious rather than deeply perturbed. Warrior officials and American ship personnel peacefully examined each other's weapons. Nonetheless, Perry's demand that the shogunate respond to President Millard Fillmore's request to establish at least limited trade and diplomatic exchange, if not an outright treaty, affected the shogunate's relationship to both the daimyo and the imperial institution.

Perry promised to return in a year's time with better-armed ships. In the interim, the chief senior advisor in the shogunate, Abe Masahiro, broke Tokugawa precedent by asking all of the daimyo, including those from the outer domains who were typically shut out of the formal decision-making process in the shogunate, for their opinions on how to respond to the Americans. Why, after a little over two hundred years of keeping them at political arm's length, would the shogunate need their voice?

The answer to that question connects to an issue that all prominent warrior families had faced since at least the beginning of the Kamakura period, and possibly earlier—the problem of succession. The Tokugawa shogun at the time, Ieyoshi, died only weeks after Perry arrived the first time, and his successor, Iesada, was weak politically and physically, having suffered from several diseases since childhood. Abe and his supporters controlled the shogunate's policies but did not do so with impunity. He needed consensus because the shogunate was weak.

Unfortunately for Abe, a consensus was not forthcoming. Daimyo response ranged from some form of "opening the country" to the Americans by engaging in trade and learning from their science and technology to an insistence that all American requests be rejected, even if doing so risked an unwinnable war. When Perry returned in 1854, Abe signed the Treaty of Kanagawa. Neither he nor the daimyo who supported a treaty embraced the West per se. The treaty did not guarantee the Americans much, and Japan avoided war, but criticism from many daimyo, politically influential nobles in Kyoto, and samurai loyalists to the emperor and its institution was swift and powerful.

When studying the Tokugawa shogunate, it is easy to forget about the other perennial issue in samurai history: every regime's interaction with the court and emperor in Kyoto. The Kyoto nobility did not influence political and social events in Tokugawa Japan to the same degree it did before the seventeenth century. The nobility and emperors remained in Kyoto, and few Japanese knew or cared about them. People encountered royalty only in history writing. But because history writing is always done with an agenda, whether the author knows it or not, people understood the imperial institution through the lens of samurai authors. Historical works published throughout the Tokugawa period had to assess Go-Daigo's Kenmu Restoration of 1333. Was his southern court the legitimate imperial line that had been wronged? Was Ashikaga Takauji a rebel who acted against the imperial institution or an admirable leader who was justified in creating a new shogunate once Go-Daigo's leadership had descended into chaos? Was Takauji to be demonized or celebrated? And what did the answers to those questions mean for warrior legitimacy as it related to the supposed divine lineage of the emperors? No single view dominated, but when Kyoto residents awoke on a late winter morning in 1863 to find the decapitated heads of three Ashikaga shoguns pilloried along the Kamo River, clearly the pro-emperor views had gained currency as never before. The accompanying placard labeled "vengeance of heaven" portended bad things to come for the shogunate. Heaven, in this act, sided with the imperial institution and not with the Ashikaga shoguns who inherited Takauji's legacy.

The Tokugawa period was the apex of warrior dominance in Japanese history and especially shogunal authority over the court. Political dominance should not be understood as a complete lack of political influence for the court, however. Respect for the emperor and the imperial legacy spread among the samurai in the latter half of the Tokugawa era, in part as a result of history writing.

In the seventeenth century, the Mito domain, led by a daimyo family tied to the Tokugawa clan itself, began an immense history-writing project titled *The Great History of Japan*; it was completed in 1906. As with much scholarly work in Japan before the twentieth century, the text was influenced by Chinese thought, in this case, Neo-Confucianism. It also followed Chinese historical style by tracing change over time through the descent of the emperor. Samurai teachers used the content as teaching materials, and its focus on the emperors influenced several generations of samurai who took seriously the twin themes of loyalty and imperial prestige. By the time Perry arrived, writers who had followed a wide range of schools of thought, from ancient Chinese learning to nativist teachings about Japan, and even those who dedicated their lives to studying imported European texts, had been convincing many that the Tokugawa clan and its shogunate ruled only at the behest of imperial grace.

Newfound respect for the imperial institution connected to foreign policy, with disastrous results. In 1846, an imperial rescript commanded the shogunate to build coastal defenses. In 1858, the emperor rejected the shogunate's attempt to seek after-the-fact approval for a commercial treaty it signed with the United States. Criticisms leveled against the shogunate by nobles, daimyo, samurai, and even some commoners culminated in unprecedented violence. In 1860, a group of rōnin from the Mito domain descended upon a senior councilor's entourage as it approached Edo Castle. They killed the guards, who had their swords tucked in the scabbards to protect against the snow, and assassinated the councilor, Ii Naosuke, still in his palanquin. Throughout the 1860s, samurai from across Japan, mostly low-ranking, underemployed men, left their domains for Kyoto to gather around the court and like-minded loyalist samurai. Meanwhile, the shogunate tried its best to pursue détente with Kyoto and its supporters, arranging a marriage between the emperor's daughter and a shogun. It also dutifully answered a summons from the court to send the shogun to Kyoto in 1863, illustrating the extent to which the warrior regime had lost its control of the emperor. Humiliated and unable to deny the emperor's command, the shogunate promised to follow an imperial order it could not keep. The shogun, in his ancient role as the general who would "expel the barbarians," agreed to force Europeans out of Japan.

While many daimyo played little role in the Kyoto-shogunate politics and did not feel directly affected by Westerners, they still faced pressure from commoners in their domains. Unlike other revolutions in world history, Japan did not experience a revolutionary movement among commoners. Peasants complained about tax hardships and the bad behavior of local officials, but they never attacked the basic structure of the daimyo–shogunate warrior regime. They drew on the Confucian concept of benevolence to plead for leniency, and if they did not receive it, they could protest. It was a risky strategy, and ringleaders were often executed, sometimes alongside their family members, children included. The most desperate villages sent men to Edo to appeal directly to the shogun himself as he traveled through the city in a covered palanquin. But it was a tactic that could work. In the best-case scenario, the shogunate would investigate a troubled area and force the daimyo to make reforms. At the very least, a protest illustrated daimyo incompetence and could lead to ridicule and punishment, such as confiscating the domain and putting another daimyo in charge.

Villagers could collectively pressure their daimyo, but merchant groups could yank purse strings. Wealthy merchants and rural entrepreneurs held sway over some rank-and-file samurai and in some cases even had access to daimyo. As moneylenders, they could advise daimyo how to enact economic reforms within the domain. Daimyo often looked to commoners to expand industries that would bring more income and tax revenue into the domain. Among middle-ranking samurai who drew their stipends and other resources from villages assigned to them in the countryside, several employed villagers in their mansions in Edo or followed demands that the family change its spendthrift ways or be cut off from future loans. And when Japan's economy encountered global capitalism, merchants in big cities profited from textile trade with Europeans. Trade was so successful that prices of goods skyrocketed throughout the 1860s, and these increases led to riots and "smashings" against warehouses where the wealthy were accused of hoarding goods. Among the many imperial loyalists were commoners, women included, who felt that they too should play a role, no matter how minor, in the future direction of Japan.

The mystique and majesty of warrior rule had dwindled by the 1860s, and those who believed in warrior notions of loyalty, obligation, and action started uprisings around Japan. They attacked what they saw as the most offensive representatives in the shogunate, such as Ii Naosuke, and enemies within their home domains and among the nobility in Kyoto. Factionalism in some domains resulted in small-scale civil wars, numbering hundreds of men on each side, in large outer domains in the south and in the smaller but politically connected domain closer to Edo.

Not a single year during the 1860s passed without some degree of political violence. The era before that decade had been relatively calm, but now the peace was destabilized by factionalism and domain civil wars, attacks against Europeans and their servants living in newly formed merchant communities in Yokohama, riots in the cities of Kyoto and Edo, and the unexpected deaths of two key political figures, the shogun Iemochi (in 1866, at age twenty) and the emperor Kōmei (1867, at age thirty-five). The new emperor, Meiji, was only a teenager and was controlled by a handful of court nobles and their daimyo supporters. The new shogun, Yoshinobu, was a reluctant successor. Not wanting to start a war with his enemies at court and no doubt fearing for his life, he "returned" the title of shogun to the emperor in 1867, setting up the "restoration" of political rule to the Meiji emperor in name, if not in reality. Yoshinobu remained the head of the Tokugawa clan, a partner with the court and emperor, and leader of the samurai bureaucrats attached to the shogunate. He mounted an attack against daimyo gathered at Kyoto who he claimed were manipulating the young emperor. His army of fifteen thousand troops outnumbered those from the southwestern domains, but the battle at the villages of Toba and Fushimi on the outskirts of Kyoto did not go his way. He retreated to Edo and surrendered the Tokugawa forces to the emperor in 1868.

Despite Yoshinobu's surrender, supporters of the Tokugawa clan, including a few French military attachés, continued to fight against the southern daimyo and their soldiers who composed the "emperor's army." The samurai holdouts did not fight out of love for the shogunate; indeed, when a few thousand men commandeered the shogunate's ships and left for Hakodate in the north, they created a republic and installed a Tokugawa family member as its president. Another thirty-eight domains in the northeast formed a military alliance to fight against the fifty thousand troops sent under the emperor's banner from the south.

For the first time since the early seventeenth century, tens of thousands of troops were being mobilized for war, but they were hardly like their predecessors. Long before the war, the shogunate had been reforming its military, arming it with Western rifles and asking the French for help reorganizing its tactics. In the south, the British and other western Europeans had been selling rifles left over from the American Civil War. Daimyo there formed "peasant" militias to help in coastal defense, although it was mostly samurai who were dispatched to fight in the emperor's name. Still, traditional weapons like swords, spears, halberds, and bows appeared on the battlefield.

The bloodiest fighting occurred in the northeast Aizu domain, ruled by the Matsudaira clan. Despite having been given up by the Matsudaira as a hostage, Ieyasu never completely abandoned them. Branch lines of the Matsudaira clan formed after Ieyasu's death celebrated the older Matsudaira–Ieyasu connection, and they remained among the most reliable supporters of the shogunate even as it fell two and a half centuries later. While Aizu samurai bore the brunt of the siege against Aizu Castle, their women inside took care of the wounded, tried to supply food, and packed gunpowder and ammunition in makeshift bamboo bazookas; when cannonballs landed on the roof, women covered them with wet blankets to keep them from setting fires. Although the men implored them not to, samurai women eventually joined them in battle with swords and halberds, the first people to use them in combat since at least the sixteenth century. Many women cut their hair to look like men, and one even donned her dead brother's clothes. In the end, nearly 200 women died in the fighting. Another 230 old men, women, and children committed suicide lest they suffer dishonor at the hands of their enemies. Years later, the Aizu domain's house elder Saigō Tanomu recounted the suicide of all the women in his family: his mother, wife, younger sister, and five daughters, the youngest of whom were four and two. Each wrote a death poem. His thirteen-year-old daughter wrote, "If you take my hand / and we go together / I won't get lost," to which her sixteen-year-old sister added, "When the time comes, I will take it / as we depart for death on the mountain road."

10. This woodblock print by Tsukioka Yoshitoshi reflects his experience as a witness to the violence of the Meiji Restoration as it unfolded in Ueno. Although the words on the 1868 print describe the life of Komagine Hachibei, a rebel fighting during the seventeenth-century Shimabara Rebellion, the clothing style clearly reflects the dress of a Shogitai member. The Shogitai was one of many groups of irregulars who fought on the side of the Tokugawa shogunate.

Post-Restoration warrior legacy

In 1872, only a few years after the Meiji Restoration, a southern ex-samurai turned modern oligarch named Itō Hirobumi delivered a speech in San Francisco. He stated, with a disregard for history, that despite a temporary civil war, the feudal system had been destroyed without "firing a gun or shedding a drop of blood." History textbooks in Japan from the late nineteenth century to the present tend to downplay the violence of the Restoration. One prominent historian in Japan went so far as to suggest that the Meiji Restoration was a unique revolution in world history because it involved relatively little violence compared to other modern revolutions and that the samurai abolished their own class. During a short presentation on the need to reconsider the violent and traumatic nature of the Meiji Restoration, this same historian, sitting in the audience, argued that local tourist boosters had been responsible for overemphasizing Restoration violence only long after the fact. He might be right, but that still does not erase the deaths of more than thirteen thousand people killed during the latter half of the 1860s, most of them during the Boshin War that began after Yoshinobu's capitulation and ended in 1869. Such is the controversy of the Meiji Restoration even 150 years later: not even the dead are given their due.

The Meiji Restoration ushered in a sweeping abolition of the shogunate, the nearly 280 extant domains, and warrior status itself. The newly formed Meiji oligarchy first asked the lords to voluntarily "return" their domains to the emperor, effectively eliminating them. Prominent daimyo with large domains who led the Restoration forfeited their domains first. Later, the government forced all daimyo to do so. Some were moved across the country to become governors in one of the seventy-two newly formed prefectures, but many were not. For the most part, daimyo did not bemoan their new status. They received payoffs that ensured them a comfortable retirement. Even before the

Restoration, a few daimyo had asked the shogunate to take control of their domains, as continuing to try to govern them had simply not been worth the effort.

Samurai response to the end of the status system was mixed. The newly formed government replaced the traditional samurai stipend with bonds that were immediately bought back by the national banks. Some lower-ranking samurai profited nicely from this transaction and used the cash to establish factories and businesses. For higher-ranking samurai, however, the stipend–bond switch fell short of providing a decent living.

Moreover, the physical vestiges of samurai privileges were eliminated; samurai could no longer carry swords or maintain their distinctive hairstyle. And they no longer monopolized the military, which was now open to all males. Ex-samurai in the government enacted these laws, but even within the bureaucracy there were widely contrary opinions. In 1869, one such official in the newly formed deliberative assembly proposed that swords no longer be carried in public by anyone but police, military, and government officials. He was dismissed from the assembly, demoted in rank, and threatened with death. This same assembly spent more time debating whether or not to abolish seppuku than on how to interact with Western countries—it voted against eliminating seppuku by 200 to 3, and the man who proposed the idea was assassinated.

With their status abolished, many samurai could not find jobs that utilized their backgrounds. Nor were they trained to handle money; being above financial dealings had been a source of pride during the Tokugawa period, a field of knowledge relegated to selfish merchants. Some former warriors were so impoverished that they sold the swords, armor, and other samurai objects that now fill Western museums, selling family heirlooms just to survive. Others were happy to be free from the bounds of their previous status, now able to pursue whatever occupation pleased them. A granddaughter of a samurai who later published a history of her family states that her grandfather, a samurai of the Mito domain, was glad to see the old system fall. He found it was easier to make a living even though he, like all samurai, lost his traditional stipend.

Far from celebrating the samurai, many Japanese in the late nineteenth century considered the samurai an anachronistic embarrassment, unproductive, and useless. Instead, a vogue for all things Western, even dress, spread throughout society. Local governments destroyed their abandoned castles. In the Aizu domain, the newly formed prefectural government sold off the land surrounding the castle, where much of the fighting had occurred. They opened the structure to local tourists for a twenty-day viewing before tearing it down and auctioning the materials. Only one person made a bid. The land around the castle was sold off to local farmers.

But by the end of the nineteenth century, samurai represented the putative strength of a unique, traditional Japan. The most famous ex-samurai turned modern intellectual, Fukuzawa Yukichi, who is featured on the 10,000-yen bill, is well known for celebrating the end of the status system and the Tokugawa shogunate. Nonetheless, he later bemoaned the disappearance of the samurai spirit represented by the "losers" of the Meiji Restoration, such as the Aizu fallen and the Tokugawa shogunate's samurai. For their part, many of those losers now worked in the Meiji oligarchy, and the Aizu men, once regarded as hated enemies of the emperor, found newfound respect from those who celebrated Japan as a martial country.

As Japan embarked on wars against China (1894–95) and Russia (1904–5), ideologues promoted the notion that now all Japanese were samurai. Kendo, a modern form of swordsmanship that used armor and point scoring, was introduced into the school system because it fostered martial spirit. Self-sacrifice and love of the emperor became a central theme in literature, film, and primary school textbooks. *Hagakure*, once a marginal text at best, was republished in the early twentieth century and enjoyed a wide readership, especially during the 1930s, at the height of Japanese fascism.

And what of the "way of the samurai?" It was not nearly as influential among the populace as it was among government officials and high-ranking military men. Most people credit Nitobe Inazō for defining *bushido* for a modern audience in his book *Bushido: The Soul of Japan*, published in 1900 in English for Americans. But nearly a decade before Nitobe, a journalist and politician, Ozaki Yukio, described bushido as Japan's version of gentlemanliness, comparable to Europe's notion of chivalry. His concept said nothing of martial prowess or self-sacrifice. Throughout the 1890s, intellectuals responded to Ozaki's writings about bushido. Some used the word to describe the vitality of commerce or argued for a Christian version of bushido, but no single definition dominated until the twentieth century. Nitobe had been living in the United States during the first bushido boom in Japan, and when his book was published in Japanese, it barely registered among anyone except interested intellectuals who deemed it too little too late. Instead, the philosopher Inoue Tetsujirō popularized the concept of bushido as a repository for nationalism, service to the emperor, and self-sacrifice. Those themes, and samurai history in general, became central to World War II propaganda. Samurai appeared in textbooks, boys learned Japanese fencing at school, and girls practiced how to wield a glaive (*naginata*), a long staff with a curved blade attached to the end.

After the Second World War, this wartime samurai image was taboo. Samurai films, a popular genre even during the silent film era, were censored by the American occupation army. Directors could still make samurai films, but they could not glorify violence, self-sacrifice, or loyalty to the emperor. A samurai film boom occurred during the 1950s after the occupation ended, when classic films such as Akira Kurosawa's *Seven Samurai* appeared, but they no longer portrayed an ultranationalist version of the samurai. The US occupation forces also banned martial arts practice, which was seen as another vehicle for disseminating dangerous bushido and fascist ideology. Even when martial arts like kendo reemerged, they emphasized cooperation and competition and deemphasized martial applicability.

During the high economic growth beginning in the 1960s, the archetypical, dark-suited "salaryman" became the new samurai. Called the "corporate warrior," such a businessman remained loyal to his company and would never abandon it for a better deal elsewhere—unlike a medieval warrior who readily switched sides or betrayed his lord. As for self-sacrifice, it was the exception that proved the rule of self-preservation for early warriors, but the business samurai was expected to sacrifice his well-being for the company. One wonders how the use of a more historically accurate image of the samurai might affect Japanese culture, business, and politics in the future.

References

Chapter 1

Bonnie Rochman, "Samurai Mind Training for Modern American Warriors," *Time*, September 6, 2009.

Yamamoto Tsunetomo, *Hagakure*, trans. Alexander Bennett (Tokyo: Tuttle, 2014), 60.

Chapter 2

For a full English translation of the law code, see David Lu, *Japan: A Documentary History* (Armonk, NY: M. E. Sharpe, 1997), 1:109–15.

Statement from Japan's 1869 government: Margaret Mehl, *History and the State in Nineteenth-Century Japan* (New York: St. Martin's Press, 1998), 1.

Chapter 3

Peter D. Shapinsky, *Lords of the Sea* (Ann Arbor: Center for Japanese Studies, University of Michigan, 2014), 6, 106.

David Lu, ed., *Sources of Japanese History* (Armonk, NY: M. E. Sharpe, 2015), 1:153–54.

Obata Kagenori, *Kōyō Gunkan jo*, ed. Koshihara Tetsurō (Tokyo: Kyōikusha, 1979), 40:69.

Donald Keene, *Yoshimasa* (New York: Columbia University Press, 2006), 15–22.

Hōjō Sōun letter: Translation my own. For alternative translation of full text, see Carl Steenstrup, "The Imagawa Letter," *Monumenta Nipponica* 28, no. 3 (Autumn 1973): 299–315.

Twenty-One Articles: Translation my own. For full version of alternative translation, see Carl Steenstrup, "Hojo Soun's Twenty-One Articles," *Monumenta Nipponica* 29, no. 3 (Autumn 1974): 283–303.

Chapter 4

Richard Cocks diary: This version from Constantine Vapori, *Voices of Early Modern Japan* (London: Taylor & Francis, 2018), 63.

Relocation of lords: Harold Bolitho, *Treasures among Men: The Fudai Daimyo in Tokugawa Japan* (New Haven, CT: Yale University Press, 1974), 8.

Advisor scolds heir: Constantine Vaporis, *Tour of Duty* (Honolulu: University of Hawai'i Press, 2016), 19.

Insults to Tokugawa: Albert Craig, *Choshu in the Meiji Restoration* (Cambridge, MA: Harvard University Press, 1961), 22.

Sumurai complains about poor warriors: Buyō Inshi, *Lust, Commerce, and Corruption* (New York: Columbia University Press, 2014), 56.

Kian dreamed of becoming a warrior: Yoshida, *Hei to nō no bunri* (Tokyo: Yamakawa Shuppansha, 2008), 97–101.

Chapter 5

Hayashi Hōkō explains the heart of being warrior: Quoted in part from *Sources of Japanese Tradition*, vol. 2, part 1, *1600–1868* (Armonk, NY: M. E. Sharpe, 1997), 361.

Buyō Inshi, *Lust, Commerce, and Corruption* (New York: Columbia University Press, 2014), 43.

Jippensha Ikku and Thomas Satchell, trans., *Shank's Mare* (Boston: Tuttle, 1960), 339.

Saitamaken, *Shinpen Saitamaken-shi Shiryōhen* (Urawa, Japan: Saitamaken, 1979), 742–43.

Translated by Anne Walthall in *Politics and Society in Japan's Meiji Restoration: A Brief History with Documents* (Boston: Bedford St. Martin's Press, 2017), 141.

Further reading

General history

Friday, Karl, ed. *Japan Emerging: Premodern History to 1850*. New York: Routledge, 2012.
Hane, Mikiso, and Louis G. Perez. *Premodern Japan: A Historical Survey*. Boulder, CO: Westview, 2015.

Warrior origins

Farris, William W. *Heavenly Warriors: The Evolution of Japan's Military, 500–1300*. Cambridge, MA: Harvard University Press, 2010.
Friday, Karl F. *The First Samurai: The Life and Legend of the Warrior Rebel Taira Masakado*. Hoboken, NJ: Wiley, 2008.

Early warrior authority

Friday, Karl F. *Hired Swords: The Rise of Private Warrior Power in Early Japan*. Stanford, CA: Stanford University Press, 1996.
Lu, David J. *Japan: A Documentary History*. Armonk, NY: M. E. Sharpe, 2005.
Mass, Jeffrey P. *Antiquity and Anachronism in Japanese History*. Stanford, CA: Stanford University Press, 1995.
Mass, Jeffrey P. *Yoritomo and the Founding of the First Bakufu: The Origins of Dual Government in Japan*. Stanford, CA: Stanford University Press, 1999.

Mass, Jeffrey P., and Takeuchi Rizo. *The Kamakura Bakufu: A Study in Documents*. Stanford, CA: Stanford University Press, 1976.

Oyler, Elizabeth. *Swords, Oaths, and Prophetic Visions: Authoring Warrior Rule in Medieval Japan*. Honolulu: University of Hawai'i Press, 2006.

War and culture

Berry, Mary E. *The Culture of Civil War in Kyoto*. Berkeley: University of California Press, 1997.

Berry, Mary E. *Hideyoshi*. Cambridge, MA: Council on East Asian Studies, Harvard University, 1990.

Conlan, Thomas. *State of War: The Violent Order of Fourteenth-Century Japan*. Ann Arbor: Center for Japanese Studies, University of Michigan, 2004.

Friday, Karl. *Samurai, Warfare and the State in Early Medieval Japan*. New York: Taylor & Francis, 2005.

Ōta, Gyūichi, trans. *The Chronicle of Lord Nobunaga*. Edited by J. S. A. Elisonas and Jeroen Pieter Lamers. Leiden: Brill, 2011.

Shapinsky, Peter D. *Lords of the Sea: Pirates, Violence, and Commerce in Late Medieval Japan*. Ann Arbor: Center for Japanese Studies, University of Michigan, 2014.

Warriors: Late sixteenth to mid-nineteenth centuries

Bolitho, Harold. *Treasures among Men: The Fudai Daimyo in Tokugawa Japan*. New Haven, CT: Yale University Press, 1974.

Hanley, Susan B. *Everyday Things in Premodern Japan: The Hidden Legacy of Material Culture*. Berkeley: University of California Press, 1997.

Katsu, Kokichi, and Teruko Craig. *Musui's Story: The Autobiography of a Tokugawa Samurai*. Tucson: University of Arizona Press, 2003.

Totman, Conrad D. *Early Modern Japan*. Berkeley: University of California Press, 1995.

Vaporis, Constantine N. *Tour of Duty: Samurai, Military Service in Edo, and the Culture of Early Modern Japan*. Honolulu: University of Hawai'i Press, 2016.

Yamakawa, Kikue. *Women of the Mito Domain: Recollections of Samurai Family Life*. Translated by Kate W. Nakai. Stanford, CA: Stanford University Press, 2001.

Warrior myth and legacy

Benesch, Oleg. *Inventing the Way of the Samurai*. New York: Oxford University Press, 2016.

Buyō, Inshi, Mark Teeuwen, Kate Wildman Nakai, Noah Arlow, and John Breen, trans. and eds. *Lust, Commerce, and Corruption: An Account of What I Have Seen and Heard, by an Edo Samurai*. New York: Columbia University Press, 2017.

Goro, Shiba, and Teruko Craig, trans. *Remembering Aizu: The Testament of Shiba Goro*. Ishimitsu Mahita, Honolulu: University of Hawai'i Press, 1999.

Jaundrill, D. C. From *Samurai to Soldier: Remaking Military Service in Nineteenth-Century Japan*. Ithaca, NY: Cornell University Press, 2016.

Index

Samurai

VERY SHORT INTRODUCTIONS are for anyone wanting a stimulating and accessible way into a new subject. They are written by experts, and have been translated into more than 45 different languages.

The series began in 1995, and now covers a wide variety of topics in every discipline. The VSI library now contains over 500 volumes—a Very Short Introduction to everything from Psychology and Philosophy of Science to American History and Relativity—and continues to grow in every subject area.

Titles in the series include the following:

Risk: A Very Short Introduction

Baruch Fischhoff and John Kadvany

RISK

A Very Short Introduction

OXFORD

UNIVERSITY PRESS

Great Clarendon Street, Oxford OX2 6DP

Oxford University Press is a department of the University of Oxford.
It furthers the University's objective of excellence in research, scholarship, and education by publishing worldwide in

Oxford New York

Auckland Cape Town Dar es Salaam Hong Kong Karachi
Kuala Lumpur Madrid Melbourne Mexico City Nairobi
New Delhi Shanghai Taipei Toronto

With offices in

Argentina Austria Brazil Chile Czech Republic France Greece
Guatemala Hungary Italy Japan Poland Portugal Singapore
South Korea Switzerland Thailand Turkey Ukraine Vietnam

Oxford is a registered trade mark of Oxford University Press
in the UK and in certain other countries

Published in the United States
by Oxford University Press Inc., New York

British Library Cataloguing in Publication Data

Data available

Library of Congress Cataloging in Publication Data

Data available

Typeset by SPI Publisher Services, Pondicherry, India
Printed in Great Britain on acid-free paper by
Ashford Colour Press Ltd, Gosport, Hampshire

ISBN 978-0-19-957620-3

Contents

Acknowledgements

For their patience, encouragement, and wise counsel, we thank our parents and our families: Andi, Maya, Ilya, and Noam (BF); Susan, Daniel, and Elena (JK).

For models of how to think, and often what to think about, we thank our teachers, especially Daniel Kahneman, Reuven Kaminer, Sarah Lichtenstein, Paul Slovic, and Amos Tversky (BF); Imre Lakatos and Paul Feyerabend (JK).

We thank our colleagues, especially Wändi Bruine de Bruin, Robyn Dawes, Julie Downs, Paul Fischbeck, and Granger Morgan (BF); friends and colleagues at Applied Decision Analysis and Carollo Engineers, Bob Righter, and Jane Smith (JK).

List of illustrations

List of tables

Introduction

Risks are everywhere. They come from many sources, including crime, diseases, accidents, terror, climate change, finance, and intimacy. They exact their price in many ways, including money, health, safety, reputation, peace of mind, and self-esteem. They arise from our own acts and are imposed on us, when societies license new technologies, site hazardous facilities, or go to war.

Although different in many ways, risks have much in common. *Risk: A Very Short Introduction* draws on the sciences and humanities to bring out those common elements. *Risk* shows how social institutions and conventions influence risk decisions, so that risks provide windows into how societies express and define themselves. *Risk* considers the challenges to human intellect and resilience, as we grapple with uncertainty about the world and ourselves.

Risk shows readers how to be critical consumers of claims about risk, from politicians, pundits, doctors, financial advisors, car mechanics, suitors, or scientists. It shows how to evaluate claims about facts (what might happen) and about values (what might matter). It shows how current controversies echo historical themes of chance, pollution, purity, and danger. It shows what science has learned about how people deal with risks, so that readers can better understand others' psychology, and their own. That science includes results that might surprise some readers, such as 'people rarely panic in disasters', 'anger produces optimism', and 'adolescents have a unique sense of vulnerability'.

By applying general principles to diverse examples, *Risk* is designed to help readers make better risk decisions in their public and private lives. The book will afford them fluency in applying its basic concepts to personal or social risk decisions of many kinds.

Risk's perspective is compatible with the quantitative methods of risk analysis. However, its focus is on the concepts underlying these methods, not their execution. Understanding what modern methods of risk analysis can and cannot do is essential for ensuring that they aid, rather than supplant, human judgement. By reducing the mystery in risk decisions, *Risk* will make readers fuller partners in those choices.

The foundations of risk and *Risk* lie in decision theory, which articulates concepts whose emergence must have begun with the first human thought about uncertain choices. Applications of decision theory have led to unique collaborations among disciplines. Natural scientists have assessed probabilities for outcomes identified by ethicists reflecting on tradition, politics, and policy dilemmas. Social scientists have devised ways to explain these prospects and help individuals decide what they want, given what they might be able to have. Mathematicians and philosophers have formulated questions about uncertainties that computer scientists and psychologists have helped to answer. Sociologists and political scientists have shown how selecting experts and defining 'risk' can highlight some issues and obscure others. These collaborations have also enriched the participating disciplines, by confronting them with issues outside their normal sphere. As a result, risk has changed sciences, as well as societies.

Chapter 1, *Risk decisions*, introduces a conceptual framework for thinking about risks, by viewing them in the context of decisions where they matter. Chapter 2, *Defining risk*, examines the science and practice of creating measures of 'risk'. Chapter 3, *Analysing risk*, describes how scientists come to understand the probabilities and multiple causes of risks, by combining historical records, scientific theories, and expert judgement. Chapter 4, *Making risk decisions*, considers how individuals move from understanding risks to making choices, paying particular attention to how their preferences are constructed in the process of making choices that pose novel trade-offs. Chapter 5, *Risk perception*, summarizes modern research on how people think and feel about risks, with a focus on judgemental biases that can, sometimes, sway choices. Chapter 6, *Risk communication*, addresses the science and politics of affording citizens opportunities to master the facts about risk decisions. Chapter 7, *Risk, culture, and society*, considers how societies reveal themselves by how they deal with dangers, including their use of risk analysis in the pursuit of their wellbeing.

Chapter 1
Risk decisions

Risks are all around us, appearing in many forms. We face risks in new technologies (nuclear power, genetically modified crops) and old ones (dams, ladders), in modern medicine (stem-cell therapy, colonoscopy) and home remedies (herbs, diets), in familiar personal relationships (heartbreak, betrayal) and novel ones (online predators, identity theft), in simple savings (inflation, illiquid pension funds) and esoteric investments (collateralized mortgages, hedge funds), in familiar violence (robbery, sexual assault) and inventive forms (dirty bombs, anthrax attacks).

Some risks have immediate effects (tainted food) and others delayed ones (saturated fats). Some affect us directly (personal losses) and others indirectly (employers' losses). Some are material (personal injuries) and others psychological (injury to loved ones). Some affect people (accidental poisoning) and others affect the natural environment that supports them (pesticides). Some are voluntary (skiing) and others are not (terrorism). Some involve one event (eating forbidden food) and others repeated events (eating unhealthy food).

Risks vary in how well they can be controlled, how equitable they are, how much dread they evoke, how reversible their effects are, how much they threaten our sacred values, and how far we trust those in charge of them. We might need help in understanding the world (how could they hate us so much? why do older people fall?) or in understanding ourselves (how much does money matter? could I live with myself, if things went wrong?).

Experts studying specific risks find their details endlessly fascinating. Non-scientists, though, can find themselves adrift in a morass of facts, values, emotions, fears, regrets, social pressures, claims and counterclaims, all vying for their attention. Experts flounder like everyone else, once outside their specialities – as when doctors or car mechanics ponder investing, and brokers wonder about unfamiliar creaking in their bodies and cars. Coping with a world of risks requires concentrating on the few things that matter most, when making decisions about risks, whether as citizens, parents, patients, employees, activists, investors, drivers, or friends.

Decision theory seeks to bring order to the world of risks. *Risk: A Very Short Introduction* uses decision theory to that end, showing how the same basic issues (assessing uncertainty, deciding what really matters, looking for better evidence) emerge in very different guises. Decision theory is not a comprehensive theory of risk. Indeed, it is not really a theory at all, but a language for describing risky decisions. Nor is it a panacea, ensuring good decisions for those who master it. Rather, it is an aid to practical reasoning, helping people to make the best decisions possible, given what they know (or could learn) about the decisions facing them.

A simple scheme

Risks threaten things that we value. What we do about them depends on the *options* we have (undergo surgery, wait and hope), the *outcomes* we value (get well, suffer lasting pain), and our *beliefs* about the outcomes that might follow, if we choose each option. The outcomes could be certain (a medical bill, eventual death) or uncertain (whether surgery succeeds, whether insurance claims are honoured). Our choices could be simple (inexpensive surgery, relieving chronic pain) or complex (experimental medical treatment, for ourselves or a loved one).

Decision theory looks at choices from three complementary perspectives. One is logical, or normative, analysis, identifying the choices that we would make, *if* we were fully informed, *if* we were fully in touch with our values, and *if* we followed consistent rules, however hard our choices are. Those are, of course, big 'ifs'. The second decision theory perspective is the descriptive study of the necessarily imperfect ways in which people actually make choices. The third perspective involves prescriptive interventions, trying to bridge the gap between the normative ideal and the descriptive reality. Thus, decision theory asks the questions that decision-makers ask themselves: What decision am I facing? How well am I facing it? How could I do better?

We begin with the stories of three very different risk decisions, focusing on the individuals forced to make them, mindful of the society that shapes their choices.

Very premature infants

Seemingly normal pregnancies sometimes go badly wrong at 23 to 25 weeks' gestation, forcing parents to choose between palliative care and intensive care for their infants. Parents choosing palliative care know that their child will die, while receiving treatment that makes their short lives as peaceful and painless as possible. Parents choosing intensive care know that their child may die in the neonatal intensive care unit or survive with developmental disabilities. These are some of the cruelest decisions that modern medicine makes possible.

Some parents, however, see no decision at all. Their faith or personal philosophy dictates their choice. Some of them will do everything possible to save a life, making intensive care their only option. Others will see limits to human intervention, making palliative care their only option.

Parents who see a decision must compare the options. With palliative care, death is certain, but other outcomes are not. For example, although pain control is well understood, some chance remains that their infant will suffer. There is also uncertainty about how they themselves will fare, when living with their decision. Even if there were extensive research into the wellbeing of parents who choose palliative care, parents cannot be sure how they, personally, will react. As a result, palliative care has uncertain outcomes, even if the main outcome is never in doubt.

There are statistics on some possible outcomes of intensive care. Figure 1 shows those offered on a public website. It has pull-down menus for five risk factors, such as the infant's gestational age and birth weight. The first row has the infant's survival probability (62%, in this example). The next two rows have probabilities for survival without severe disability (44%) and without moderate-to-severe disability (27%). The final three rows have complementary probabilities for dying and disability. These are grim statistics, but not so grim that many hospitals do not offer intensive care as an option, for cases like this one.

The right-hand column in Figure 1 gives the same statistics for infants who receive mechanical ventilation as part of their intensive care. These infants fare a little better than all infants (left-hand column). However, it is hard to imagine these small differences mattering enough that parents would switch from palliative to intensive care after being told 'Your child will receive mechanical ventilation, raising the survival probability from 62% to 64%.' If a normative decision analysis showed that this information has no practical value, then the second column could be eliminated, as needless clutter. Without such analysis, well-meaning experts can drown their audiences with pointless facts.

NICHD Neonatal Research Network (NRN):
Extremely Preterm Birth Outcome Data

Based on the following characteristics:

Gestational Age (Best obstetric estimate in completed weeks): 24 weeks
Birth Weight: 700 grams
Sex: Male
Singelton Birth: Yes
Antenatal Corticosteroids: Yes

Estimated outcomes for infants in the NRN sample are as follows:

Outcomes	Outcomes for All Infants	Outcomes for Mechanically Ventilated Infants
Survival	62%	64%
Survival Without Profound Neurodevelopmental Impairment	44%	46%
Survival Without Moderate to Severe Neurodevelopmental Impairment	27%	29%
Death	38%	36%
Death or Profound Neurodevelopmental Impairment	56%	54%
Death or Moderate to Severe Neurodevelopmental Impairment	73%	71%

1. Probabilities of major outcomes for extremely premature infants who receive intensive care, given the five risk factors at the top (gestational age, birth weight, sex, single birth, mother's receipt of corticosteroids)

Once they know the gist of the risks, many parents will find that the deepest uncertainties lie in themselves, as they ponder what they want, faced with this wrenching choice. Does a 27% chance of a healthy life outweigh a 56% chance of death or profound impairment? Should their own wellbeing matter? Should that of siblings? Should the opinions and experiences of other parents? If they struggle with these questions, then, in effect, they do not know what they want.

In such situations, people can search fruitlessly for the critical fact that will tell them what to do. When that search fails, they may seek advice. When doctors offer it, parents must still assess its relevance. Are doctors saying what they imagine that they would do, if they faced this choice in their own lives – or what they think the parents would want to do, if they fully grasped the situation? Are the doctors factoring in how well they think the parents can handle the decision and its aftermath? Are they saying what their employer wants them to say?

Explicit advice invites asking such questions. Less obvious pressures may be hidden in how decisions are *framed*. For example, instead of 'palliative care', some doctors use 'comfort care', a term that may evoke different images or social norms. Figure 1 presents just statistics, perhaps suggesting that just statistics matter, perhaps suggesting that the experts are deliberately silent about ethical issues, deferring to parents' wishes. Presenting the two columns of statistics may suggest that the decision is so close that a 2% difference in survival probability could matter. Presenting the same information in terms of good outcomes (top three rows) and bad ones (bottom three rows) may suggest that parents need to look at it both ways.

Descriptive research can discipline such speculations by assessing how people actually respond to different ways of framing choices. For example, a study posing hypothetical decisions found that intensive care was more attractive when described in terms of good outcomes, rather than bad ones. In decision theory terms, people who are unsure about what they want 'construct' their preferences from whatever perspectives come to mind, which can be different with positive and negative frames. It is hard to manipulate people with clear values. Indeed, in that study, framing had no effect on people who described themselves as at least moderately religious; they chose intensive care, however the options were described.

Societies express themselves in how they make life and death decisions. This one invites reflection on why society has invested so much in creating the technologies that sometimes save these precious lives. Has it made comparable investments in preventing premature births – or in controlling environmental stressors that increase those risks? Which families have access to such intensive care? Who pays for it? Who decides when parents, rather than doctors, choose? Why is so little known about the experiences of parents who choose palliative care? Who collected the statistics in Figure 1? Who decided to make them so readily available?

> ### Risk and uncertainty
>
> In 1921, before the great financial crash, economist Frank Knight argued that:
>
> Uncertainty must be taken in a sense radically distinct from the familiar notion of risk, from which it has never been properly separated ... The essential fact is that 'risk' means in some cases a quantity susceptible of measurement, while at other times it is something distinctly not of this character; and there are far-reaching and crucial differences in the bearings of the phenomena depending on which of the two is really present and operating ... A measurable uncertainty, or 'risk' proper ... is so far different from an unmeasurable one that it is not in effect an uncertainty at all.

Vehicle insurance risks

In the United States, Pennsylvania and New Jersey require vehicle insurance companies to offer drivers a 'limited tort' option. Drivers who take that option pay lower premiums, but give up the right to sue for 'minor pain and suffering' after an accident. Drivers who purchase limited tort insurance know, with certainty, how much they will save in their premium payments. They are uncertain about the risk they are taking if they give up that right to sue. That risk depends on their chances of having an accident and their chances of suing and winning.

Figure 2 depicts this choice in a *decision tree*, a graphic format that some people find helpful. (Readers who do not can skip to the next paragraph.) On the left, the tree has drivers' two options, full tort (buying insurance with the right to sue for 'minor injuries and suffering') and limited tort (buying insurance without that right).

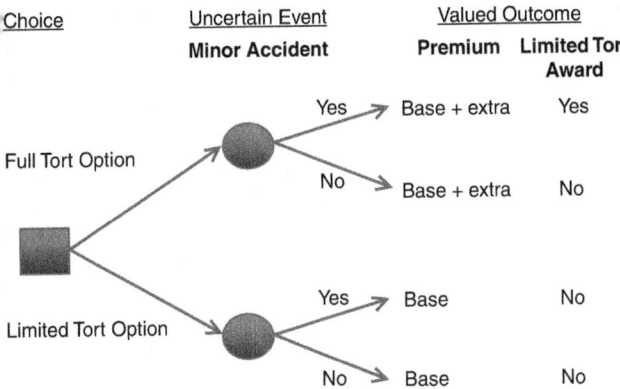

| Choice | Uncertain Event | Valued Outcome | |
| | **Minor Accident** | **Premium** | **Limited Tort Award** |

Full Tort Option

Yes → Base + extra — Yes
No → Base + extra — No

Limited Tort Option

Yes → Base — No
No → Base — No

2. Decision tree for limited tort decision. On the left is a square choice node, with two options, *limited* and *full tort*. On the right are two valued outcomes, the *premium* (a cost) and *limited tort award* (a benefit). In the middle, the circular *event nodes* represent the main uncertainty, whether drivers have a *minor accident* that allows suing successfully. Each pathway, read from left to right, represents a different future. In the top one, drivers buy full tort, experience minor accidents, and win their suits. Paying the extra premium makes them poorer; receiving the limited tort award makes them wealthier. All drivers have the same decision tree, but with different probabilities (some have lower accident risks) and values (some have a greater need for money)

On the right, the tree has two outcomes that depend on this choice (the premium and the limited tort award, if any). In the centre is the key uncertainty, the probability of having an accident for which drivers could sue and win. Each pathway through the tree describes a different scenario. In the top one, the driver first chooses the full tort option, then experiences a minor accident and receives a limited tort award, along with paying the larger premium (base + extra). Drivers' personal scenarios depend on their choices and the events that follow.

Assessing event probabilities is one province of *risk analysis*. Few risks have been analysed as thoroughly as car accidents. Most drivers would benefit from knowing about those analyses, rather than relying on their own intuitive risk perceptions. Although often sensible, risk perceptions are also often biased. For example, most drivers believe that they are safer than average, which could be true only for half of all drivers. One reason for this bias is that other drivers' mistakes are more visible than our own. We see when they cut us off in traffic more readily than we see ourselves doing the same. We see their misfortunes reported in the news and not our own. We also fail to see the cumulative risk from all the trips we take. Each individual trip seems so safe that driving as a whole seems safer than it is. In the US, an average trip has about one chance in ten million of ending in a fatal accident. However, an average person has about one chance in 200 of dying in a car accident – on one of their many lifetime trips.

Information about average accident risks should help drivers to make better insurance decisions. However, that average underestimates the risks for those who drive fast, in small cars (especially when colliding with larger ones), late at night, on country roads, or after drinking. The average overstates the risks for drivers without these risk factors. Whether drivers need more precise, personal risk estimates depends on how 'sensitive' their decisions are to their accident risk. If they would make the same choice for risks anywhere near the statistical average, then all they need is the average. With close decisions, better estimates might help. For the limited tort decision, an attorney friend claimed that 'In the US, you can always sue. So, take the limited tort option and save the extra premium.' If his advice is correct, then any accident probability leads to the same choice (buy limited tort), making the decision completely insensitive to accident risks.

If more precise accident risk estimates could help drivers to choose among insurance options, then they must decide how hard to look for them. Unless they expect to learn something useful, with a reasonable effort, they might as well save the bother and decide right away. There are formal methods for calculating the 'value of information' – and the return on investing in it. Energy companies sometimes use these methods in deciding whether to drill test wells when exploring oil fields. So do health economists, in deciding whether tests, such as mammography and colonoscopy, produce enough information to be worth the cost and risks. However, anyone can ask, 'Could I plausibly learn anything that would change my mind?' If not, then one might as well decide already.

Limited tort decisions are a private matter. However, like other risk decisions, they also reveal how societies deal with risks. For example, the limited tort option exists only because insurance interests successfully lobbied for it, as a way to reduce 'nuisance' suits for minor pain and suffering, arising in a litigious society. Yet, despite having common goals, the two states defined drivers' decisions differently. In New Jersey, limited tort is the 'default' option, forcing drivers to 'opt out', if they want full tort. In Pennsylvania, full tort is the default, forcing drivers to 'opt in', if they want limited tort. Given the psychology of risk decisions, defaults matter because people tend to stick with them. Indeed, drivers were about twice as likely to end up with limited tort in New Jersey (where it was the default) as in Pennsylvania (where it was not). Drivers are also much more likely to be organ donors, when that is the default, compared to when they must opt in to being donors. Sometimes people stick with defaults because they can't figure out what else to do. Sometimes they stick with defaults because they assume that the framing reflects a social norm, hence what they are supposed to do.

How well limited tort insurance programmes work depends on how well drivers understand the risks and benefits – and on how well they resist the 'moral hazard' of gaming the choice. A programme will fail if drivers accept limited tort, but sue anyway, as our attorney friend suggested. The term 'risk homeostasis' is used for another moral hazard: drivers pay for the right to sue (full tort), then drive less safely, expecting compensation for any minor pain and suffering, thereby keeping their overall risk level constant. Doing so need not be irrational, any more than it is irrational for rock climbers or skiers to push harder with better equipment. They pay more and get greater benefit in return – even if that behaviour frustrates those who would like them to be safer drivers, climbers, or skiers.

Risk and insurance

Societies manage many risks by sharing the costs of protection through insurance.

Suppose that a million homes have, on average, one chance in ten thousand (1/10,000) of a fire, with an average damage of £200,000. The expected number of fires is 1/10,000 × 1,000,000 homes = 100 fires per year. The expected damage is 100 fires × £200,000 = £20 million.

If each household pays a £20 annual premium, there will be enough money to cover the expected damages for 100 devastated households. By pooling unpredictable individual risks, insurance protects people against catastrophic losses that they cannot bear alone, allowing them to live relatively stable lives.

With fire insurance, moral hazard might mean being more careless with flammables. Deductibles reduce that threat, by making insured people pay, say, the first £1,000 of damages. So do required home inspections and the physical risks that insurance cannot cover. Insurers must also avoid 'adverse selection', whereby people forgo insurance, expecting others to pay their costs, through disaster relief or bank rescues. Banks holding vehicle loans and mortgages reduce this threat by requiring insurance.

Although decisions about premature infants and car insurance are different in many ways, understanding them requires the same three perspectives: normative analysis, organizing the relevant facts; descriptive research, seeing where people need help; and prescriptive interventions, providing that help. For the insurance decision, that help entails providing drivers with critical facts about accident risks. Unfortunately, drivers often get incomprehensible insurance policies, with nothing about risk levels. As a result, they stumble through their choices, relying on the framing that defaults provide.

Sex education

US schools that provide comprehensive sex education sometimes allow parents to remove their children from lessons that will consider options other than abstinence, such as condoms and birth control pills. Many parents see no decision here, happy for whatever schools can teach their teens. However, parents who strongly favour abstinence face a decision with two options: letting their children participate in these lessons or removing them. Their choice has one certain outcome: they will feel better if they remove their children. It has two uncertain outcomes: how it affects their teens' risks of pregnancy and of sexually transmitted infections (STIs).

Parents who remove their teens hope to reduce those risks by encouraging abstinence. So do parents who let their children participate, hoping that the course encourages safer sex. Parents who make different decisions may disagree about values (the importance of abstinence) or about facts (the effectiveness of abstinence education). Parents who oppose comprehensive sexual education often believe that it increases those risks, by accepting the possibility of teen sex. Other parents believe that teaching teens how to handle sexual situations reduces risks that are going to arise anyway. That teaching includes 'social skills', such as how to rebuff unwanted advances, use condoms, and evaluate sexual partners' claims of being STI-free. Teens who master these skills should have safer and less coerced sex. More might even be abstinent, if they have only the sex that they want.

The major uncertainty in this choice is, therefore, teens' decision-making, with and without comprehensive sexual education. Studies of adolescent decision-making can reduce that uncertainty. They generally find that, by the mid-teen years, adolescents' (cognitive) ability to think about decisions resembles that of adults. Teens know more about things that they learn in school, less about things that require experience to master. However, teens also face social and emotional pressures that can keep them from acting on what they know. As a result, teens should benefit from lessons teaching them how to make sex-related decisions, how to handle social and emotional pressures, and how to avoid situations producing those pressures. Indeed, studies find that such (social-skills) training reduces teens' risks from STIs – and those of fighting and smoking as well. 'Graduated' drivers' licence programmes protect teen drivers from social pressure by prohibiting them from having teen passengers until they have had experience coping just with traffic (after which they 'graduate' to taking friends along).

In contrast, abstinence education appears to have little lasting effect on American teens' sexual activity. STI and pregnancy risks will, then, increase for teens less able to handle sexual situations when they arise. If so, then keeping teens from comprehensive sexual education implicitly places a higher value on making a moral statement than on reducing teens' risks of pregnancy and STIs.

Whether parents perceive that trade-off depends on what they believe about the programmes' effectiveness. If they believe that abstinence education is more effective, then removing their teens from other classes is a 'dominating alternative', both more moral and less risky. Although studies of programme effectiveness indicate otherwise, strongly held beliefs often have great staying power, partly because people typically associate with others who share their beliefs. People are also good at explaining away inconvenient evidence. Thus, parents who favour abstinence education might argue that the research does not apply to their teens or that strong moral statements will eventually make premarital abstinence a social norm. Were the tables turned, defenders of comprehensive sex education might produce analogous arguments, going beyond the available science.

There is nothing irrational about requiring strong new evidence before relinquishing strong existing beliefs. Orderly discourse does, however, require saying what evidence would change one's mind. If the parties to a dispute can agree about the meaning of new evidence, then their beliefs should increasingly converge, even if they never see things quite the same way. Without the possibility of such convergence, disagreements over risks are about ideology, not evidence. In the US, debates over evolution, stem-cell research, and the historical climate record have suffered this fate, with political disputes couched in science-like language.

People who agree about the facts of a risk decision need not make the same choices. Abstinence advocates might accept that there is little evidence demonstrating its effectiveness, yet still oppose letting schools countenance premarital sex. Were the tables turned, advocates of comprehensive sex education might argue that it sends a vital message of empowerment, however it affects STI risks.

The debate over abstinence education reflects the confluence of three American political principles: majority rule, separation of church and state, and local control over education. Science might seem to offer a neutral, even objective, way to resolve such deadlocks. However, emphasizing science can force advocates to cast moral arguments in scientific terms. Science itself may suffer, if it becomes just another political tool, rather than a special way to assess and reduce uncertainty. Eventually, electoral politics resolved this dispute. The G. W. Bush administration supported only abstinence education. The Obama administration reversed that policy, supporting programmes with demonstrated effectiveness, which were versions of comprehensive sex education.

The social context of risk decisions

Each of these three private risk decisions reflects public risk decisions, occurring over many years and involving many decision-makers.

Those public decisions made it possible for parents to have a say in the fate of very premature infants, for drivers to have the limited tort option, and for parents to remove teens from non-abstinence lessons. Public decisions also set the terms of the private ones. For example, the probability of premature birth depends on public decisions that affect pregnant women's health, by determining the availability of prenatal exams and healthy foods. An infant's survival probability depends on public decisions that affect the quality of intensive care, by determining investments in research and facilities. The probability of car accidents depends on public decisions about road construction, vehicle inspections, driver education, and drinking and driving laws. The probability of teen STIs depends on public decisions regarding the availability of medical screening, treatment, and barrier contraceptives.

These public decisions are also subject to normative, descriptive, and prescriptive analyses, asking what the decisions were, how decision-makers perceived them, and how they might have been made better. Those analyses assume that public decision-makers (legislators, regulators, executives, doctors, financiers, military officers) are people, too, subject to biased risk perceptions and letting their emotions run away with them. Thus, those analyses would ask whether the officials who approved limited tort insurance considered all three options (opt in, opt out, no change); whether they focused on outcomes that the public values (premiums, compensation, safety) or on other ones (insurance company profits, their own job prospects after leaving office); whether they understood the factors determining those outcomes (defaults, moral hazards); and what additional information would have had value to them (briefings on safety research or on other ways to reduce nuisance suits).

Officials often claim to represent 'the people'. However, that claim is empty unless officials have the right implicit decision tree, focused on the outcomes that 'the people' value and the uncertainties that they face. However well officials do their work, its value depends on how well it is communicated to those who depend on it. The most thoughtful insurance reform does little good if drivers treat it as some new chicanery, produced by people they never trusted anyway. Figure 1's statistics are wasted if parents find them inscrutable and the display callous. Sex education cannot help teens unless it addresses their misconceptions, such as how the risks of sexual acts accumulate over time (like the risks of car trips or workplace safety shortcuts).

People tend to exaggerate how well they understand others and how well others understand them, meaning that seemingly sensible communications often fail without either side realizing that. It takes research or continuing two-way communication to ensure that people understand one another. A commitment to the public's right to know is a tenet of many political systems. Fulfilling that commitment requires a comprehensive (normative, descriptive, and prescriptive) approach, so that the public receives the information that it needs in a comprehensible form.

Given the complexity of many risk decisions, there are many possible accounts of how people think about them. Without evidence, it is easy to speculate about the roles played by lay people's beliefs, values, emotions, and social pressures, when they respond to risks. It is equally easy for the public to speculate about political actors' judgements, biases, incentives, and malfeasance. When those speculations are wrong, they can needlessly cloud already difficult decisions. As a result, *Risk: A Very Short Introduction* emphasizes what is known about human behaviour regarding each aspect of making risk decisions.

Conclusion: risks derive their meaning from risk decisions

All risk decisions have the same basic elements as these three examples: options, outcomes, and uncertainties, set in a social context, framed in language highlighting some ways of looking at the decision. For each decision, normative analysis can organize the relevant knowledge and uncertainties. Descriptive research can contrast decision-makers' intuitive views with the normative analysis. Prescriptive interventions can help people to make better choices. Together, these approaches afford lay people and experts alike ways to think about public and private risk decisions, whether as active participants or interested observers.

Thinking about risk decisions in these terms treats decision-making as an exercise in practical reasoning. Thus, decision theory provides a toolkit for identifying and organizing knowledge that might be helpful in making risk decisions. It helps one to sort through statistical analyses of risks and find the most relevant estimates, to extract the critical uncertainties revealed by expert debates, to follow risk communications, to seek cultural traditions that deal with danger, and to know when emotions are aiding or clouding judgement. Thus, decision theory provides a general approach to making sense of the world of risks, posing threats to outcomes that we value.

No one is expert in all aspects of any of risk decision, much less all risks. Technical specialists' knowledge of risks is limited to their areas of expertise. Our knowledge of ourselves is limited by our insight into our own beliefs, desires, and blinders. Chapter 2 provides the first step towards better understanding of risk decisions, defining risks in clear, common terms expressing underlying values. Chapter 3 examines how risks (and benefits) are assessed, once they have been defined. Chapter 4 considers ways in which risk decisions can be made, based on those assessments. Chapter 5 addresses barriers to understanding decisions, with Chapter 6 offering ways to overcome them. Chapter 7 discusses how societies define and express themselves in how they deal with risks.

Chapter 2
Defining risk

Risks involve threats to outcomes that we value. Defining risk means specifying those valued outcomes clearly enough to make choices about them. For some valued outcomes, there are widely accepted measures, such as annual mortality rate and gross national product. For other outcomes, such as wellbeing and sustainability, there is no such agreement. For yet other outcomes, such as threats to justice and nature, the very idea of measurement is controversial, with some people agreeing with legal scholar Laurence Tribe that measurement can 'anaesthetize moral feeling' and others agreeing with physicist Michael Faraday that, 'if you cannot measure it, you cannot improve it'. Defining risks clearly enough to measure them means bringing value issues into relief.

There are two ways to gain insight into those issues. One is to look carefully at the values embedded in possible definitions. The second is to observe what people implicitly or explicitly value when they make judgements and decisions about risks. We apply both approaches, beginning with the seemingly simple task of defining the risk of dying. We then proceed to more diffuse risks, such as threats to the integrity of ecosystems and societies. A common goal is defining diverse risks and their valued outcomes in common terms, helping us to tell which are, or perhaps should be, our biggest worries.

Are all deaths equal?

Table 1 shows statistics for a familiar definition of the risk of dying: the annual death toll. If American society based its public health risk decisions on this definition, then it would focus its resources on reducing the risks on the top of the list. The first four are problems affecting older people: heart disease, cancer, stroke, and chronic respiratory diseases. Focusing on them means accepting the value implicit in this definition: all deaths are equal and only the total number matters. Another possible guiding value places a premium on deaths of younger people. That value requires a definition of risk that worries more about accidental deaths (#5 in the list), which affect young people disproportionately. That measure would see greater benefit in eliminating all 121,599 deaths from accidents than all 124,583 deaths from chronic lower respiratory diseases (#4) or perhaps even all 631,636 deaths from heart disease (#1).

If age matters, then there is an alternative definition for the risk of dying: 'expected life-years lost'. When an otherwise healthy 20-year-old dies in a road accident, about 60 years of expected life

Table 1. Leading causes of death in the United States (2006)

1. Heart disease: 631,636
2. Cancer: 559,888
3. Stroke (cerebrovascular diseases): 137,119
4. Chronic lower respiratory diseases: 124,583
5. Accidents (unintentional injuries): 121,599
6. Diabetes: 72,449
7. Alzheimer's disease: 72,432
8. Influenza and pneumonia: 56,326
9. Nephritis, nephrotic syndrome, and nephrosis: 45,344
10. Septicaemia: 34,234

Source: Centers for Disease Control and Prevention (National Vital Statistics Report, 2008)

are lost (before something else would prove fatal). When an 80-year-old succumbs to a heart attack, 'only' a few years of expected life are lost. Estimating the exact loss requires nuanced statistical analyses, asking questions such as 'How vulnerable are people with heart conditions to other diseases?' However, the value question is stark: is it especially bad if young people die? There is no way to avoid this question. Any definition treats young and old either similarly or differently. Risk analysts will use some definition when they calculate the 'risk of dying'. They need guidance on which outcomes matter to decision-makers. Without it, their procedures will determine societal values.

'Life-years lost' counts years. A logical next question is whether all years are valued equally. When health economists answer that question, they typically assume that unhealthy years are worth less than healthy ones. Thus, when older people suffer heart attacks after protracted cardiovascular illness, they lose relatively few years of relatively poor health. A common unit for measuring those years is the Quality-Adjusted Life Year, or QALY (pronounced 'kwallie'), which puts less value on years in the lives of unhealthy people.

The definition of 'risk of dying' could make other distinctions as well. It could assign different weights to men and women, to mothers and non-mothers, or to citizens and non-citizens. The definition could also give extra weight to deaths from specific sources, such as medical X-rays, radon in homes, sunlight, car exhausts, pesticides, asbestos insulation, damaged genes, endocrine disruptors, heat, cold, carbon dioxide, carbon monoxide, salt, gangs, alcohol, aspirin, or sources with any other attribute deemed to make a death special.

Thus, with risks of dying, it matters what is counted and how. Sometimes these issues are buried in seemingly prosaic procedures. For example, in 2007, the *US Standard Certificate of Death* was revised to add three attributes deemed worthy of

Table 2. Alternative measures of the risk of dying

Deaths per million people in the population
Deaths per million people within x miles of an exposure source (e.g. air pollution, plant explosion)
Deaths per unit of toxic concentration (e.g. nuclear radiation, pesticide toxicity)
Deaths per facility (e.g. coal mine, chemical plant, office building)
Deaths per ton of air toxic released
Deaths per milligram of air toxic absorbed by people
Deaths per kilowatt of electric power by nuclear, hydropower, coal, gas
Deaths per mile of transportation by airline, car, train

Source: Adapted from P. Slovic (ed.), *The Perception of Risk* (Earthscan, 2000), p. 397

attention: race, pregnancy status, and tobacco use. However, the committee revising the certificate chose not to add (or care about) whether the deceased was homeless, had health insurance, or suffered from diabetes. In the Vietnam War, US body counts were criticized for reducing people to numbers. In the Iraq War, the lack of US counts for Iraqi civilian casualties was taken to indicate indifference to their suffering. Table 2 shows yet other definitions of risk, each expressing a position on the relative value of different deaths.

Revealed preferences for risk–benefit trade-offs

Figure 3 adopts the second strategy for defining risks, trying to discern the factors that guide people when they make risk decisions in their lives. Published in 1969, it had a seminal role in discussions of risk. Its creator, the late nuclear engineer Chauncey Starr, sought a formula for determining whether risks were socially acceptable. He idealized society as a rational agent that 'revealed' its preferences in the risks and benefits that it accepted from different 'hazards'. His challenge was to identify those preferences.

Starr proposed that society defined 'risk' as deaths per hour of exposure to a hazard (e.g. while on the job or travelling) and 'benefit' as economic activity per person involved with it. Applying these measures to the hazards in Figure 3 shows that hazards with greater risk tend to have greater benefit, as seen in the points being generally arrayed from lower left to upper right. From this rough pattern, Starr concluded that society 'accepts' greater risk from hazards that provide greater benefit. However, he also concluded that the pattern was so messy that his definition of risk must be incomplete. That is, people must consider more than just deaths per hour of exposure, if they accept so much greater risk, say, from general (private) aviation than from commercial aviation, two hazards having roughly similar economic benefits.

Starr proposed that people accept greater risk from general aviation because they assume it voluntarily, when they decide to travel in private planes; in contrast, the risks of commercial

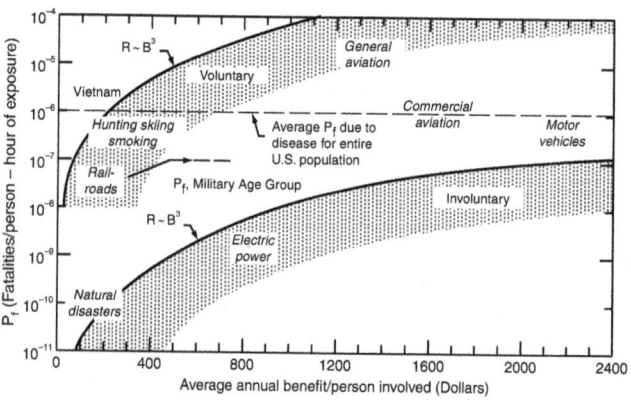

3. **Risk–benefit trade-offs 'revealed' in statistical estimates of risk and benefit levels from eight hazards. 'R~B³' means that risk (defined as probability of fatality) increases approximately in proportion to benefits raised to the third power. Shaded areas are Starr's informal uncertainty bands**

aviation are involuntary, for people who must fly that way. Starr argued further that aviation was typical of a general double standard, whereby, for any level of benefit, society accepts greater risks from voluntary hazards (hunting, skiing, smoking) than from involuntary ones (natural disasters, electric power, motor vehicles). As a result, the points in Figure 3 do not fall on a single risk–benefit curve, but on two curves, one for voluntary risks (top) and one for involuntary risks (bottom). If true, this pattern means that a hazard's social acceptability could be determined by assessing its risk, benefit, and voluntariness, then seeing whether it fell above or below the relevant curve.

As a sign of those times, Starr attributed some of Americans' opposition to the war in Vietnam to the large involuntary risks that it imposed on draftees, compared to the baseline risk for the 'military age group'. He saw no economic benefit to the war, putting it in the upper left-hand of Figure 3. The involuntary curve ignores the war because so many Americans found its risks unacceptable.

Starr's analysis made three strong assumptions, typical of revealed preference analyses, which try to read people's minds based on their actions. One assumption is that the people making these decisions defined 'risk', 'benefit', and 'voluntary' as Starr did. The second is that those people saw each hazard as having the same degree of risk, benefit, and voluntariness as he did. The third is that they found these risk–benefit trade-offs acceptable.

Each of these assumptions is questionable. Consider natural disasters (such as floods and earthquakes). Starr treated them as involuntary risks with no compensating economic benefits. However, one could argue that people voluntarily choose to live in harm's way, on flood plains, barrier islands, and earthquake faults. If so, then this point belongs on the voluntary curve. Where it falls on that curve depends on how one calculates the economic benefits of living in those risky places. For example, is money spent on flood protection and recovery a cost or a benefit, given that someone makes a living from it?

Even when people define risks and benefits similarly, they may not perceive them similarly. People often lack good information, even for big decisions, such as where to live. For example, the geographer Gilbert White found that people living in areas protected from minor floods underestimate the risks of major ones, not realizing the limits to that protection. If so, then they accept a lot more risk than they realize, when they choose to live behind levees or downstream from dams – and the statistics do not reveal the choices that they think they are making.

Other hazards raise similar definitional questions. Are the risks of smoking voluntary, based on individuals' initial decisions to experiment, or are they involuntary, based on the difficulty of stopping? Do first-time smokers perceive the risks in Starr's statistics or do they see them as irrelevant because they believe that they could always stop? Does the amount of money spent on smoking capture its benefits or underestimate them, given that smokers will often spend more when prices rise? Is money spent on smoking cessation programmes and lung cancer treatment an economic benefit, just as money spent on waste disposal is counted in nations' gross national product? Do smokers think or care about such costs, which lie far in the future and may be borne by others? Thus, although risk decisions reveal something about how people define risks and benefits, extracting that lesson requires much more knowledge about how they make decisions than is captured in aggregate statistics like Figure 3.

Dimensions of risk

Although Starr's analysis revealed a somewhat murky lesson about individuals' preferences, it captured the insight that intuitive definitions of risk reflect more than just death statistics. Following Starr, bioethicist William Lowrance proposed eight additional 'attributes' that might affect how people define risks and make decisions about them. His attributes included whether risks are relatively *unknown* to science, evoke a feeling of *dread*, and take many lives *catastrophically*, rather than one at a time. Subsequent lists had many more attributes. One review found 39 attributes for ecological risks alone.

One way to make sense of so many attributes is to ask people questions such as 'How voluntary are the risks of nuclear power?', then see which attribute ratings go together. Figure 4 summarizes such ratings for 30 hazards on variants of Lowrance's risk attributes. (These results are from members of a Eugene, Oregon, civic group, in the late 1970s. Many other studies, with different people, hazards, and procedures, have produced generally similar pictures.)

A statistical procedure (factor analysis) found two dimensions underlying the nine attributes. Hazards high on the vertical dimension, such as food colouring, pesticides, and nuclear power, have risks that are seen as relatively involuntary, delayed, unknown to the exposed, unknown to science, uncontrollable, new, catastrophic, and dreaded. Hazards high on the horizontal dimension, such as nuclear power, handguns, and general aviation, have risks that are seen as relatively dreaded, catastrophic, and certain to be fatal, if something goes wrong. Thus, as different as handguns and general aviation are in many other respects, they have similar risk attributes. On the horizontal dimension, both hazards are high because their risks seem relatively dreaded, fatal, and catastrophic. On the vertical dimension, they are more average. If these ratings capture important aspects of risks, then where hazards fall in the risk space should predict how society deals with them. Indeed, both handguns and general aviation are moderately regulated in the US, although not as much as nuclear power and pesticides, two hazards that are high on both dimensions.

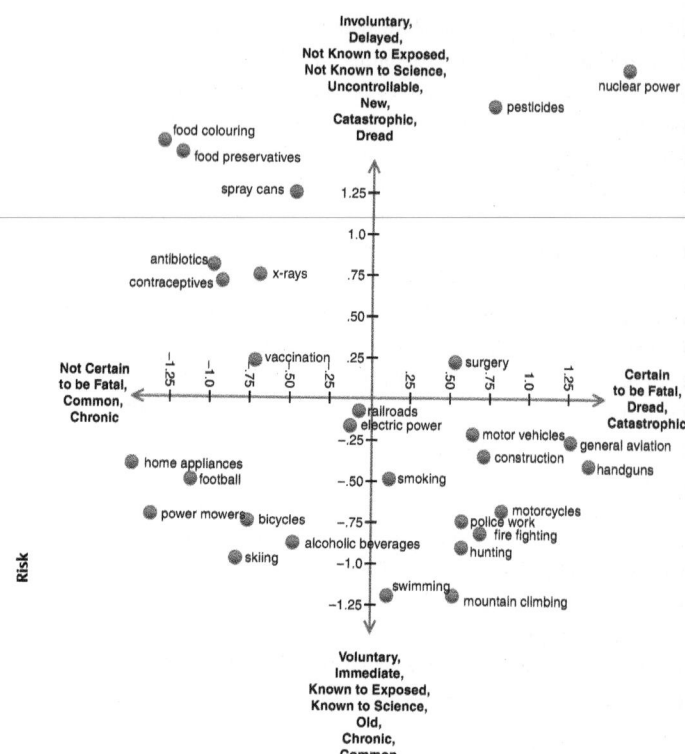

4. A risk space based on ratings of 30 hazards on 9 risk attributes

Whether these attributes should affect risk decisions is a separate question. One might argue that having a 'double standard' for voluntary and involuntary risks unfairly demands more from industry (nuclear power, pesticides, food preservatives) than from oneself (skiing, hunting, alcoholic beverages). Setting higher standards for new technologies might seem like opposition to progress. Considering the dread that hazards evoke might seem like letting emotions rule risk decisions.

However, because these attributes are correlated (as seen in Figure 4), it is not easy to disentangle their effects. Involuntary, new, and dreaded hazards also tend to be unknown and potentially catastrophic. Demanding more from dreaded hazards might seem irrational; however, it also means demanding more from unknown hazards, which seems prudent. Demanding more from hazards with catastrophic potential might express a dubious aversion to multiple-death events, compared to single-death ones (300 people in one plane crash versus 300 in single-car accidents). However, it could also reflect aversion to the uncertainty that is part of hazards that can produce such tragedies. Involuntary risks also tend to be distributed inequitably, meaning that people who demand more from them might be exercising a right (to be treated fairly), rather than acting on emotion.

Thus, asking people to rate risk attributes (Figure 4) reveals more about how they define risks than do revealed preference analyses, which try to infer motives from their behaviour (Figure 3). However, like all surveys, such studies limit how fully people can express themselves. The next section considers ways to engage people in deliberative discourse over how risks should be defined.

Ranking risks

In the early 1990s, the US Environmental Protection Agency (EPA) convened dozens of citizen panels, asking each to identify the risk outcomes most important to its region (including, in one case, 'the Vermont way of life'). After each panel had defined 'risk' this way, environmental scientists summarized the evidence about regionally relevant hazards in those terms. The panels then used those summaries to rank the hazards by their risk level.

For the EPA, these 'risk-ranking exercises' had two major goals. One was empowering people to take on regional problems in a scientifically informed way. The second was refocusing the EPA's own definition of 'risk', largely set by national concerns at the time of its creation 20 years earlier. Like other well-designed citizen participation processes, these panels often produced fruitful dialogue, connecting 'stakeholders' with technical experts and one another. However, because the panels emphasized regional needs, each created its own definition of 'risk', making it hard to compare their priorities.

In order to achieve greater comparability, a British government initiative created a standard set of risk attributes to use when evaluating any project (real-estate development, green energy source, hazardous facility). As seen in Figure 5, the scheme includes (on the left) results from cost–benefit analyses (CBA) estimating the economic costs of expected deaths and other harms. People should be willing to pay (WTP, an economics term) at least that much to eliminate those risks. On the right are six risk attributes, representing the dimensions in Figure 4. The two

Concern Assessment Framework

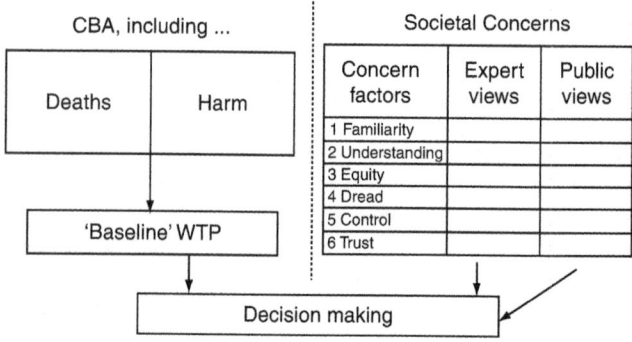

5. A standard method for defining risk. The attributes on the left are calculated. The ones on the right are measured with judgements allowing five levels for each attribute. For *dread*, these levels are: (1) trivial, temporary, and commonplace; (2) potentially serious, but treatable; (3) serious, long-term, but natural; (4) serious, permanent, and unethical; or (5) catastrophic, permanent, and highly feared

columns acknowledge that experts and lay people might see hazards differently on these attributes. Defining risks this way does not tell decision-makers how to weight the attributes or what choices to make, after comparing risks and benefits. However, it does legitimate considering a wide range of public concerns.

The US EPA and British methods are explicit approaches to the priority setting that people do implicitly all the time. On a given day, a parent might wonder how much to worry about a child's cough, a car's rattle, an ageing parent's fall, a wave of burglaries, a worrisome skin rash, and a shrinking investment portfolio. At a given meeting, a school board might wonder how much to worry about school bus seatbelts, playground fights, pandemics, broken stairs, and student obesity. Farmers, truckers, teens, parliaments, and others grapple with their own lists of risks, trying to focus on the big ones and 'not sweat the small stuff'.

People often berate themselves for how poorly they set their risk priorities. However, it is hard to rank risks without a clear, common definition of risk, expressing one's basic values, like those offered by the EPA and Her Majesty's Treasury. Without such a definition, thinking about many risks simultaneously means thinking about none of them thoroughly. In life, people typically 'muddle through', waiting until an event (e.g. a flood or heat wave) draws a risk to their attention. After thinking about it, they raise or lower its priority, then move on, without ever explicitly defining risk. Thus, seeing an accident might convince a driver to decide whether a car's rattle is just annoying or serious enough to need immediate repair. An alarming news report might induce a school board to figure out whether pandemic preparedness is urgent or can be put off indefinitely, in deference to the other risks it faces (food poisoning, violence, truancy).

How well such sequential priority setting works depends on which risks draw attention. People will get their priorities right if they notice risks that threaten outcomes that they value. They will get their priorities wrong if life focuses them on minor risks. Parents can neglect their own health while managing minor kid, car, and house problems. Nations can ignore their future health needs while concentrating on immediate economic stresses. School boards can neglect looming disasters while addressing everyday crises. People chained to the 24/7 news cycle can be endlessly distracted by uninformative coverage of minor issues. Priority setting can be easier in traditional cultures, where stable, consensual definitions of risk draw everyone's attention to dangers that threaten shared valued outcomes.

Risk indicators

Although defining the risk of death has many nuances, at least it deals with a distinct outcome, as found with many disease, accident, and financial risks. However, some valued outcomes are too complex to capture with any simple, direct measurement. These risks must be defined with 'indicators' that serve as proxies for the most valued outcomes. Healthy ecosystems and human societies involve such complex outcomes.

Aquatic ecosystems are threatened by many pollutants (road salt, pesticides, oil, faecal bacteria, water purification by-products, excreted drugs, fertilizer run-off, decomposing plastics), affecting many organisms (plankton, kelp, fish, marine mammals) in many ways (direct poisoning, compromised immune and navigation systems, confused social behaviour). Even when these individual effects can be assessed, those measures do not capture the complex interdependencies that constitute 'ecological health'. Measuring the health of fish populations, one key aspect of aquatic ecosystems, faces similar problems. Because those populations can fluctuate widely, depending on predation, weather, disease, and other factors, no single number captures the quality of their health.

One way to capture that complexity is with a suite of indicators addressing different aspects of ecosystem health. For example, water quality at a treated sewage outfall might be measured by dissolved oxygen available to aquatic life, peak water temperature, dissolved and suspended solids, alkalinity (pH), and pesticide residues. As with risk of dying, different measurement procedures express different values. For example, making observations over finer timescales (hours rather than years) and areas (ponds rather than regions) increases the chances of exceeding an action level (high temperature or turbidity) and of spotting problems ('we're losing rich foraging for age one and older Coho salmon'). Suites of measures at different biological scales approximate the flexible rulers that ecologists use to evaluate ecosystems and habitat quality.

A second kind of indicator is the health of keystone species that are essential to ecological balance. For example, sea otters eat sea urchins that destroy kelp forests by nibbling at tiny root structures. As a result, sea otter populations are an indicator for many aspects of ecosystem health. When the Pittsburgh area de-industrialized after 1980, the return of river otters signified nature's rebound. Amphibians and invertebrates provide early warning of ecosystem decline, as do deaths of corals and their symbiotic algaes when ocean waters warm.

A third kind of indicator is biodiversity, which keeps small problems from cascading into catastrophes. A rich ensemble of plant and animal species has more ways to perform the essential functions of purifying water, decomposing litter, recycling nutrients, providing food, and protecting habitat. As a result, biodiversity provides a kind of biological insurance against adversity. Valuing it means valuing a scientifically sound measure of ecosystem resilience.

A fourth imperfect indicator of an ecosystem's health is its economic value. Ecosystems provide the photosynthesis, nitrogen conversion, oxygen formation, and other processes on which human life depends. We need the food and shelter provided by healthy water, land, and forests; the flood control and filtration provided by wetlands; and the pollination provided by birds and insects. 'Ecosystem service' indicators measure the monetary cost of replacing natural systems, for example by substituting levees and water-purification plants for wetlands. Another approach from environmental economics seeks to 'monetize' nature's intrinsic value, independent of any such instrumental benefit. The usual indicator is how much people say they would pay to protect part of the natural world. Such monetization gives standing to environmental outcomes that would otherwise be neglected. However, while it can win battles where there is a clear economic case for environmental protection, it may be losing the war to treat the natural world as valued in its own right.

Risk to the human condition

Aristotle's measure of human wellbeing was living the 'good life'. Indicators for that rich concept parallel those for ecosystem health. Some measures cover minimal conditions for wellbeing, such as sustenance, clean water, primary healthcare, educational opportunities, and physical protection. Figure 6 shows one such set. Focused on the world's 'bottom billion', living on less than $1 per day, it uses routinely collected statistics that are directly linked to ways of improving wellbeing. For example, the Education Index includes school enrolment and literacy, two common statistics and targets for social programmes.

The equivalent of keystone species is found in indicators of healthy human societies. One is a low rate of subsistence agriculture, whose low productivity prevents accumulating the surplus food needed to free labour for generating wealth. A second is a low rate of multiple early pregnancies, which limits women's access to the education needed for economic autonomy and social power. A third is robust infrastructure (roads, sanitation,

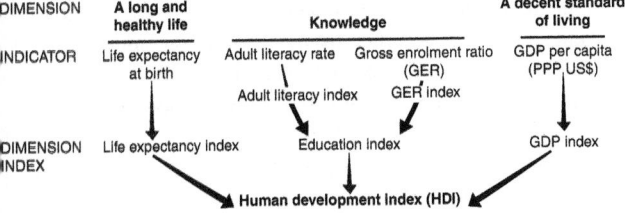

DIMENSION	A long and healthy life	Knowledge		A decent standard of living
INDICATOR	Life expectancy at birth	Adult literacy rate / Adult literacy index	Gross enrolment ratio (GER) / GER index	GDP per capita (PPP US$)
DIMENSION INDEX	Life expectancy index	Education index		GDP index

→ Human development index (HDI) ◄

6. United Nations Human Development Index

electrical power), making labour more productive and resources more available.

As with ecosystem indicators, these measures are only as good as the science showing their importance and guiding their application. The relationships between women's education, family size, and wellbeing are well established. Demographers know how to apply measures of family size such as the Total Fertility Rate (TFR), which ranges from below 2.0 in ageing European countries (just below that needed to maintain a population) to 6.0 in some developing ones. Sociologists have developed a measure of 'violent outbreaks' that captures threats like armed conflicts, population displacement, and genocide. That measure is related to the prevalence of unemployed young men, who may turn to violence, in societies sometimes described as 'too poor for peace'. Here, as elsewhere, defining risk places science at the service of values, identifying threats to valued outcomes and ways to assess them.

Is it safe?

However defined, 'risk' is not a dichotomous (either/or) variable, but one that ranges from 'smaller than can be measured' to 'as high as possible'. Often, though, decision-makers must treat risks categorically, as being above or below an action threshold. Thus, they may need to decide whether an investment is safe enough for retirement accounts, whether a bomb threat is large enough to evacuate an airport, whether a snow forecast warrants closing schools, whether a drug's side effects require a 'black-box' label warning, or whether a solvent is too toxic for home use.

Comparing a specific risk to a general threshold is a job for risk analysts. However, setting that threshold is a task for policy-makers, who must decide, for example, what risk of terrorist attack justifies the certain economic loss from closing an airport. When policy-makers leave such thresholds vague, they force others to infer or invent them. Table 3 describes the inferences required from climate scientists, when applying the 'dangerous anthropogenic interference' (DAI) metric of the Intergovernmental Panel on Climate Change (IPCC).

Any single indicator (like DAI) confronts a famously thorny value question: how to compare costs and benefits experienced over time. When everything is reduced to money, economists have a widely accepted solution: 'discount' the future by the current interest rate. If that rate is 5%, then £100 today is worth £105 next year, about £110 the following year, and, by the magic of compound interest, very large sums in the distant future (about £1,150 in 50 years). That logic leads to concluding that saving £100 today, by not protecting the environment, outweighs much larger damages in the future (up to about £1,150 in 50 years).

However well this logic applies to private investments, it can be questionable for public ones. When people save for themselves, they can expect to receive the deferred benefits. However, future generations may not benefit from money that is saved today by neglecting the environment. If those savings happen to be invested in ways that make future generations wealthier, then the proceeds might be used to undo the damage or taken as compensation for irreversible losses. However, if that money is spent solely to benefit people today, then discounting the future means writing it off. Whatever is done with money, there is no obvious justification for

Table 3. Defining 'dangerous climate change'

The Intergovernmental Panel on Climate Change (IPCC) creates research summaries of the form 'if CO_2 concentrations stabilize at 580 ppm, *then* there are two chances in three that temperature will increase by 1.5° to 4.5°C, compared to 2005'. (The table below shows a set of such estimates.) These summaries reflect scientific judgements, integrating data from many sources. However, the IPCC charter also requires it to assess the risk of 'dangerous anthropogenic interference' (DAI). 'Dangerous', like 'risky', requires a value judgement, regarding which impacts are intolerable. In response, IPCC scientists rated future global warming levels, from 'low' to 'high', based on five 'reasons for concern': *1*) ecosystem threats, *2*) extreme weather events, *3*) varying distributions of impacts, *4*) cumulative impacts, and *5*) large-scale 'discontinuities' (e.g. in ocean currents or sea levels). They did not, however, set an explicit threshold. Climatologists Stephen Schneider and Marcello Mastrandrea argued, however, that IPCC reports had revealed an implicit threshold of about +2.85°C. Their colleague James Hansen argued that the IPCC had so underestimated damages that its threshold should be +1°C. He argued, further, that +1°C was an objective 'danger' threshold, as it exceeds the maximum temperature since the last ice age, taking us 'outside the range of human experience'.

Stabilization level of CO_2 and other greenhouse gases	+2°C	+3°C	+4°C	+5°C	+6°C	+7°C
450 ppm	78%	18%	3%	1%	0%	0%
500	96%	44%	11%	3%	1%	0%
550	99%	69%	24%	7%	2%	1%
650	100%	94%	58%	24%	9%	4%
750	100%	99%	82%	47%	22%	9%

Looking at the top row: if concentrations stabilize at 450 ppm, there is a 78% chance of at least 2°C increase (compared to 1850), an 18% chance of at least 3°C increase, and so on. 560 ppm roughly doubles pre-industrial concentrations. (These calculations translate the impacts of other greenhouse gases, such as methane, into the equivalent effects of CO_2.)

Source: M. Mastrandrea and S. Schneider, 'Probablistic Integrated Assessment of "Dangerous" Climate Change', *Science*, 304; 2004, 571–575
N. Stern, *The Global Deal: Climate Change and the Creation of a New Era of Progress and Prosperity* (New York: Public Affairs, 2009), p. 26.

discounting future lives, other than valuing people today more than people in the future. Otherwise, a life (or QALY) should have the same value, whenever it is lost.

'Acceptable risks'

Risks are sometimes presented in lists like Table 1, with many hazards expressed in terms of a single attribute. One popular version shows the dose of a hazard estimated to increase the chance of premature death by one in a million. Such lists encourage 'risk comparisons' such as that between the one-in-a-million cancer risk from both living 50 years at the boundary of a nuclear power plant and eating a tablespoon of peanut butter (from aflatoxin). Those comparisons lead, in turn, to the inference that people who accept one risk should accept the other.

Such comparisons are flawed in three fundamental ways. One is in assuming that 'risk' is defined by that one measure of the risk of dying (whose limits are discussed above). The second is in assuming that risk decisions are about risks alone. However,

A one-in-a-million chance of death

The annual death rate in affluent countries is about 1 per 100 people (0.8%). A year has about 10,000 hours, making about 1 death per million hours of living (= 100 x 10,000). Thus, a person in these countries has an average chance of one in a million of dying each hour; in effect that is the risk of being alive. Of course, that risk varies considerably, as a function of age, sex, socioeconomic status, and other factors. The average roughly holds for infants up to one year and 55–64 year olds, with members of both groups having roughly 1 chance in a 100 of dying in the coming year.

Source: Adapted from V. Smil, *Global Catastrophes and Trends*, p. 226

people do not voluntarily accept risks without some compensating benefit. If the benefits differ in the two cases, there is no reason for similar risks to lead to similar choices. Thus, a person may feel that the great taste of peanut butter justifies its aflatoxin risk, but see no benefit in having a nuclear neighbour. Finally, such comparisons assume that accepted risks are acceptable. A person may find peanut butter uncomfortably risky (due to aflatoxin, Salmonella, etc.), but see no better way to get its nutritional benefits while finding alternatives to nuclear power.

From this perspective, the everyday term 'acceptable risk' is often a misnomer. Whatever choices people make, they accept some risks. However, those risks need not be acceptable, if people wish that they had options with lower risks. Even when risks are acceptable, that is conditional on their benefits. One could equally say that the benefits are acceptable, given the risks. There is nothing inconsistent about rejecting a small risk and accepting a large one, if it has sufficient benefits. Moreover, a risk that is acceptable to one person might not be acceptable to another, who defines risk and benefit differently.

Conclusion: how risk is measured depends on what we value

Risk entails some chance of losing something of value. If people value different outcomes, then they define 'risk' differently. As a result, defining risk is an exercise in value-focused thinking. It can be informed by reflecting on which outcomes really matter and by examining past decisions for what they reveal about what people value. Risk definitions are sometimes debated publicly and sometimes buried in technical details. Once 'risk' is defined, its causes can be understood and its magnitude estimated, the topics of Chapter 3.

Chapter 3
Analysing risk

Once a risk has been defined, describing which outcomes decision-makers value most, analysts can begin their work, determining how large the risks are and what causes them. Risk analyses are intricate constructions, often integrating diverse sciences and forms of evidence. However, their basic logic is straightforward: observe or infer as much as possible about the magnitude of risks, then use scientific knowledge about their causes to extrapolate from known situations to unknown ones. In this chapter, we show how that logic emerges in increasingly complicated analyses, going from simple counts to statistical analyses and computer simulation models – and how it sometimes drives basic science, such as the research unravelling the HIV virus or tobacco's powerful effects. However simple or complex the analysis, expert judgement plays a vital role, in identifying the processes that create and control risks, in using the evidence available about those processes, and in assessing the residual uncertainty. The chapter concludes with research regarding the quality of the expert judgement that is part of all analysis. Risk analysis emerges as a kind of applied science or engineering, using decision theory to integrate results from whichever sources prove useful.

Counting casualties

Societies have recorded the grim toll of cholera since antiquity. Modern statistics evolved, in part, to study the devastating, dreaded epidemics that swept Europe in the 19th century. Cholera has such distinctive symptoms (acute diarrhoea and dehydration) and kills so quickly that creating reliable casualty records is straightforward. Anyone can record who has fallen ill and died, then tally their number. These counts alone, however, tell little about cholera's causes and remedies. Going beyond counts requires understanding the chains of physical and social processes that determine cholera risks. In a famous analysis, physician John Snow showed how careful observation and astute judgement could clarify those causes, even with the limited health science of his day.

During the 1854 London outbreak, Snow created a map of cases in Soho (Figure 7), revealing a concentration around the Broad Street pump. Snow guessed that cholera was transmitted through drinking water and not, as many believed, through 'bad air' or

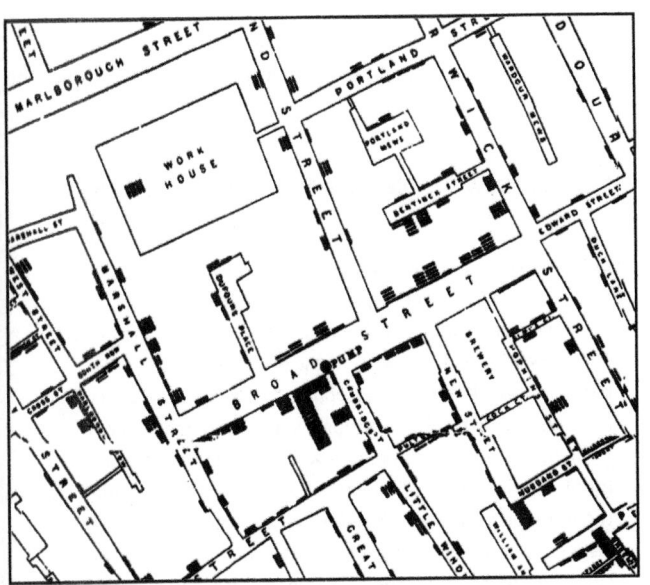

7. **Sir John Snow's map of cholera in Soho, London, 1854**

'miasma' (an ancient theory of disease). However, even though Snow found nothing in the pump's water that directly supported his hypothesis (the cholera bacterium was not discovered until 1866), he still convinced the local water board to remove the pump handle. The disease abated. Although that change supported Snow's theory, it was not conclusive, as the outbreak might just have run its course (as suggested by historical analysis). However, Snow supported his case for the cause of the outbreak with other evidence, including the lack of disease among inmates of a workhouse that had its own water supply and among drinkers of beer made with other water.

Snow's study showed what is possible with thoughtful observation and counting, informed by weak hypotheses about causes. It was also good enough for decision-makers, showing them what to do: stop using the suspect water. Although scientific understanding of cholera has advanced greatly since then, when outbreaks occur risk analysts use the same basic approach: count the casualties, identify possible causes, and try to alter them, hoping to reduce the

Sir John Snow's cholera analysis in modern terms

Cholera-infected water was the risk *source* (or *hazard*) and the pump was part of its *pathway* to the exposed *populations* of users. They experienced *health effects*, whose *outcomes*, or *consequences*, include diarrhoea, rapid dehydration, and death. The *probability* and *severity* of these effects depend on the bacterial *dose*. Individuals' *responses* to a given dose depend on their body size, health, nutritional status, and behaviour, including whether they boil the water and how they ingest it (drink, food, bathwater). Bacterial *concentrations* depended on the *transport* of sewage through the pathways to drinking water (sewers, water pipes, Thames tidal flows) and other factors (sunlight, water chemistry) affecting the *fate* of the contaminant.

danger. If such 'risk management' works, then the problem is solved and the theory supported. Snow's work presaged modern risk analysis with its varied methods for integrating uncertain knowledge from multiple sources.

Correlating doses and health effects

Snow succeeded, in part, because cholera casualties are easy to count and its causes relatively simple. Although cardiovascular (heart) disease (CVD) causes many more deaths (Table 1), its risks are much harder to analyse, because it has so many causes (smoking, obesity, stress, diet, genetics), often intertwined with other health problems (diabetes, cancer, emphysema).

Epidemiologists use statistical methods to analyse such risks, typically requiring large quantities of data collected over many years. For CVD, the mother lode of such data is the Framingham Study, which has followed the health and habits of thousands of Massachusetts residents since 1948. It produced some of the first strong evidence finding that heart disease was correlated with smoking and high cholesterol levels in the blood, while high blood pressure was uncorrelated with ageing *per se* (absent other risk factors). These results stimulated research into the causal mechanisms underlying them, eventually leading to public health programmes capable of reducing the risks.

In 1948, the annual US death rate from CVD was 146 cases per 100,000. It increased to 220 in 1963, reflecting post-war lifestyles with heavy food and smoking. It declined to 87 in 1996, partially due to behaviour changes arising from Framingham's insights into healthy living (smoking less, exercising more). The recent worldwide rise in obesity shows the roles of other causes, such as stress and the availability of unhealthy food. Over this time, there has been no change in the *dose-response relationships*, between, say, a 'dose' of good diet or aerobic exercise and the 'response' of CVD. However, the doses have changed, as people first ate less and exercised more, then reversed those trends.

Clarifying causes

The importance of dose-response relationships was recognized 500 years ago, when the Renaissance physician Paracelsus stated the 'first law of toxicology': 'All things are poison and nothing is without poison, only the dose permits something not to be poisonous.' Thus, even beneficial drugs are poisonous, if the dose is too large, whereas even small doses of toxic venom and bacteria can induce protective responses, as with vaccination. As a result, risk analysis depends on measuring doses and responses well enough to establish the relationships between them.

As far back as the 1930s, German scientists hypothesized smoking's role in cancer. Yet the US Surgeon General's *Report on Smoking and Cancer* appeared only in 1964, after which 45 more years passed until Congress gave the Food and Drug Administration the authority to regulate tobacco. One scientific barrier to faster action was the difficulty of inferring the causes underlying these correlations. A second was the difficulty of identifying the 'effective doses' of the many chemicals in tobacco smoke, whose absorption and 'fate' depend on complex physiological processes.

The tobacco industry's vigorous defence highlighted those uncertainties in the science and proposed other reasons why smokers might have more cancer, such as weighing more or working with chemicals. Even increased longevity was sometimes invoked as a possible cause, with tobacco's defenders arguing that longer life-spans provided more time for lung cancers to emerge. Better measurement and statistical methods gradually eliminated these other causes as possibilities and isolated smoking's role. These epidemiological analyses were further supported by research into the physiological mechanisms linking smoking and health (e.g. how smoke carries chemicals to the lungs, then to vulnerable organs via the lungs' natural processes for oxygenating blood). Although tobacco has long been known to contain carcinogens, such as tar laced with benzene, the US mandated full disclosure of those chemicals only in 2010.

Complex exposures

As complex as smoking's risks may be, they come from a single source. In contrast, many organic (carbon-containing) chemicals (e.g. fuels, plastics, pesticides) are so pervasive that it is hard to measure their doses – and, hence, responses to them. For example, the amount of pesticide that people absorb when eating fruit depends on how much was applied to that fruit, how it degrades over time, how the fruit is prepared and processed, and how their bodies process such chemicals.

One research strategy for clarifying dose-response relationships involves looking at people who receive large doses, then extrapolating downward to the effects with smaller doses. For organic chemicals, workers in poorly regulated chemical plants are an obvious focus. However, studies often find that they actually live longer than their peers. That seemingly paradoxical result reflects a 'healthy worker effect': people must be fairly healthy in order to be in the workforce, healthier still to work in facilities requiring vigorous labour. Statistical procedures that 'control' for overall health often find higher cancer rates for chemical workers (three to eight times higher among workers in one study of arsenic mines, smelters, and oil refineries). Yet, there are always other possible causes that might account for the difference, such as chemical workers' body weight or smoking habits.

As with smoking, physiological research complements statistical analyses, by measuring chemicals' effects directly. That research often gives measured doses to animals, sometimes using ones bred for their susceptibility to cancer. That research measures toxicity in terms like LD_{50} (the Lethal Dose needed to kill 50% of test animals), NOAEL (the No Observed Adverse Effect Level), and MTD (the Maximum Tolerated Dose, not causing death, whatever other harm it does). Table 4 shows how widely LD_{50} values can vary for different substances.

Table 4. Examples of LD_{50} = lethal dose needed to kill 50% of test animals

LD_{50} values are often used in setting safety standards for accident risks, which create sudden large exposures. For example, the estimates below imply that one half milligram of mercury(II) chloride will kill 50% of laboratory rats weighing one-half kilogram. LD_{50} values can depend on the animal used, the exposure route, and other factors that complicate extrapolating experimental results to humans. Except where noted, the estimates reflect oral ingestion by rats.

Substance	LD_{50} milligrams/kilogram
Sucrose (table sugar)	29,700
Vitamin C (ascorbic acid)	11,900
Cadmium Sulfide	7,080
Grain alcohol (ethanol)	7,060
Table Salt	3,000
Paracetamol (acetaminophen)	1,944
THC (psychoactive agent in Cannabis)	1,270 males; 730 females
Metallic Arsenic	763
Aspirin (acetylsalicylic acid)	200
Caffeine	192
Cadmium oxide	72
Nicotine	50
Strychnine	16
Arsenic trioxide	14
Mercury(II) chloride	1
Aflatoxin B1 (from *Aspergillus flavus*)	0.48
Venom of the Inland Taipan (Australian snake), subcutaneous	0.025
Dioxin	0.020

Source: 'Median Lethal Dose', Wikipedia

What these estimates mean for humans is uncertain. Species vary in how they absorb, metabolize, and excrete chemicals. Toxicity studies typically deliver much larger doses than people ever experience. As a result, they sometimes overwhelm the body's natural defences. For example, formaldehyde is a strong irritant that can damage nasal linings. If large doses reduce the protection that those linings normally provide, then formaldehyde toxicity might be overestimated. Some scientists question the very idea of extrapolating from the high doses in studies to the lower ones in everyday life, arguing, for example, that living organisms must be able to repair the damage from very low doses of naturally occurring radiation (in soils, from outer space). As a further complication, the same total dose can have different effects when delivered at a constant rate or a variable one (with peaks and valleys over time). Faced by such uncertainties, regulators often define 'safe' human exposures as a 'conservative' fraction of animal toxicity levels (NOAEL, LD_{50}, etc.), perhaps with different safety standards for average and peak exposures.

Table 5 sketches the kind of calculation that risk analysts might make when extrapolating from animal experiments to human cancers. It gives the probability of premature cancer death for an individual with a given dose, weight, and so on. If all individuals have the same risk, then multiplying that probability by the number of people in the exposed population gives the total number of expected deaths. When individuals' sensitivity varies (e.g. with dose or weight), the choice of average value can make a big difference in population estimates. One common compromise is performing separate calculations for average adults and the average of sensitive populations (e.g. children, the elderly). A fuller solution is to conduct sensitivity analyses, seeing how much risk estimates vary with variations in 'inputs', like weight, dose, and dose-response relationship. One common summary of such sensitivity analyses is a probability distribution with assessments such as 'there is a 10% chance that fewer than 300 people will die and a 90% chance that no more than 5,000 will die'.

Table 5. Calculating cancer risk for chloroform in drinking water, based on data from animal experiments (for a 70-kilogram adult, who ingests 2 litres of water per day, with 0.050 milligrams/litre)

Background: Chlorinated water has chloroform residues
Typical concentration in source: 0.050 mg/litre (typical US regulated limit = 0.1 mg/litre)
Total daily dose: 0.1 mg (milligram) = 0.050 mg/litre x 2 litres/day
Daily dose per kilogram of body weight: 0.1 mg/day ÷ 70 kg = 0.0014 mg/kg/day
Additional cancer risk for 1 mg per kg/day (based on animal data, extrapolated to 70 years of human ingestion): 6/1000 (0.006)
Additional lifetime cancer risk: 0.000008 = 0.006 × 0.0014
Bottom line: approximately 8 of one million people consuming such water will develop cancer over a 70-year lifetime. With 300 million people in the US, that would mean 2,400 such deaths.

Source of calculation: J. Rodricks, *Calculated Risks* (New York: Cambridge University Press, 1992), p. 197

If decision-makers need greater precision, then they may sponsor research to 'tighten' the distribution (so that the 10%–90% range becomes, say, 1,000–3,000 deaths).

Complex pathways

Estimating exposures requires identifying the 'pathways' creating them. That is relatively straightforward for the pipes that spread cholera or the cigarettes that cause cancer. It is much more complicated for exposures that accumulate from multiple, identifiable 'point sources', such as the cars and fossil-fuel power plants that emit carbon dioxide, the landfills and feedlots that produce methane, or second-hand cigarette smoke. Estimating exposures is more complicated still with diffuse 'non-point' sources, such as the run-off of petroleum residues from streets and fertilizer from fields into water bodies. Some chemicals are not emitted at all, but emerge from complex chemical reactions. For example, smog is created by the interaction of nitrogen oxides (NOx), mostly from point sources such as car exhausts, with volatile organic compounds (VOCs), mostly from non-point sources such as forests. These chemicals 'cook' in the sun and disperse in the air, often being transported great distances. Individuals' doses depend on how heavily they exercise, while their responses depend on whether they are aged or asthmatic.

Nature has its own complex pathways, often deeply intertwined with our social world. For example, malaria risks depend on both biology (mosquito species, reproductive habitat, weather, time of day) and behaviour (bed-netting, anti-malaria drugs, healthcare). Insects are the 'vector' that transmits malaria. Humans are the vector that transmits HIV, with bodily fluids (blood, sperm) as pathways. HIV risks, too, depend on both biology (the prevalence and virulence of virus strains) and behaviour (sex, intravenous drug use, partner notification, needle-exchange programmes, healthcare). So do pandemic flu (H1N1-swine, H5N1-avian) risks, with biology including unpredictable mutations and behaviour including whether people trust vaccines and obey quarantines.

Analyses of such risks typically use computer 'simulations' that examine many possible 'scenarios', each making different assumptions about biology (e.g. how transmissible and lethal the disease is) and behaviour (e.g. how mobile and hygienic people are). Climate change models follow a similar logic. They break land, sea, and air into three-dimensional grids, then use formulae based on physics to compute changes in climate variables (temperature, precipitation) over time, with scenarios making different assumptions (e.g. about carbon dioxide emissions, airborne particulate matter). The result is probability distributions for possible climate futures, like those in Table 3. In addition to assessing overall risks, these analyses show opportunities for interventions, such as ways to slow an outbreak.

Accidents

Human behaviour affects most risks. It affects how pollutants are used, when people get vaccinated, and who receives mosquito netting. With accidents, behaviour is typically centre stage. Risk analysis treats human behaviour as it treats everything else, starting with counts that reveal where problems lie, then proceeding to study correlations, causes, and remedies, drawing on whatever science proves relevant. For example, in the US, statistics find that two-thirds of deaths from falls involve people over 75, while half of drowning deaths involve children under 4. Once such patterns are observed, causal analysis can begin. It finds, for example, that older people may not realize when they can no longer navigate familiar home hazards or how much osteoporosis increases their risk from falls, both causing them and slowing recovery. It also finds that parents may not realize how deeply they can get lost in conversation, or how quickly small children can wander off, when supervising them poolside.

As elsewhere, the factors that create risks may offer opportunities to reduce them. How well any intervention works, though, is an empirical question. For example, warnings are an obvious way to prevent accidents. However, research finds that they often are ineffective, unless people already are looking for them or they somehow grab attention. Estimating the effectiveness of safety measures follows the same strategy as other risk analyses, combining direct observation with scientific knowledge. For example, the effects of improved lighting on falls can be informed both by studies in places where the elderly live and by basic research into how vision and balance deteriorate with age. The effects of banning mobile phone use while driving can be informed both by field experiments and by brain-imaging studies into how attention is divided.

Sometimes the research identifies situations that pose unavoidable risks, such as unfenced pools, hidden intersections, and sunken living rooms. Indeed, many safety researchers dislike the terms 'accident' and 'operator error' because they encourage blaming victims for their misfortune in situations that demand unreasonably great care. Those 'operators' might be workers on an oil platform, patients struggling with complex medical devices at home, or truck drivers on extended shifts. With poorly designed systems or inadequate instruction, the accidents are waiting to happen, adding the insult of blame to the injury they cause.

Risk analyses of complex technologies decompose them into components small enough to be observed directly or analysed theoretically. Analysts then reassemble the pieces to understand the technology as a whole. For example, in aviation safety, that means examining the navigation, fuel, communication, and other systems separately, then seeing how they interact. Analysts look for the 'redundancy' that allows one system to pick up when another fails, as in planes that can fly with a dead engine or incapacitated pilot. In order to improve the quality of their observations, aviation authorities often create incentives for candid reporting, such as not punishing pilots if they report their own mistakes before anyone else does, and putting prevention of future problems ahead of punishment for past ones. In order to reduce hindsight bias, which exaggerates how avoidable problems were, aviation safety analysts use black-box recordings that often capture flight crews' confusion before crashes. These analysts painstakingly reconstruct accidents, sometimes leading to surprising findings, such as the possibility that flight crews can get so absorbed in malfunctioning warning lights that they forget to 'fly the plane' or that co-pilots can so fear pilots' authority that they fail to warn them about imminent problems (as with the collision of two jumbo jets on the taxiways at Tenerife). In order to have larger samples, risk analysts study near-accidents, looking for both the actions that prevented them and the actions that could have doomed them. The aviation industry's remarkable safety record reflects this commitment to looking for problems, then addressing those that are found. The text boxes show less happy examples in other industries.

The Piper Alpha disaster

In 1988, a vapour release started a fire on the Piper Alpha oil platform in the North Sea, killing 165 workers and 2 rescuers, and costing billions of pounds in property damage. Blame was initially placed on the platform manager, who had commanded poorly and left the platform leaderless (and later died). However, subsequent investigations revealed what sociologist Charles Perrow calls a 'normal accident', caused by the conjunction of poor management practices that undermine the overprotectiveness that complex technologies require in order to cope with the problems that inevitably arise. One such practice was a design in which seemingly redundant safety systems all depended on the same electrical supply, allowing a *common mode failure*. A second flawed practice was allowing night-shift workers to remove two of three critical vapour pumps for repair without notifying day-shift workers, who then unwittingly used a valve without a safety seal, releasing the vapours that started the fire. A third was using less well-qualified replacement workers when regular employees were temporarily unavailable. A fourth was not training operators well enough for them to understand the implications of turning off an automatic fire-suppression system in order to avoid sucking divers into its underwater pumps. A well-managed technology would have had the 'defence in depth' needed to keep individual problems from cascading out of control. Nearby Norway achieved better safety with the same technology, showing that such management is possible.

Sources: M. Elisabeth Paté-Cornell, 'Learning from the Piper Alpha Accident: A Postmortem Analysis of Technical and Organizational Factors', *Risk Analysis* (1993), 13:2, 215–32; Charles Perrow, *Normal Accidents: Living with High-Risk Technologies* (Princeton: Princeton University Press, 1999)

Risk

The financial crisis of 2008

The crisis of 2008 was, in its way, a normal accident in which management practices in the financial industry gradually eroded the redundant safety systems needed to keep complex financial markets from spinning out of control. Those practices allowed the unsupportable proliferation of *collateralized debt obligations* (CDOs) combining pieces of many loans. According to sophisticated financial analyses, CDOs promised attractive, predictable risks and rewards, but only if there were relatively few of them, assembled from relatively safe loans, and with no real estate bubble to inflate the values of the underlying properties. However, CDOs' very attractiveness undermined those assumptions, both by increasing their number and by creating incentives to include pieces of unsafe loans, which unscrupulous lenders obligingly provided in the form of 'subprime' mortgages to individuals with little chance of repaying them.

The ensuing collapse revealed other flaws in financial markets. The credit-rating agencies that evaluated CDOs were paid by the very firms that offered them, creating incentives for overestimating their safety. Working in an anti-regulation environment, government agencies had little authority to intervene. Like many banks and investors, they struggled to understand these complex investments. Once the weakest holders of subprime mortgages began to default, a chain reaction ensued, with CDO markets collapsing, lenders panicking, interest rates rising, and housing prices declining, leading to additional defaults.

Proposals for strengthening financial markets include making investments less complex (so that they are easier to evaluate), separating finance and savings operations (so that conservative investments do not subsidize risky ones), limiting mortgage leverage (so that bubbles are less likely), paying rating agencies from public funds (so that they are independent), disclosing more

Accident risk analyses often create step-by-step scenarios for how a dangerous sequence of events might unfold. Analysts assess the probability of each step, then combine them to get a probability for the overall scenario. For example, the steps in a house-fire scenario might include using a toaster-oven for a grilled cheese sandwich, setting the oven on 'high', getting called away, having dead batteries in the smoke alarm, having other combustibles nearby, having no fire extinguisher, and so on. Each step offers a chance to break the accident sequence (like never using a toaster-oven or regularly testing the smoke alarm). When these steps are independent, the overall probability equals the product of the component probabilities. Often, though, they are correlated, as when people with dead smoke detectors also lack fire extinguishers and get easily distracted.

The probability of any specific scenario, occurring exactly as described, is typically so small that one can hardly worry about it. But that's not a reason to ignore it. If many scenarios share the same element, then it becomes a general risk factor, worth analysing for ways to control it. Malfunctioning smoke alarms and inattentiveness are such risk factors, with different opportunities for control. Resolving 'never to get distracted while cooking' is cost-free, but unlikely to happen. 'Having a working smoke detector' is both feasible and moderately effective at reducing some fire risks (burning toast, but not bad wiring). When no single intervention can eliminate a risk, redundant measures are needed, such as having both smoke detectors and fire extinguishers, and encouraging family members to comment (politely) on one another's safety lapses. However, it requires as much persistence for parents to keep nagging their kids as it does for hospitals to use checklists for surgical procedures or factories to empower workers to report safety problems.

Disciplined judgement

Risk analyses are abstractions which often ignore many features of problems in order to understand a few features well. At their best, such analyses can reveal hidden features of complex problems. For example, simulations showed how needle-exchange programmes could greatly reduce HIV transmission rates among intravenous drug users, how inexpensive mosquito netting could reduce malaria risk, and how closing schools would not reduce pandemic flu risk for strains with long latency periods (allowing transmission by asymptomatic individuals).

Each facet of these analyses requires judgement. With pandemic flu risks, judgement is needed to select risk factors (disease transmissibility), assess possible exposures (interactions in schools), evaluate the accuracy of observations (incentives for reporting), translate basic research into applied contexts (closing schools), and make simplifying assumptions (using monthly rather than daily observations). Even though made by experts, these are still judgements, using general knowledge to interpret incomplete and uncertain data.

As a result, in order to use risk analyses, decision-makers need to know how far to trust the judgements underlying them. To that end, there is no substitute for evaluating experts' judgements in the light of experience, in order to assess how much the experts know and how well they can assess the limits to their knowledge. Figure 8 shows one such evaluation. It compares US energy consumption in 2000 (the grey line at the bottom) with predictions made by

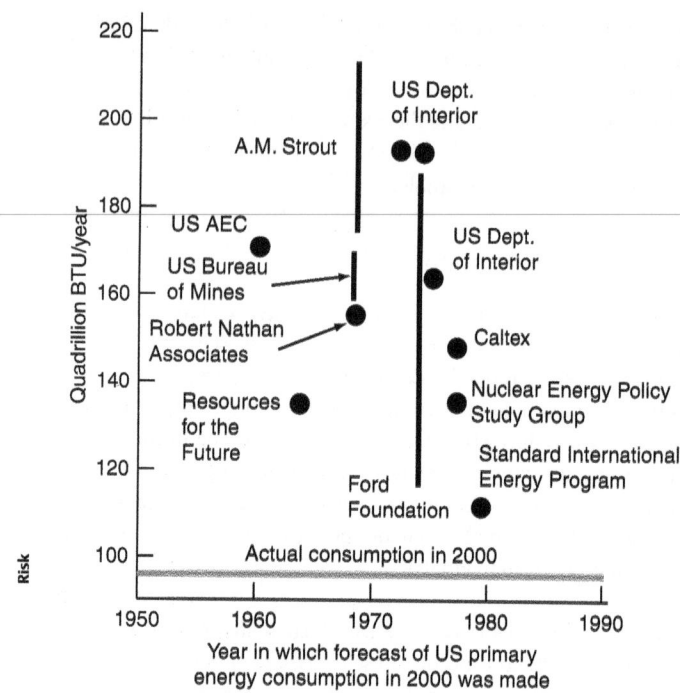

8. **Forecasts of US primary energy consumption**

several groups of experts between 1960 and 1980. Each group overestimated future consumption, often by a wide margin. In hindsight, a major source of these experts' error was not anticipating how much the oil price shocks of the 1970s would increase energy efficiency and reduce energy consumption. Most of these analysts gave just a single best guess (the black dots), making it impossible to tell what they saw as the range of possible values. Three analyses did provide such ranges (the vertical bars). In each case, the actual value (in 2000) was outside that range, meaning that these experts' overestimates (of what consumption would be) were also overconfident (because they treated the actual value as implausible).

Figures 9 and 10 present two other sets of expert judgements, expressed precisely enough to be evaluated in the light of subsequent experience. Figure 9 has judgements of the probability of the avian flu virus (H5N1) becoming transmissible among humans, in the three years following November 2005, when they were made. The medical experts were leading public health figures; the non-medical experts were leaders in other fields, mostly communication technologies that might help keep society running during a pandemic. The medical experts were divided. Most saw a low probability (around 10%); a minority saw a high one (around 70%). The non-medical experts mostly saw high probabilities, presumably reflecting what they had inferred from the saturation media coverage of the time. Given that there was no pandemic, the medical experts' generally low probabilities seem relatively

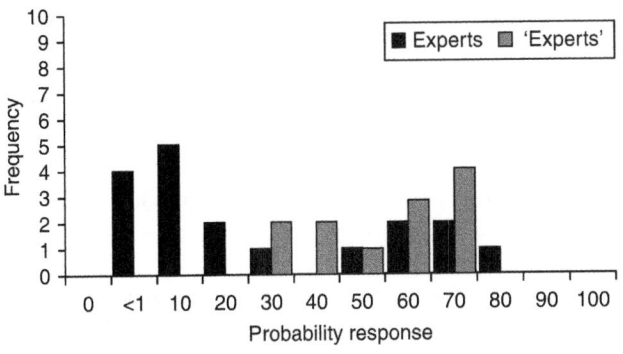

9. Judgements by medical experts (dark bars) and non-medical 'experts' (grey bars) of 'the probability that H5N1 will become an efficient human-to-human transmitter (capable of being propagated through at least two epidemiological generations of humans) some time during the next 3 years'; data collected October 2005. Median judgements: medical experts (15%); non-medical experts (60%)

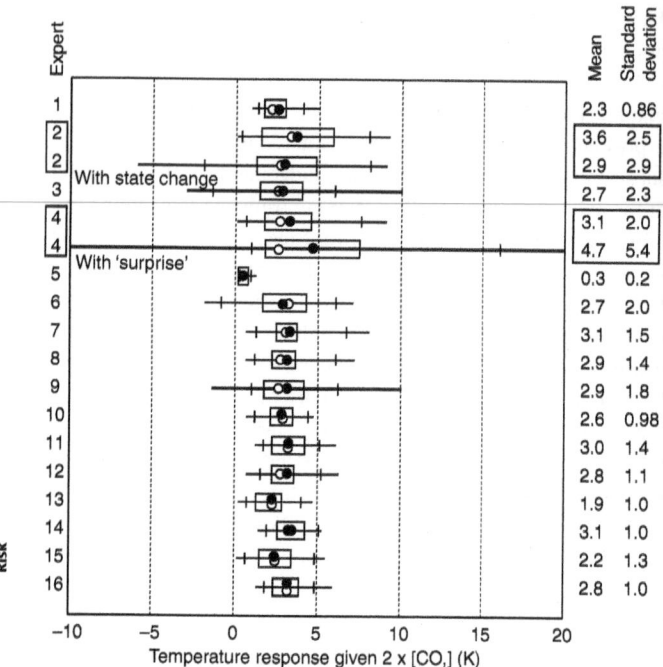

10. Climate experts' judgements of the probabilities of changes in globally averaged surface temperature, if atmospheric CO_2 doubles

accurate, whereas the non-medical experts' much higher probabilities seem alarmist.

Giving a high probability to an event that does not occur does not, in itself, prove that one has poor judgement. Events with a 70% chance of happening should still *not* happen 30% of the time. Evaluating experts' judgements requires multiple predictions, expressed in clear, consistent ways. Weather forecasters make such predictions with their probability-of-precipitation forecasts. They prove to be remarkably 'well calibrated', in the sense that it rains about 70% of the time when they say there is a 70% chance. One secret to weather forecasters' success is that they receive large quantities of prompt, unambiguous feedback about whether it rains, helping them to learn how confident to be. A second secret is that weather forecasters are rewarded for candour – and for avoiding 'umbrella bias', that is, overstating these probabilities so that people are rarely caught unprotected.

Such intensive feedback is, however, uncommon for most experts. For many years, psychologist Philip Tetlock has had experts assign probabilities to political events – and has consistently found them to be overconfident, based on what actually happened. Some errors are inevitable when predicting uncertain events. However, overconfidence is not inevitable. If experts know the limits to their knowledge, then events will happen 70% of the time, when they are 70% confident. Tetlock observes that experts could keep the records needed to create the feedback that would allow them to evaluate and improve their probability judgements. However, few do.

Unless experts express their beliefs in explicit, consistent ways, it is also hard to know how much they agree. Figure 10 shows judgements expressing sixteen experts' beliefs about the expected change in mean global temperature given a doubling of atmospheric carbon dioxide. The small vertical lines show 90% *confidence intervals*, with a 5% chance of the actual value being below the left one and 5% chance of it being above the right one. The box shows 50% confidence intervals (25% chance below, 25% chance above). The dots are two kinds of 'best guess'. Some experts are more confident than others, seen in the narrower ranges of their lines, bars, and boxes. The most confident expert (#5) is an avowed 'climate sceptic', certain of a tiny increase. Two experts (#2, #4) made two predictions, depending on whether a 'surprise' or 'state change' occurred, such as the Gulf Stream collapsing. Most of the experts' best guesses are around +2°C warming. No expert saw much chance of cooling. These judgements could be evaluated, one day, if carbon dioxide does indeed double.

How should these judgements be viewed today, when decisions must be made? If experts are like other people (Chapter 5), then their confidence intervals are too narrow, reflecting overconfidence. Experts might have more appropriate confidence levels if they receive systematic feedback, as do the weather forecasters, or if the give and take of scientific discourse exposes their views to rigorous criticism. On the other hand, experts could be more overconfident if they rely too heavily on their own discipline when the analyses require broader perspectives. As much as they might disagree among themselves, members of any community (scientific or otherwise) share tacit, mostly unexamined, assumptions about the world. For example, engineering risk analyses often neglect human behaviour, considering it too hard to quantify and distrusting the social sciences needed to provide relevant evidence. Such analyses would miss the psychological and organizational risk factors critical to the events discussed in the text boxes.

Analysing the risks of nuclear power

The 1974 Reactor Safety Study (WASH-1400), led by physicist Norman Rasmussen, was a landmark attempt to analyse the risks of a famously complex technology, nuclear power plants. The controversy that it sparked prompted the American Institute of Physics to conduct an independent review led by Harold Lewis. It found no systematic bias, as some industry critics had alleged. However, it also found the Study's conclusions much too confident, given the nature of the technology and the limits to the evidence.

The Study demanded an extraordinary degree of expert judgement because it tried to quantify nuclear power's overall risk level, as an answer to the political question of whether the technology was sufficiently safe. A more modest goal is to answer the engineering questions of how best to deal with specific design issues. Relative risks are much easier to assess than absolute ones. As it happened, the industry's fortunes were substantially undone by a risk factor largely absent from these analyses, the kinds of human behaviour that led to Three Mile Island and Chernobyl. Although there have been attempts to quantify the risks of 'operator error', design flaws, and weak management practices, the industry's primary response has been improving operators' training and reactors' operability.

Explicitly expressing uncertainty is necessary, but not sufficient, for letting decisions-makers know how much faith to put in risk analyses. Decision-makers also need to know how well calibrated those confidence assessments are; that is, how well experts can tell how much they know. Empirical evaluations often find overconfidence, meaning that experts should broaden their confidence intervals. Philosophers Jerome Ravetz and Silvio Funtowicz recommend that experts disclose the maturity (or 'pedigree') of their science, reporting features such as its quality and standards of evidence.

Conclusion: risk analysis synthesizes knowledge from multiple sources

Risk analyses integrate knowledge from diverse sources in order to assess risks to valued outcomes. The simplest analyses involve counts, such as falls, drowning, and cholera cases. Interpreting those counts requires thinking about possible causes of the risks, which include risk sources, pathways, exposures, and population characteristics. Clarifying the strength of these causal relationships can involve the statistical methods of epidemiology, experimental studies of dose-response toxicology, and scenario-based simulations of possible futures. These methods allow tracking the evolution of risks from their sources, through their pathways, and to their effects on valued outcomes. Risk analyses often summarize their results with probabilities capturing the residual uncertainties. Whatever methods are chosen, they require the exercise of judgement. These methods' practical value depends on risk analysts' ability to identify, assemble, and integrate the relevant pieces, then assess the confidence that their conclusions warrant. The better job they do, the better they can inform risk decisions, the topic of Chapter 4.

Chapter 4
Making risk decisions

Risk decisions can seem so easy that we barely notice making them (how fast to drive, whether to lock our home windows). They can also seem so hard that we wish they would go away (how to deal with a school bully, whether to leave our home for assisted living). In all cases, they involve applying beliefs about risks (Chapter 3) to the pursuit of valued outcomes (Chapter 2).

Decision-making research approaches these processes by contrasting abstract rules, specifying how people *should* make decisions, with behavioural studies, seeing how people actually *do* make decisions. If people do not follow the rules, then either they need help or the rules need revision. This chapter uses this interaction of theory and reality to illuminate different kinds of choices, starting with simple ones, then adding layers of complexity.

Simple decision rules

With the simplest choices, each option is certain to produce some amount of a single valued outcome (money, days off, wetland acres). The logical decision rule goes without saying: choose the option that promises the most of what you want. Given an orderly list of options, all characterized in terms of a single outcome, most people can easily choose the best, as they do when they shop online for the cheapest product. If people struggle with such simple choices, then their problem may be literacy or numeracy, not decision-making ability. Without an orderly list, though, applying this simple rule becomes much harder. Even diligent shoppers may have trouble finding the cheapest soap, mozzarella, or towelling among the products arrayed on supermarket shelves.

Decision rules and human behaviour become more complicated when the outcomes are uncertain, so that each option has some probability of producing some amount of the valued outcome. For example, one lottery ticket might have 10% chance of winning £20, whereas another has 25% chance of winning £10. One emergency rescue plan might have a 10% chance of saving 20 lives, whereas another has 25% chance of saving 10.

For such cases, decision theory offers the *expected value* decision rule. First, multiply the outcomes by their probabilities, then choose the option with the largest product (or 'expected value'). For the first lottery, the expected value is £2 (= 10% × £20); for the second, it is £2.50 (= 25% × £10). The expected value of the first rescue plan is saving 2 lives; for the second, it is 2.5. Obviously, the second option will not save 2.5 lives; that number is the average of the two possible outcomes, saving 0 or 10 lives, weighted by the probability of each occurring. Given an orderly list of expected values (like Table 1, in Chapter 2), applying this decision rule is simple, too. A philanthropist or medical student could decide, 'I want to work on the risk with the largest number of expected deaths, which is cardiovascular disease, at the top of the list.' However, the mental arithmetic needed to compute expected values is hard for most people, even with fairly simple options. For example, a lottery ticket with 20% chance of winning £20, 50% chance of £10, and 30% of £0 has an expected value of £9, because $9 = (0.20 \times 20) + (0.5 \times 10) + (0.3 \times 0)$. Even people who can do the maths might not trust themselves to set the problem up correctly, then bet their life or fortune on the answer. However, given a proper set-up, expected values perform a kind of magic, combining probabilities and values into a single number – which could be expected costs, expected lives, expected goals, or expectations for any other valued outcome.

Expected value is all that matters, if all options cost the same, as would happen if all lottery tickets are £2 or all rescue missions imperil the same number of rescuers' lives. If the costs differ, then the logical decision rule is: 'choose the option with the lowest cost per unit'. For many groceries, that might mean 'buy the product with the lowest cost per ounce'. For term life insurance, that might mean 'get the largest death benefit per premium pound'. If these numbers are readily available, then applying the *unit-cost* rule is easy, too.

In this spirit, policy-makers often evaluate health and safety programmes in terms of their *cost per expected life saved*, using estimates like those in Table 6. If these estimates are taken literally (and some are controversial), then the unit-cost rule shows some clear 'best buys'. If policy-makers can spend money on anything, then the top six options look attractive (costing little to save an expected life). If policy-makers can regulate benzene emissions in only one industry, then it should be rubber and tyre, not service (petrol) stations. If decision-makers can pursue only one screening programme for colon cancer, then it should be colonoscopy, not extra stool tests. If intensive care funds are limited, then they will save more expected lives with patients experiencing acute respiratory failure than with very ill patients undergoing major vascular operations. Whether policy-makers can act on such analyses depends on whether their resources are fungible; that is, whether they can move money from poor buys (benzene controls on underground tanks) to best buys (supplemental nutrition programmes).

Table 6. Estimates of costs per expected life saved (in the United States)

Chlorination of drinking water	$3,100
Supplemental food programmes for women, infants, and children	$3,400
Mandatory motorcycle helmet laws	$2,000
National 55 mph speed limit on highways and interstates	$6,600
Screening blood donors for HIV	$14,000
AZT therapy for people with AIDS	$26,000
Benzene exposure standard of 1 (versus 10) ppm (part per million) in the rubber and tyre industry	$76,000
Benzene emission controls on service station storage vessels	$91,000,000
Colonoscopy for colorectal cancer screening for people age 40+	$90,000
Six (versus five) stool guaiac (blood tests) for colon cancer screening for people age 40+	$26,000,000
Intensive care (including mechanical ventilation) for acute respiratory failure	$4,700
Intensive care for patients with multiple trauma	$26,000
Intensive care for very ill patients undergoing major vascular operations	$850,000

Source: Adapted from T. Tengs et al., 'Five hundred Life-Saving Interventions and Their Cost-effectiveness', *Risk Analysis*, 15 (3), 1995, pp. 369–90.

Utilities

Expected value calculations treat each unit of the valued outcome (money, life, wetlands) as equally valuable. Often, though, some units are more valuable than others. An extra pound usually means more to a person when poor than when wealthy, and when the stakes are small (£1 versus £2) than when they are large

(£1,000 versus £1,001). How much an amount of a good is worth is often called its *utility*. Decisions about utilities can use the same rules as decisions about values: with certain outcomes, choose the option with the greatest utility; with uncertain outcomes, choose the option with the greatest expected utility. Expected utility is a mathematically consistent way to combine probabilities and subjective values.

Distinguishing (subjective) utility from (objective) value was an intellectual breakthrough by Daniel Bernoulli (1700–82), trying to understand why seemingly reasonable people might both gamble and buy insurance. Bernoulli reasoned that large losses hurt so much that they have disproportionate (negative) utility. As a result, people are 'risk-averse', in the sense of willingly paying a premium (£1,500) that is greater than the expected value of a potential loss (£1,000 = 1% × £1,000,000). Conversely, people might value a gambling prize so much that they are 'risk-seeking', in the sense of willingly paying more for a chance to win (£10) than the gamble's expected value (1% × £500 = £5).

Building on Bernoulli's insight, modern theorists (including Frank Ramsey, John von Neumann, Oskar Morgenstern, and Leonard Savage) made a remarkable discovery: *if* people's preferences among simple gambles follow a few apparently reasonable rules, *then* they will choose the option with the greatest expected utility, no matter how complicated the choice. One of those rules is *comparability*; people who follow it can compare any two options, meaning that they prefer A to B, B to A, or are indifferent between them. A second rule is *transitivity*; meaning that if A is preferred to B and B to C, then A is preferred to C. Another rule is having a *certainty equivalent* for any gamble, a guaranteed pay-off (or loss) that would be just as good (or bad) as that of the gamble with the probabilities. The theory shows, further, that when people consistently violate the rules, it is possible to create bets with guaranteed losses, a fact exploited in finance and risk 'arbitrage'.

Some academics, especially economists, find these rules (the ~~choice axioms~~) ~~so appealing that they equate following them~~ with being 'rational'. Other academics question defining rationality in terms of axioms with no obvious place for emotion, intuition, or overriding cultural, ethical, and religious values. In addition, the 'consequentialist' perspective of utility theory considers just the outcomes (or consequences) that follow choices and ignores the decision-making process that precedes them. Yet, sometimes people will accept less expected utility in return for the thrill of gambling or the right to make their own decisions. The axioms themselves sometimes seem inappropriate, as with many life-and-death risk decisions. For example, critical care decisions, as in Figure 1 (Chapter 1), can leave people paralysed, violating the comparability axiom, because they cannot express preference or indifference. The book and film *Sophie's Choice* involved immoral comparisons. The same may be true for accepting any certain payment as 'equivalent' to risking one's life or that of a loved one deliberately. The text box discusses deliberate violations of the choice axioms in intergroup conflicts, seen through the eyes of anthropology and political science.

Sacred values in intergroup conflict

People believe that devotion to essential or core values – such as the welfare of family and country or commitment to religion, honour, and justice – trump trade-offs with other values, particularly economic ones. Matters of 'sacred honour', when they are enforced to a degree out of proportion to any material pay-off, are often seen as defining 'who we are'. After the Vietnam War, successive US administrations resisted Hanoi's efforts at reconciliation until Hanoi accounted for the fate of American soldiers missing in action.

[It] is often hard for members of one culture to understand another's [sacred values]; however, acknowledging [those] values may help to avoid or resolve the hardest of conflicts. For example, in 1945, the American government realized that preserving, and even signalling respect for, the emperor might lessen the likelihood that Japanese would fight to the death to save him.

In a series of experiments, [we] measured emotional outrage and propensity for violence in response to peace deals involving compromises over issues integral to the Israeli-Palestinian conflict, [such as] exchanging land for peace (with 601 Jewish settlers); sovereignty over Jerusalem (with 719 Palestinian students); [and] the right of Palestinian refugees to return to their former lands and homes inside Israel (with 535 Palestinian refugees). We found that use of material incentives may backfire when adversaries treat contested issues as sacred values, and that symbolic concessions of no apparent material benefit may help to solve intractable conflicts.

For Israel's former chief hostage negotiator, Ariel Merari, 'Trusting the adversary's intentions is critical to negotiations, which have no chance unless both sides believe the other's willingness to recognize its existential concerns.' Overcoming moral barriers to symbolic concessions and their emotional underpinnings may pose more of a challenge, but also [may] offer greater opportunities for breakthroughs for peace than hitherto realized.

Excerpt from S. Atran, R. Axelrod, and R. Davis, 'Sacred Barriers to Conflict Resolution', *Science*, 317, (2007), 1039–40 [ellipses omitted in quote]

The Ellsberg paradox: uncertain probabilities

Daniel Ellsberg is famous for leaking the Pentagon Papers, a secret US government history of the Vietnam War, in 1971. He was also a pre-eminent decision theorist. The 'Ellsberg paradox' arises when people compare ambiguous and exact probabilities.

Suppose you are shown an urn with 30 red balls and 60 other balls that are either black or yellow, but you are not told how many there are of each colour.

Which gamble do you prefer?

Gamble A	Gamble B
You win $100 if you draw a red ball.	You win $100 if you draw a black ball.

Most people prefer Gamble A (with a probability of winning equal to exactly 30/90, or 1/3) over Gamble B (with a probability of winning somewhere between 0/90, or 0, and 60/90, or 2/3).

Now which gamble do you prefer, with the same two urns?

Gamble C	Gamble D
You win $100 if you draw a red or yellow ball.	You win $100 if you draw a black or yellow ball.

Most people prefer Gamble D (with a probability of winning equal to exactly 60/90, or 2/3) over Gamble C (with a probability of winning somewhere between 30/90, or 1/3, and 90/90, or 1).

These preferences are inconsistent if you have an opinion about the numbers of black and yellow balls. Imagine you think that there were no black balls. If so, then the chance of winning with Gamble B is 0, making Gamble A more attractive. However, that would also mean that the chance of winning with Gamble C is 1, making it more attractive than Gamble D.

When Ellsberg discovered this paradox in 1961, it was interpreted as showing flawed choices. Today, however, many scholars interpret it as showing a flaw in utility theory, which ignores how people reason with partial knowledge (about the urn's contents). Theories of 'ambiguity aversion' now consider how people deal with uncertain probabilities, a reason that they dislike Gambles B and C.

In the 1960s, the mathematician Benoit Mandelbrot observed similarly deep uncertainties in the sometimes wild fluctuations of commodity prices, whose swings were unlike the more orderly variations assumed by financial models like those that did so poorly in the 2008 crash.

Uncertain values

When people know what they want, they may often follow the axioms. An investor who strongly prefers stocks to bonds and bonds to cash should also prefer stocks to cash – hence be transitive. A late-night walker who feels much safer moving from an alley to a side street and then to a main street should not feel safer moving back to an alley – hence be intransitive. However, people cannot always know what they want for all of life's decisions, especially the novel, painful choices that risks can create. As a result, people are often forced to 'construct' their preferences, inferring what they want in specific situations from the 'basic' values that generally guide them in life. If people stumble in that process, then they may violate the axioms and be irrational (in that sense).

Consider a couple buying a car, who both hate to spend money and love to protect their children, but haven't figured out just how important these two conflicting values are. Sensing that uncertainty, an adept car salesperson will keep suggesting models with additional safety features, trying to increase the sales price. That sales strategy will work unless the couple suddenly realizes that the total 'safety package' is too expensive for them and reverts back to preferring a cheaper, riskier, stripped-down model. In that case, the salesperson loses the bigger sale and the couple violates transitivity, going back to an option that they have already rejected. If the couple is still uncertain, the salesperson might start the process again, hoping to sell some extra safety, just not quite as much.

Utility theory says nothing about which trade-offs people should make, only that their trade-offs should be consistent. Research has documented many violations of that consistency, like the intransitivity in the car decision and the wildly varying cost-effectiveness of the different safety programmes (Table 6). Such violations are practically important because they show that people need help in making better choices. They are theoretically important because they reveal something about why people are not always 'rational'. Is something wrong with them or with the rules of rationality?

Because of their importance, inconsistent preferences are a central research topic. Psychologists call them 'context effects', showing how changing a decision's context can change what people choose, even when the expected outcomes stay the same. One 'classic' example is that fewer people will forbid an activity (handgun ownership, abortion) than will not allow it, even though the outcome is the same. Reportedly, a key British vote on EU membership was formulated as 'staying in Europe', rather than as 'joining Europe', in order to evoke a more favourable context for a public uncertain about its preferences.

One large class of inconsistent preferences arises when people cannot predict their own reactions to future events. People expect winning the lottery to solve their problems, then are disappointed. They expect a misfortune to crush them, then adapt fairly well. They make bold investments when in a bold mood, then feel sick when they must live with bad outcomes. They expect to use a health club when buying a membership, then rarely feel like going. They buy new food, wanting to be adventurous, then just cook familiar dishes. They commit to palliative care, should they fall mortally ill, then want aggressive care when that happens.

Such inconsistencies vanish when people know what they want. One path to stable preferences is holding uncompromising values. Firm supporters of religious freedom (or the right to bear arms) would no more forbid that activity than they would refuse to allow it. People whose faith precludes organ donation are insensitive to whether it is the default. People will have consistent preferences, however options are presented, if they firmly believe that no amount of money can compensate for wilfully risking human life, that no amount of success can justify violating professional ethics, or that no risk to a mother can condone abortion. Such deeply held preferences will, however, be 'irrational' in a utility theory sense because they violate the choice axiom of *continuity*, which holds that everything has a price, even if a very large one, such as requiring £1 million to accept a one in a million risk of death. Consciously rejecting the utility theory axioms is one way to create stable preferences that obey other rules.

Prospect theory

A prominent account of context effects and inconsistent preferences is *prospect theory* created by psychologists Daniel Kahneman and Amos Tversky. It holds that the choice axioms often fail to describe human behaviour because they ignore basic psychological principles. One such principle is that people evaluate an option by how they expect it to change their lives, not by where they expect it to leave them (in terms of their overall wealth), as held by utility theory. As a result, people 'sweat the small stuff' (of changes), unlike rational actors who always see the big picture (and count their blessings). A second behavioural principle neglected by utility theory is that people care more about losses than about same-sized gains. As a result, they may prefer a sure gain to a gamble with the same expected value, while rejecting a

Prospect theory framing experiment

One group of people is asked to imagine that a rare disease is expected to kill 600 people in a community. Two programmes can address this risk. With Programme A, 200 people are certain to be saved. With Programme B, all 600 people are saved with probability 1/3 and nobody is saved with probability 2/3. The expected value of Programme B is 200 lives (= 1/3 × 600 + 2/3 × 0), which is the certain value of Programme A. In the original experiment, 72% of people preferred Programme A, favouring certainty over uncertainty.

A second group received a different formulation of the same choice. With Programme C, 400 of the 600 people are certain to die. With Programme D, all 600 people die with probability 2/3 and nobody dies with probability 1/3. The expectation of Programme D still equals that of Programme C. However, now 78% of people favoured the gamble (Programme D), over the certainty (Programme C).

Thus, people are risk-averse with 'lives saved', but risk-seeking with 'lives lost'. Prospect theory accounts for this framing effect in terms of how differently people feel about losses and gains.

sure loss in favour of a gamble whose gain has the same positive expected value. A third principle is that people place extra value on certain outcomes, so that going from 90% to 100% means much more than going from 40% to 50%.

According to prospect theory, people evaluate gains and losses relative to a *reference point* – which could be where they are now, where they expect to be, or where someone else is. As a result, changing reference points can change preferences, even when the outcomes stay the same, by changing whether outcomes are seen as gains or losses. For example, a 3% raise makes people happier if they compare it with their current wage than if they compare it with a 3% average raise or with the top employee's 5% raise. When compared to current wages, the raise feels like a 3% gain; when compared to the average raise, it feels like no change; when compared to the top employee's raise, it feels like a 2% loss. Reference points are often highly malleable, as seen in experiments in which letting someone hold a coffee mug increases its value, because surrendering it feels like a loss. Merchants try to exploit this 'endowment effect' when they ask customers to try on new clothes or 'get behind the wheel' of a new car.

Feeling losses more intensely than gains leads to 'loss aversion'. One of its expressions is 'status quo bias', whereby people resist making beneficial changes because they care too much about what they will give up, relative to what they will gain. Another expression is the sunk cost bias, whereby people throw good money after bad, so as to avoid acknowledging losses. During food recalls, some people will not throw out suspect products that they would no longer buy. Investors let their portfolios stagnate because they hate to part with their current holdings, especially when that means booking losses. Dam construction rarely stops after the first concrete is poured regardless of the problems that are encountered.

Experimental demonstrations of context effects often can ensure that nothing changes except the context variable (e.g. whether one holds the coffee mug). In life, though, context can convey valuable information, as when people infer social norms from defaults ('why would they make me opt into organ donation, unless that was uncommon?') or politicians advocate allowing abortion, rather than not forbidding it, in order to cast it as a right; or when developers continue an ill-advised project, in order to avoid admitting to poor judgement.

Heuristic decision rules

People can handle only so much information at once. A psychological maxim, proposed by George Miller, is that people can think only about 7±2 things (i.e. between 5 and 9) at once. Above that, things start slipping out of mind and focus. Context effects are one result. When decisions become too complex, some elements get lost and the most salient ones dominate preferences.

Nobel Laureate Herbert Simon described various general strategies that people use to simplify overly complex decisions, reflecting the more realistic aspiration of *bounded rationality*. One strategy is *approximate optimization*, which entails ignoring enough elements of the decision that one can think systematically about those that remain. For example, investors may limit themselves to evaluating exchange-listed securities, suggestions from their investment advisor, or short-term gains. National leaders may focus exclusively on diplomatic options or domestic politics. Patients may ignore alternative medicine treatments. In each case, people hope that understanding some issues well compensates for neglecting others altogether.

Simon's second general strategy is *satisficing* (from an old Scots word). It entails ignoring nothing, but abandoning the search for the very best choice. Satificers examine options until they find one that is 'good enough' in terms of critical valued outcomes. Thus, investors might buy the first security that outperformed the market last year, has a decent yield, and is in a familiar industry. A leader might pick the first strategy that she can sell to her supporters, defend in public, and keep from imploding during her term in office. A patient might adopt the first treatment that he can afford and that no one criticizes too strongly. Satisficing decision-makers know that better options may be 'out there', but are willing to make do with the ones they choose.

In this view, people are expert decision-makers to the extent that they have good *heuristics* (or rules of thumb), knowing which elements to ignore (for approximate optimization) or how to search for good options (for satisficing). Thus, politicians who optimize approximately know which outcomes lack strong constituencies (hence can be ignored). Politicians who satisfice know how to find options that will not enrage any constituency (hence might fly).

How well heuristics work, even in the hands of experts, depends on the decision. Some decisions are more forgiving than others. For example, many decisions with continuous options (drive at X miles per hour, invest £Y) are fairly insensitive to exactly what one chooses. Thus, driving is roughly as risky whatever speed one chooses within a given range. Nor does it matter much exactly how many minutes one exercises or exactly what percentage of one's portfolio goes into stocks. Many decisions with discrete options, such as which job (or holiday) to take, are also fairly insensitive to how different expected outcomes are weighed. Indeed, it is often enough to evaluate an option by subtracting the number of bad outcomes from the number of good outcomes (a rule sometimes known as 'Benjamin Franklin's Prudential Algebra'). Simple rules often do as well as professionals in predicting events as diverse as medical school success, criminal recidivism, trial settlements, and bankruptcy. For example, as complex as romantic relationships can be, the fate of student couples has been predicted by comparing how often they fight with how often they make love. Doctors can assess damage from head injuries with the Glasgow Coma Scale, which adds up simple ratings of eye, verbal, and motor responses, with scores ranging from 3 (deep coma or death) to 15 (fully alert). The ABC (Adaptive Behavior and Cognition) Group of Gerd Gigerenzer and his colleagues has examined the robustness of heuristics in areas as diverse as law, medicine, and partner choice.

Simple rules do well, in part, because they are so reliable. Unlike people, rules do not have bad days, get distracted, or forget things. Recognizing this, pilots, doctors, and other professionals use checklists in order to get all the simple things right. Experts sometimes treat such routines as an affront. However, these rules codify, rather than replace, their knowledge. Relying on them also frees experts for tasks that only they can do, such as talk with patients or negotiate with air traffic controllers.

Rules and regulation

Risk regulations are a form of bounded rationality, applying the same rule to many hazards, while ignoring differences among them. How well regulations work depends on how well their bounds are set. One aspect of those bounds is how regulatory categories are defined. For example, regulatory rules in the US are less strict when (a) a herbal remedy is classified as a dietary supplement, rather than as a drug; (b) a cheese pizza has pepperoni, so that it is regulated by the Department of Agriculture rather than by the Food and Drug Administration; or (c) investments are deemed unsupervised hedge funds, rather than regulated securities.

Applying general rules requires translating them into specific terms. For example, in the US, 'new' electric power plants are regulated more strictly than existing ones. However, 'new' and 'existing' are sufficiently ambiguous terms that electric companies sometimes rebuild plants almost completely in order to stay under the more lenient old rules. Some nuclear power plants still rely on huge 'old' cooling water intakes that kill billions of fish eggs and larvae, rather than deploy 'new' technology. Looking at risk outcomes, terms like 'adverse environmental impact' (the brief phrase long used in the US) have so many interpretations that regulations using them are hardly rules at all. Sometimes, the vagueness is deliberate, leaving regulators with discretion that belies the promise of standard rules; sometimes, it is inadvertent, as with the cooling water language that emerged from frantic, last-minute negotiations in the US Congress.

As seen in Chapter 2, definitions express values. For example, decision rules often invoke 'fairness'. However, that term will have different winners and losers, if it means (a) dividing water equally among all farmers versus first honouring the oldest water rights; (b) requiring new housing developments to pay for their infrastructure (roads, sewers) versus charging everyone in a jurisdiction; (c) imposing toxic clean-up costs on all 'responsible parties' versus only current property owners; or (d) applying carbon emission limits on all nations versus just developed ones, in so far as developing nations have not had the benefits of historic energy use.

Once assigned to a regulatory class, hazards must be bounded to some portion of their life cycle. For example, the risks from a solvent may be very different if regulators consider just the health and environmental impacts of its direct usage or also those of its 'downstream' fate (waste transport and disposal), 'upstream' sources (mining and transport), occupational exposures, and those of the intermediate chemicals used in its production. As another example, the benefits of chlorination far outweigh its risks, when regulated just for its use in controlling microbial diseases in drinking water (dysentery, hepatitis, giardia, cholera); that balance can be less clear when regulations also consider carcinogenic by-products, such as chloroform.

Unless regulatory rules are enforced, the trade-offs they embody will not be achieved or remain highly uncertain. For example, lax supervision can allow farm labourers to re-enter fields too soon after pesticide use. Strict regulations can also prompt evasion, as with the illegal dumping of asbestos removed from old buildings or solvents used in manufacturing furniture and surfboards. The Soviet Union had strong worker protection regulations, reflecting its ideological commitments, and weak enforcement, reflecting its actual priorities.

Evolving decisions

If the world changes, then the meaning of decision rules can change, too. For example, regulations that ban 'detectable' toxins become more stringent as detection technology improves, sometimes to the molecular level. Medical treatments are used more often when they are triggered by more subtle suggestions of trouble. Food recalls become more frequent when electronic health records detect possible disease outbreaks more quickly. With imperfect tests, just doing more tests will produce more false positives (cases where there is no real problem). One US healthcare system finds it most efficient to do many standard tests on all blood samples, but report only those results that doctors specifically request – knowing that the other tests will have too high a rate of false positives, requiring needless follow-up procedures. Defensive medicine, conducting tests in order to avoid being sued, also increases false positives and overtreatment.

Rules can change the world that they govern. Regulations formulated in terms of *performance standards* impose stringent goals ('increase fuel efficiency to 37 mpg') in the hope of stimulating innovative ways to meet them. *Technical standards* specify solutions ('use catalytic converters'), in the hope of making it easier to monitor compliance, but discourage innovation because new solutions require new technical standards. *Adaptive management* combines the two, revising rules as experience accumulates. Its advocates, who include many ecologists, argue that conventional regulation is too focused on evaluating existing options, rather than on creating new ones.

US acid rain laws, limiting sulphur dioxide emissions, are a notable performance standard, with both the problem and compliance costs decreasing rapidly. These laws include tradable permits, granting some firms the right to create some pollution. If those firms can devise ways to pollute less, they can then sell the rights to other firms, which find emission control more costly. The result is reducing total pollution in the most cost-effective ways. Capping the total amount of pollution allowed under all permits, as currently proposed for carbon dioxide, limits overall damage while leaving firms free to find the most creative solutions.

The Montreal Protocol is a notable technical standard, enacted just 15 years after scientists discovered that chlorofluorocarbons (CFCs) deplete the Earth's protective stratospheric ozone layer. The Protocol committed 23 nations to reducing CFCs in refrigerants and aerosols, while specifying some allowable uses and creating a Multilateral Fund to subsidize the transition to other technologies.

Market-like mechanisms for managing risks require careful design, lest their rules be gamed. Insurers worry about moral hazard, whereby individuals buy policies when claims are imminent (just before major surgeries or adventure holidays) (see Chapter 1). Insurers incur their own moral hazard, when they select clients with less-than-average risks and then charge population-average rates. Countries without universal healthcare push uninsured (or underinsured) people into the commons of hospital emergency rooms that treat everyone. People who neglect their health put themselves and the commons at risk, should they need expensive care. In the US, a form of risk shifting occurred when employers stopped guaranteeing pensions, choosing instead to sponsor retirement accounts that employees had to fund (at least partially) and invest on their own.

When pro-social norms are internalized, people often discipline themselves, as when they use recycling bins, feed wild birds, buy Fair Trade products, and help strangers in distress. However, protecting a commons often requires overt coordinating mechanisms, not just individual goodwill. In competitive markets, civic-minded firms can be undercut by less responsible rivals, resulting in a 'race to the bottom', as each firm exploits the commons (dumping waste, exploiting workers) in order to survive. Regulations can slow the race by imposing minimal standards on all firms. Lawsuits can punish firms that behave badly. Industries can promote best practices, hoping to avoid collective punishment.

When uncertainty makes decisions hard, it may be possible to obtain information that makes them easier. To that end, doctors conduct blood tests, scans, and clinical interviews; environmental scientists sample soil, water, and air; geologists perform test drills and seismic tests (artificial earthquakes that reveal underground structures). The benefits of collecting any data must be weighed against the direct costs of getting them, the indirect costs created by their false signals, and the opportunity costs incurred while waiting for their results. For example, mammograms and prostate cancer tests have false positives that can lead to additional tests, treatment, and worry. Genetic tests for partners contemplating marriage or women considering in vitro fertilization can create difficult new risk decisions.

Testing to inform risk decisions: HIV

Positive results from HIV tests often have surprisingly weak decision-making implications. For example, in some Western European countries, the 2007 infection rate was about 1 in 10,000 among adults aged 15–49. One test correctly reports the presence of the virus 98.5% of the time for infected people (true positives). For people who are not infected, the test incorrectly reports the virus 0.015% of the time (false positives). Although a positive test is always worrying, the virus is so rare that such a result raises the probability of having the virus only from 1 in 10,000 (the base rate) to about 1 in 16. As a result, a second test is advised. Getting two false positives is very unlikely.

People can also reduce uncertainty by learning from experience, about the world and about themselves ('I didn't realize how much satisfaction it would give me'; 'I couldn't stop worrying'; 'I never should have gone'). The conditions for learning are well known: receiving prompt, unambiguous feedback, with appropriate rewards. Without those conditions, people can acquire much painful experience, without learning much. They can find themselves wondering, 'Why do I feel so bad about that investment? Is it because I wasn't as much a risk taker as I thought? Because I succumbed to sales pressure? Because winning did not change my life as much as I had expected?' Hindsight bias leads people to blame unhappy outcomes on folly, rather than on ignorance. Outcome bias leads people to confuse the quality of decisions with the quality of their outcomes, so that they experience regret over sound decisions with unlucky outcomes, while taking unwarranted pride in unsound decisions with lucky outcomes. People lose sight of smart choices that are hidden from view (airbags, vaccines), while obsessing over minor mistakes that are painfully salient. Driving provides good conditions for learning to make wise choices, and most people live to improve. Investment and diet decisions typically do not teach clear lessons, and many people reel from one poor choice to another.

In the 1960s, scientists considered seeding hurricanes, hoping to reduce their velocity and, thereby, storm damage. Experts at the time predicted that seeding would most likely reduce wind velocity, but might increase it, with unknown effects on storm paths. The decision tree in Figure 11 shows the choices on the left, followed by the probability judgements from hurricane experts for five possible changes in sustained wind speed, each associated with two key outcomes: property damage and government responsibility cost. Combining probabilities and costs shows lower expected costs with seeding. Thus, based on these expert judgements, seeding is the rational choice, *if* money alone matters *and* one can ignore who pays the costs and who receives the benefits. However, lives are at stake, too, with both winners and losers. A 'successfully' seeded

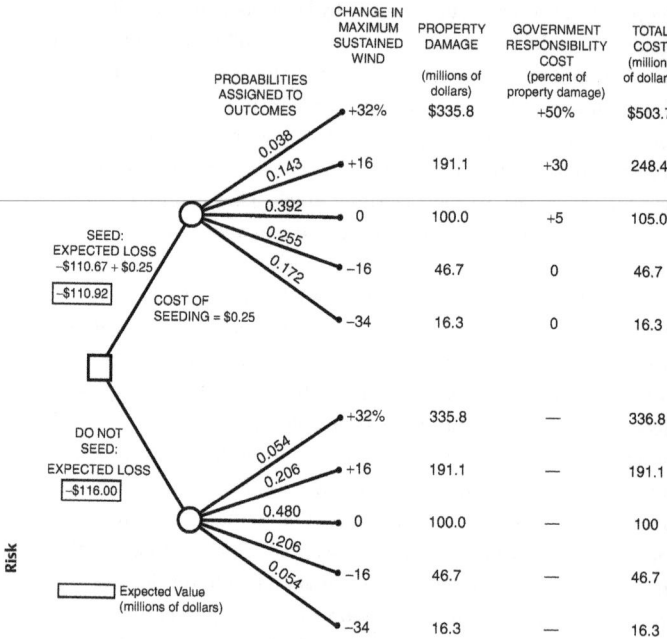

11. A risk decision: hurricane seeding

storm might change course, watering fields in a drought-stricken area, while taking out a bridge elsewhere. With no politically feasible way for the winners to compensate the losers, the seeding proposal died. Even deeper uncertainties and more complex equity issues accompany proposals for 'geoengineering', proposed planetary interventions to reduce the risks of climate change (sunshades in space, iron fertilization of the oceans).

Conclusion: Choices integrate beliefs and values

Sound choices require understanding the world's uncertain facts and one's own uncertain values. Utility theory offers one standard for 'rational' choice: assuming very orderly preferences, select the option with the greatest expected utility. That standard is appealing because people would achieve it if their preferences followed a few seemingly simple rules, like comparability and transitivity, and because it helps to structure and simplify many choices. However, utility theory ignores aspects of real-life choices, often making it a poor description of actual decisions, or even a legitimate aspiration. In life, people face novel decisions, forcing them to construct preferences that often are unstable. They face complex decisions, forcing them to use simplifying heuristics that often produce reasonable choices. People face unfamiliar outcomes, forcing them to predict their own experiences, learning only later what they value. People face conflicting social roles, forcing them to decide which 'hat(s)' to wear. People have abiding concerns (sacred values) that preclude the trade-offs central to utility theory. People can be distracted by how decisions are framed, and make different choices even when outcomes remain the same.

The bad news about making risk decisions is that uncertainty about values (understanding what an individual or society wants) can be as challenging as uncertainty about facts (understanding what can be had). The good news is that these difficulties can be reduced by trial-and-error experience, by learning efficient heuristics, by hearing multiple perspectives, and by holding values that cannot be manipulated. Also good news, in a way, is the fact that when decisions seem hard, they probably are. As a result, one need not add feeling bad about having trouble making decisions, to the trouble itself.

Chapter 5
Risk perception

Experts have the luxury (and obligation) to analyse specific risks in depth. Everyone else must deal, as best they can, with whatever risks come their way – as must experts, when making decisions about the risks in their everyday lives. On a given day, one might need to know how the HIV virus is transmitted (for a sexual encounter), how close the financial system is to collapse (for an investment), and where clean drinking water is most scarce (for a charitable contribution).

Obviously, lay people cannot know as much as experts – nor need they. For practical purposes, they just need to know enough to make effective decisions. As with experts, that means knowing how big risks are, in order to decide which risks are worth taking. It also means knowing what factors cause risks, in order to have some basic understanding of what can (and cannot) be done about them. Without that, lay people are left taking experts' claims on faith and puzzling over disagreements (e.g. about nuclear power, genetically modified crops, or electromagnetic fields).

Individuals' personal fates depend on how well they understand risks. Their place in society depends on how others perceive their ability to understand risks. If the public seems competent, then a stronger case can be made for free markets and participatory democracy. If the public seems incompetent, then a stronger case can be made for paternalistic institutions that protect them from themselves and from those who might exploit them. Three examples will illustrate the importance and difficulty of understanding lay risk perceptions without conducting behavioural research like that described in this chapter. Such research is needed because we have no direct access to how other people perceive risks. All we have is observable behaviour (choices, judgements), from which we must infer beliefs, fears, and uncertainties. The science can guide those inferences.

Perceptions of risk perceptions

Fly or drive?

After the 9/11 attacks, some observers argued that some Americans had so exaggerated the risk of flying that they increased their travel risk by driving instead. (Similar claims followed London's 7/7 bus and underground attacks.) These observers relied on statistics showing that flying is usually safer than driving. That comparison assumes that those statistics were still valid after the attacks. However, at that time, the risk of flying was so uncertain that US officials grounded the fleet, eliminating flying as a travel option. When air travel resumed, some sceptics wondered how safe it really was – and whether US officials were gambling with travellers' lives, hoping to return national life to normal. Over the next two months, civil aviation was unusually unsafe, with a major crash near JFK airport in New York. The following two years saw unusually few accidents.

Of course, travellers had no way of knowing what the risk would prove to be. The wisdom of their choices depends on what they believed when deciding whether to drive or fly (once the latter became possible). Unfortunately, no one studied those travellers' risk perceptions, meaning that no one really knows what they were thinking. Without that evidence, speculation is easy – and easily biased. People who distrust the public can claim that drivers overestimated the risks of flying and their own driving ability. People who trust the public can claim that drivers prudently avoided uncertain risks and distrusted officials who urged them to fly. They could also argue that travellers chose to drive because it was cheaper, more convenient, and easier on family members' nerves. Without evidence, though, choices reveal as little about perceptions as about preferences (see Chapter 2).

Adolescent (in)vulnerability

Popular wisdom holds that teens have a unique sense of invulnerability. That belief can seemingly explain many dubious teen risk decisions: 'They think that nothing can happen to them.' Here there is evidence that suggests more complex explanations. As noted (Chapter 1), by age 15 or so, teens' reasoning skills are much like those of adults, with similar biases. One such bias is feeling relatively invulnerable, in the sense that most people (of all ages) see themselves as better than average at avoiding risks over which they have some sense of control.

However, given that this 'optimism bias' afflicts both adults and teens, other factors must explain any differences in their decisions. One such factor is that, contrary to the myth of perceived invulnerability, many teens exaggerate their chances of dying young, so much so that they might take risks because they do not expect to live, rather than because they do not expect to die. A second factor is that teens learn and experience different things than adults, producing different risk perceptions. A third factor is that teens often face intense social pressure to act against their better judgement. A fourth factor is that teens have less of the emotional control needed to think clearly and act responsibly. Not only are teens' brains still developing, but their lives are full of maddeningly difficult decisions – about drugs, smoking, intimacy, identity, and more. Being unsure about decisions can mean drifting into situations where emotions rule, such as resolving disputes on the street corner or negotiating sex when hormones are flowing. Faced with so many hard decisions, teens are bound to get some wrong, whatever their decision-making abilities. Understanding teens' risk decisions requires a full account of their perceptions, abilities, and circumstances, not just folk wisdom.

Don't panic!

In emergencies, agitated officials often caution against panic. However, panic is actually quite rare, except when visibility and escape routes are limited, as in nightclub fires or stadium stampedes. Thus, even when people feel panicky, they usually behave otherwise, indeed often acting heroically. Although rescue squads do vital work at great personal risk, survivors are more likely to be saved by 'ordinary' people who happen to be at the scene: family, neighbours, and even complete strangers. Bystanders' brave reactions at the 2011 Tucson, Arizona shooting of Representative Gabrielle Giffords and others are surprisingly the norm.

According to sociologist Kathleen Tierney, the 'myth of panic' has several sources. Officials sometimes talk up the public's irrationality in order to assert their own authority. News media feature emotional responses, finding pathos rather than heroism in scenes of 'villagers risking their lives going through rubble'. People who expect to see panic find exactly that in the images of people running in the streets on 9/11 – and not a remarkable evacuation that saved many lives. We forget that we have seen panic scenes in movies (*War of the Worlds*, *Independence Day*), not newscasts. We worry about whether we personally would rise to such occasions, perhaps unnerved by predictions of panic.

In each of these examples, the perception of lay risk perceptions has a kernel of truth. People sometimes exaggerate small risks enough to incur larger ones. Teens sometimes underestimate their vulnerability. We sometimes feel like we might lose it in stressful situations. How people actually perceive risks in any specific situation, however, is an empirical question. Answering it requires research translating those perceptions into observable, interpretable behaviour, so that we are not left trying to read others' minds.

Judging the risk of dying

An obvious first question about lay risk perceptions is how much people know about the chances of dying from different causes. The simplest way to find out is by asking questions like, 'How many people in the US die each year from lightning strikes (diabetes, cancer, etc.)?' Figure 12 shows results from one of the first studies to do so. It shows some common patterns, observed in many studies. One is that lay people can distinguish big risks from small ones (as seen in the points rising from left to right). A second common pattern is that people do not seem to appreciate how much bigger the big risks are than the small ones. The biggest statistical estimate (all diseases) is a million times larger than the smallest one (botulism), whereas the biggest lay estimate (all diseases) is just 10,000 times larger than the smallest one (smallpox vaccination). A third pattern is that for any statistical frequency, some risks seem much bigger than others (e.g. homicide versus diabetes, tornado versus lightning).

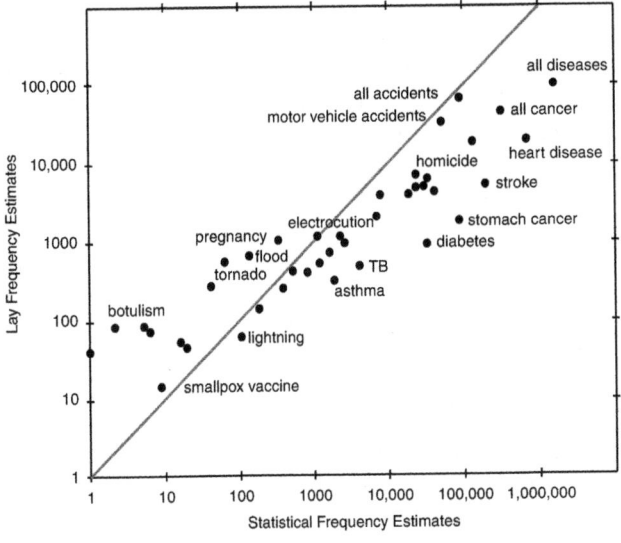

12. **Lay judgements of the annual US death toll from 41 causes (not all labelled). The horizontal (x) axis shows statistical estimates, ranging from *botulism* (on the left) to *all diseases* (on the right). The vertical (y) axis shows average judgements made by a group of educated adults**

One pattern that Figure 12 does not show is how sensitive the answers are to how the question is asked. 'Annual deaths from homicide' is a clear concept. However, many people have no idea what kind of numbers to give. Telling them that there are 1,000 deaths each year from electrocution makes it much easier to estimate the other risks. However, that information also exposes those answers to 'anchoring bias'. When people see a number, their judgements are pulled towards it, as though they spontaneously think of reasons why it might be true. In an extreme example, people give higher estimates for the mean summer temperature in San Francisco, after being asked (absurdly) if it is higher or lower than 554°F. Negotiators exploit the power of anchors by making a bold opening bid, hoping to get the other side to make sense of it.

In Figure 12, the anchor of 1,000 electrocution deaths pulled judgements towards it, making higher ones lower and lower ones higher – thereby reducing the differences between judgements of big and small risks. Figure 12 is often cited as showing that people exaggerate small risks and underestimate large ones. Although that is literally true, it is also an artefact of how the questions were asked. A second group, told that 50,000 people die annually in motor vehicle accidents, gave risk judgements that were in the same order, but were about twice as high. Thus, people have a fairly good feeling for the relative sizes of these risks. However, their judgements of absolute size depend on how they are asked.

Clear questions; clear answers

If people have trouble using numbers, why not have them express their risk perceptions with everyday words like 'very likely' or 'rare'? Indeed, when asked, people prefer using words. However, they also prefer having other people use numbers. Thus, they want to know just what a doctor means when saying that a treatment is 'likely to work' or 'not likely to hurt very much'. Is 'likely' 50% or 90%? Is 'not likely' equal to 100% minus 'likely'? However, when the tables are turned, people are more comfortable using words to express themselves. Unfortunately, that leaves their beliefs as unclear as the meaning of those 'verbal quantifiers'. 'Likely' might mean '40%' to one person and '70%' for another, who would use 'probable' for the same expectation. Indeed, 'likely' might imply different probabilities for the same person, when applied to different events, such as rain, disappoint, score a goal, and fall ill.

Understanding how people perceive risks requires asking clear questions, then eliciting answers with numbers that they are comfortable using. Probabilities are everyday numbers which can apply to any well-defined event, good or bad. Table 7 shows the results of asking teens to give probabilities for twelve significant events in their lives. The first column shows how well these judgements predict their futures. The high correlation (0.64) in the

Table 7. Probability judgements for 12 significant life events, from a large representative sample of American 15- and 16-year-olds

What is the percent chance that you will....	Correlation with outcome	Mean response (%)	Observed outcome rate (%)
1. Be a student in a regular school a year from now?	.64	92.5	79.6
2. Have received a high school diploma by the time you turn 20?	.60	94.5	92.0
3. If you are in school a year from now,... work for pay more than 20 hours a week?	.29	57.7	27.2
4. If you are not in school a year from now,... work for pay more than 20 hours a week?	.31	80.5	43.9
5. Become pregnant within 1 year from now? (female)	.37	8.9	20.1
6. Get someone pregnant within the next year? (male)	.35	9.4	7.9

(continued)

Table 7. Continued

What is the percent chance that you will....	Correlation with outcome	Mean response (%)	Observed outcome rate (%)
7. Become the parent of a baby sometime between now and when you turn 20? (female)	.38	16.0	25.7
8. Become the parent of a baby sometime between now and when you turn 20? (male)	.27	19.1	13.4
9. Be arrested, whether rightly or wrongly, at least once in the next year?	.41	10.3	8.2
10. Serve time in jail or prison between now and when you turn 20?	.29	5.4	2.8
11. Die from any cause (crime, illness, accident, and so on) in the next year?	ns	18.7	0.1
12. Die from any cause (crime, illiness, accident, and so on) between now and when you turn 20?	ns	20.3	0.5

Source: W. Bruine de Bruin, A. Parker, and B. Fischhoff, 'Can Adolescents Predict Significant Events in Their Lives?,' *Journal of Adolescent Health*, 41, 2007, 208–210.

Note: A correlation of 1.0 means a perfect match, while 0 means not correlated. 'ns' means that the correlation was not statistically significant (and should be treated as 0) first row shows that teens who gave higher probabilities to being in school a year later were also more likely to have that happen. Indeed, teens who gave higher probabilities to each event were also more likely to experience it (except for dying, in the last two rows). Thus, teens who see bigger risks also face bigger risks.

Comparing the second column (the probability judgements) and the third column (how often each event happened) shows how accurately teens perceive these risks, in an absolute sense. For example, as a group, young women underestimate their chance of becoming mothers (16.0% versus 25.7%; row 7), whereas young men overestimate their chance of becoming fathers (19.1% versus 13.4%; row 8). These results are consistent with other studies finding that young women exaggerate their control over sexual situations and young men exaggerate their sexual prowess. For these two events, and most others in the table, teens' judgements (column 2) and reality (column 3) are close enough that better information about risk levels might not affect their decisions. One exception is their tendency to exaggerate how easy it is to find work (rows 3 and 4). Better knowledge might help keep teens in school.

A second exception is that teens greatly overestimate their risk of dying in the next year (18.7% versus 0.1%, row 11) or by age 20 (20.3% versus 0.5%, row 12), expressing the unique sense of vulnerability mentioned earlier. Figure 13 shows these judgements in greater detail. About half of these teens gave a probability close to 0%. The others gave probabilities that are much too high. Among those teens, many said 50%, a completely unrealistic judgement, for all but a very few. Such '50 blips' are, however, fairly common in studies that ask about threatening events, such as dying from breast cancer or lung cancer (for smokers). When people are unable or unwilling to give a probability, saying '50', in the sense of 50/50 (or 'I don't know') satisfies the survey's need for a number without really committing themselves. Thus, for whatever reasons, many of these teens can't, or won't, give a probability of dying and say '50' instead. Presumably, they don't

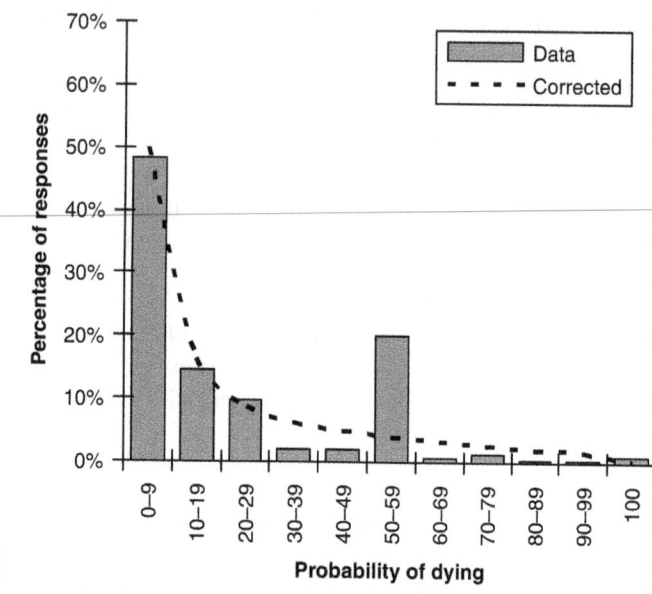

13. **Judgements of the probability of dying in the next year, from a large representative sample of American teens**

think that the probability is 0%. However, treating their judgements literally (as 50%) overstates how much they exaggerate their risk of dying – which is still worryingly high.

Observations and inferences

Studies that ask sufficiently clear questions to compare lay risk perceptions with expert analyses find a mixture of strengths and weaknesses (as in the examples above). One lay strength is that people know roughly how often they have observed events, so much so that keeping a mental tally seems automatic and unconscious. For example, one study asked people to find rhymes for many words, then surprised them by asking for the number of words starting with different letters. Although people in the study were looking at the words' ends (for rhymes), they produced good estimates of how often they had seen each beginning letter. Psychologists have two accounts for how people assess such frequencies. One is that people remember every road accident or blisteringly hot day, then review these separate memories, when they need a frequency estimate. The second account is that people have a single memory for each kind of event, which gets stronger each time they see it, and they infer its frequency from the strength of that memory.

Amos Tversky and Daniel Kahneman proposed that people trust their powers of observation enough to rely on an event's 'availability', when assessing its probability. Specifically, people judge an event as probable, to the extent that instances easily come to mind. Given how well people keep track of frequencies, this heuristic (or rule of thumb) should produce good judgements as long as they see and hear about events as frequently as they actually occur. The heuristic will produce biased judgements if people observe unrepresentative samples of events and cannot compensate for the bias in them.

Reliance on availability can partially account for the major patterns in Figure 12. People can distinguish large risks from small ones, in part because they see many more of the large ones. However, people do not see so many more of the frequent events that they fully appreciate the difference between very big and very small risks. Some causes of death are disproportionately available, leading people to exaggerate their relative frequency. For example, half as many people die from homicide as from diabetes, yet homicides were judged four times as frequent as diabetes deaths. However, homicides are much more available, with news media reporting all local homicides, while rarely mentioning diabetes even in obituaries, preferring terms like 'lingering illness' or 'natural causes'. Media reporting biases are no secret. However, undoing their effects requires, first, thinking about them, then estimating their size, and finally imagining an accurately reported world. That's asking a lot from lay judgements.

Risk

1. Estimate the number of heads in 1000 flips of a fair coin (500)
2. Convert 1 in 1000 to a percentage (0.1%)
3. Convert 1% into a proportion (10 in 1000)

'Place an "X" in either the magnifying glass or the lower part of the scale to describe the chance of each event happening to you'

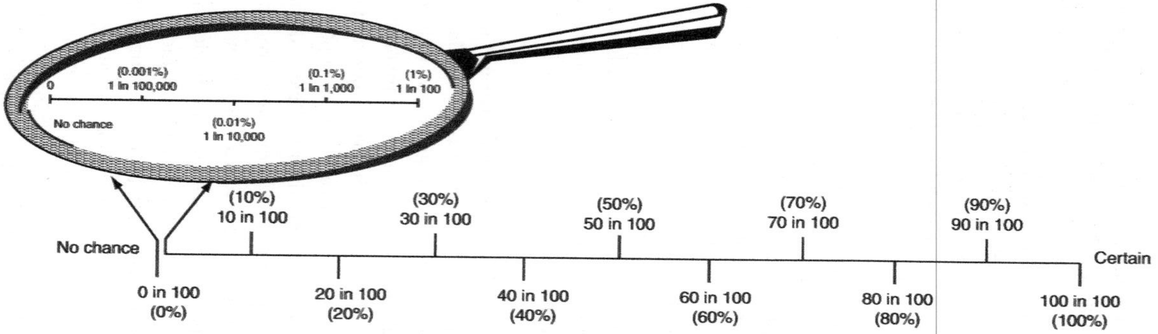

(0.001%)   (0.1%)   (1%)
0   1 in 100,000   1 in 1,000   1 in 100

No chance   (0.01%)
1 in 10,000

No chance

| (10%) | (30%) | (50%) | (70%) | (90%) |
| 10 in 100 | 30 in 100 | 50 in 100 | 70 in 100 | 90 in 100 | Certain |

| 0 in 100 | 20 in 100 | 40 in 100 | 60 in 100 | 80 in 100 | 100 in 100 |
| (0%) | (20%) | (40%) | (60%) | (80%) | (100%) |

14. A scale for eliciting very small probability judgements and a three-item scale for testing individuals' numeracy. The magnifying glass allowed orderly judgements, even from people who got all three numeracy questions wrong

A variant of availability, called the 'simulation heuristic', entails judging an event as likely if it is easy to imagine it happening (simulating it in one's mind). This heuristic, too, offers insight and pitfalls. A barely imaginable risk should not be that likely. However, imagination can fail, as when catastrophic accidents happen with supposedly safe technologies and financial systems. Conversely, implausible risks can make great, easily imagined stories. Advertisers play on our imaginations when they create vivid images of risks that their products promise to reduce (preventing disease, thwarting home invaders, avoiding social embarrassment). Even fiction can affect risk perceptions, by making real-life counterparts easier to imagine (*Jaws*, *The China Syndrome*, *Outbreak*).

Availability is one of many heuristics that people use to judge uncertain events, providing serviceable, if imperfect, judgements when people lack needed knowledge and the resources to secure it. As with choice heuristics (Chapter 4), their results can vary. For example, availability works better for people who have seen a lot and who scour their memory for relevant instances, compared to people who have more limited experience and less motivation to probe it.

The anchoring bias mentioned earlier (with respect to Figure 12) arises from relying on another heuristic, called anchoring and adjustment. People using it start with a salient number (1,000 electrocution deaths, gold at £10,000 an ounce, 100 sleeper cells), then think of reasons to adjust it, until they reach a value that seems right. Typically, they adjust too little and end up too close to the anchor. As a result, anchoring works better when the salient number is close to the needed one and when people focus on reasons why it might be wrong, rather than on reasons justifying it. One can imagine how different the adjustment processes might be for these three (true) anchors, describing a 2010 US recall: 550 million eggs, 1,300 cases of Salmonella, less than 1% of eggs.

People using the 'representativeness' heuristic judge an event as likely to the extent that it 'represents' the salient features of the process that might produce it. Thus chemical plant accidents seem less likely when their most salient features are safety systems rather than dangerous chemical stocks. One feature of many events that is rarely salient, but greatly affects their risk level, is how often they occur. People tend to think about the risk of a single car ride, sexual encounter, subprime loan, or 'permanently capped' oil well. If those risks seem small, then the event seems safe. However, even very small risks mount up, if repeated often enough (as with a lifetime of driving or sexual encounters and with industries having many subprime loans or oil wells).

Another feature that people often fail to 'represent' in their risk judgements is the quality of the evidence that they have. That insensitivity can lead to people being as convinced by fragmentary analyses as by elaborate ones. That fact can be maddening for scientists who perceive their life's work being outweighed by isolated observations, such as a cold winter's day being taken as refuting long-term climate change. A corollary of that insensitivity is 'belief in the law of small numbers': treating small samples as though the statistical 'law of large numbers' applies to them. (The latter law holds that, as representative samples grow larger, they come to resemble the 'population' from which they are drawn.) Medical researchers are required to conduct formal statistical power analyses, establishing the size of the sample needed to produce meaningful results – rather than relying on their intuitions or statistically unreliable experience.

The ultimate neglect of sample size is relying on a single example. If many people are happy with a car, medical treatment, or investment, it should not matter much if one person is not – unless that person is especially knowledgeable. When a patient's symptoms suggest an exotic disease, doctors are reminded 'think horses, not zebras, when you hear hoof beats'. Evidence should be

Misperceptions of randomness

Random processes often produce patterns that do not look random, leading people to find illusory causes. For example, clusters of bomb hits during the London Blitz appeared to indicate specially chosen targets, spawning theories about when and where to seek shelter. However, an analysis by mathematician William Feller found random clustering, by dividing the city into a grid and counting the number of hits in each cell.

There are so many forms of cancer and ways to look for patterns (families, neighbourhoods, workplaces) that worrisome clusters can appear at random. Here, too, statistical analyses are needed to determine which clusters have a common cause (pesticides? electromagnetic fields?) and which reflect no more than tragic coincidence. In a more benign setting, analyses have found that basketball players' apparent 'hot hand' streaks are about what would be expected by chance.

Even people who accept a statistical analysis demonstrating randomness may struggle to give it intuitive meaning. One possible strategy is thinking about the many causal factors that combine to make an event unpredictable. For the Blitz, those factors might include the effects of weather, navigation, and ground defences. For basketball, those factors might include the effects of shot selection, substitutions, and defenders' assignments.

very good, before one ignores the usual risks. In this light, statistical averages can make very useful anchors.

Meta-cognition: knowing how much you know?

However much people know about a risk, sound decision-making requires knowing how much they know. Overconfident people can unwittingly take risks and overlook signs of trouble.

Underconfident people can be needlessly cautious, gathering information and ruminating when they should be acting. Insensitivity to the quality of evidence is one source of overconfidence.

Figure 15 shows typical results from a common test of how well people can assess the extent of their knowledge. The test poses questions with two possible choices, such as: which is more

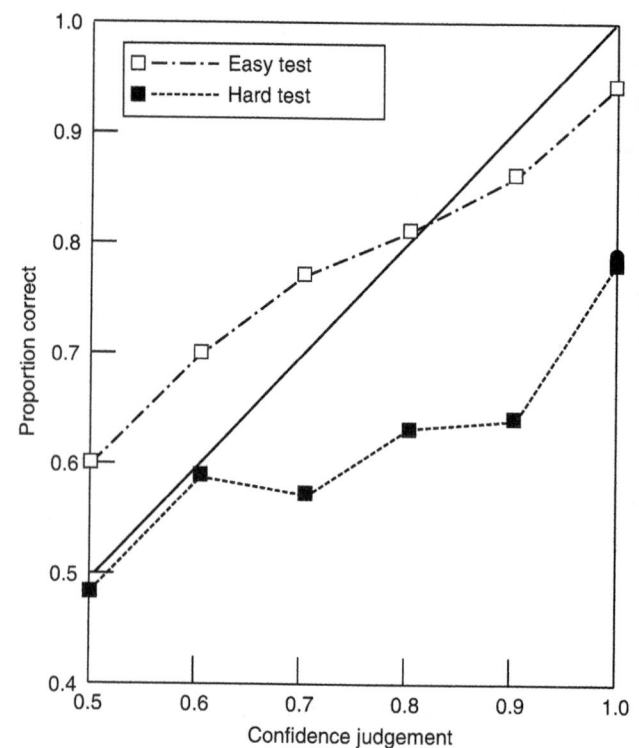

15. The appropriateness of confidence judgements, showing how often people are correct, when they give each probability of being correct. People answered questions such as 'Which cause of death is more frequent: (a) homicide or (b) suicide?'

frequent: (a) homicide or (b) suicide? Is absinthe (a) a liqueur or (b) a precious stone? After choosing an answer, people give the probability (from 50% to 100%) that it is right. Ideally, people are right 50% of the time when 50% confident; 60% of the time when 60% confident; and so on.

In Figure 15, the horizontal (x) axis shows the probabilities that people gave for being correct. The vertical (y) axis shows how often they were, in fact, correct. The top curve is for an easy test (80% correct, overall); the bottom curve is for a hard test (60% correct, overall). With both curves, there is good news: people are more accurate (moving up) when they are more confident (moving to the right). The bad news is that people are often wrong when they are 100% confident. With the easy test, absolutely confident people are right only about 90% of the time; with the hard test, only about 75% of the time. Indeed, the hard test shows consistent overconfidence. For each probability (except 50%), people overestimate how often they are correct.

Such overconfidence is often observed, even with experts (Figure 8). If it were universal, then 'doubt yourself' would be good general advice. However, underconfidence also happens, as with the easy test in Figure 15. Here, when people say 50%, they are right 60% of the time, somewhat underestimating how much they know. Adding doubt would aggravate that underconfidence. Generally speaking, people are overconfident with hard problems and underconfident with easy ones, not fully appreciating when they know a little and when they know a lot.

People assess confidence by reviewing reasons that support and oppose their chosen answer. That review can mislead them if those reasons include unrecognized errors. In judgements about risks, such errors often take the form of errors in 'mental models' of the underlying causal processes. The first text box shows examples of errors that contribute to people not knowing how much they know about risks. The second text box shows an example of medical

Mental models

When people make inferences about physical processes, they draw on *mental models* assembled from whatever they've learned, observed, and inferred over their lifetimes. These intuitive theories often have many correct elements, but are undermined by 'bugs' (in the sense of flaws in computer software), caused by misconceptions that can be corrected by providing missing facts. For example:

Temperature control
Bug: Turning a thermostat past the desired temperature will make one's home heat up or cool down faster. Missing fact: The system works at capacity until it reaches the target temperature. Setting the wrong target creates the risk of overshooting it.

Radon
Bug: Homes with radon gas are permanently contaminated. Missing fact: Tiny radon concentrations are dangerous because these radioactive isotopes decay very quickly, causing immediate damage, but then vanishing. Once radon influxes (from radioactive rocks) are stopped, the problem is gone.

Climate change
Bug: Abnormally cold winters prove that our climate is not warming. Missing fact: Destabilized climate systems will produce many weather abnormalities, but with a general trend towards warming.

Landscaping
Bug: Smooth green lawns reflect a healthy environment. Missing fact: Nature flourishes through complex interactions among multiple species.

Indoor pollution

Bug: Having a fan blow air inwards reduces risk from domestic chemicals. Missing fact: The fan just blows chemicals around inside; reversing the fan sucks them out.

Physicians' mental models

In 1847, Ignac Semmelweis hypothesized that often fatal childbed (puerperal) fever was due to physicians and medical students carrying infections from autopsies to pregnant women. He tested his theory and reduced risks by implementing new hand-washing procedures. Nonetheless, the medical establishment rejected his theory because it contradicted prevailing conceptions of disease. Faced with the tragedy of needless deaths, Semmelweis committed suicide. His view was accepted years later along with the germ theory of disease. Without an alternative theory of disease spread, though, his contemporaries could (or would) not acknowledge his evidence.

experts unable to accept clear-cut evidence at odds with their mental model of a disease.

Risk perceptions and emotions

Studies of heuristics, mental models, and overconfidence are threads in psychology's 'cognitive revolution' begun after World War II. These studies examine normal ways of thinking by seeing how they can lead people astray, much as study of optical illusions reveals normal ways of seeing. Some of those errors arise from honest, often useful, boundedly rational attempts to get things right, such as relying on the availability of examples. Other errors reflect the 'motivated cognition' of people who let their minds play tricks on them, as when drivers go easy on their own mistakes, patients hear greater hope than their doctors intend, or voters make excuses for their favourite candidates' gaffes.

Spurred by brain-imaging technology, research is increasingly revealing the roles played by emotions, such as fear, disgust, pleasure, and anticipation. Sometimes the research reveals neural mechanisms underlying effects observed in earlier studies, showing how attuned people are to emotion-related signals. For example, briefly seeing a happy face leads people to rate whatever they see next more positively. An angry face does the opposite. Other research examines those factors that make experiences positive or negative. For example, the 'mere exposure effect' refers to the tendency to like things more, the more often we have seen them.

Psychologist Paul Slovic and his colleagues proposed an 'affect heuristic' whereby people infer risk levels from their feelings. In such accounts, emotion is not antithetical to thought but essential to it, directing attention and helping people to interpret what they observe, guiding perceptions and preferences. Like other heuristics, it can help or hinder. 'Trust your gut' might be good advice with sexual predators, but not with adroit con men. Slovic argues that we must overcome our emotions lest we be overwhelmed by problems, such as distant genocides, where 'psychic numbing' can induce feelings of helplessness.

Behavioural economist George Loewenstein has described an emotional context effect, whereby people view decisions differently when in hot states (anger, passion) and cold ones (quiet, torpidity). In hot states, people may make brave decisions (about investments, conflicts, travel) that feel wrong after they cool down. In cold states, people may not mobilize themselves for actions needing intense involvement (pursuing a lover, crying for help). When feeling energetic, people make promises that are hard to keep when they feel less so.

Emotions affect risk perceptions, in part, by how they direct attention. For example, anger focuses people on threatening individuals, leading them to blame their problems on people (Osama bin Laden), rather than on situations (globalization). Anger also makes people more optimistic, by obscuring factors that could thwart their plans. A November 2001 study used video clips and a writing exercise ('What aspect of the terrorist attacks makes you most ANGRY?' 'Why does it make you ANGRY?') to increase feelings of anger, fear, or worry. Participants who were made more angry gave probabilities that were about 6% lower to risks such as being injured in a terror attack and losing sleep over terror, compared to participants made more fearful.

How important are emotions in risk decisions? A long-term view looks at their evolutionary value, asking whether being attuned to others' emotions or being more optimistic when one is angry increases reproductive success. A narrower view asks whether emotions are so powerful that they keep people from thinking clearly or distort their judgements enough to affect specific decisions. Some decisions are close enough that 6% greater optimism could tip the scales, as might shifting between hot and cold states. With other decisions, those changes would hardly be felt. Some decisions are so emotion-laden that people hardly think at all. In others, people deliberately manage their emotions, as when they resolve to control their temper or find a designated driver before alcohol makes them underestimate the risks of violence or driving.

How good – or bad – are our risk perceptions?

As seen in the examples opening this chapter, anecdotal observation can create misleading perceptions of others' risk perceptions. Behavioural research provides one source of evidence. However, applying its results requires understanding how the decisions that it poses differ from everyday decisions. Research decisions usually have these four properties:

1) They are clearly described, so that researchers can see how people make them. That clarity can produce better decisions, if it removes the clutter of everyday life, or worse decisions, if that clutter provides vital context, such as what choices other people are making.

2) They have low stakes, reflecting researchers' limited budgets. That can produce better decisions, if it reduces stress, or worse decisions, if it reduces motivation.

3) They are approved by university ethics committees. That can produce better decisions, if it reduces participants' worry about being deceived, or worse decisions, if it induces artificiality.

4) They are focused on researchers' interests. That can produce worse decisions, if researchers are studying biases, or better decisions, if researchers are seeking decision-makers' secrets of success.

How well people understand risk decisions depends on the people and the decisions, whether in research or in life. Behavioural research illuminates their strengths and weaknesses by revealing the many factors that can affect that understanding. These factors represent small truths, rather than sweeping statements about the human condition. They depict people who are neither uniformly wonderful nor terrible when dealing with risks.

Conclusion: lay risk perceptions reflect sensible, but imperfect inferences

Risk decisions force people to be experts in everything that comes their way. They meet those challenges by relying on intuitions that can produce both accurate and biased risk judgements. Those intuitions are often guided by heuristics that allow imperfect, boundedly rational answers to questions when people lack needed knowledge or decision-making resources. These judgements parallel those made by risk scientists when they, too, must go beyond hard data and rely on inference (Chapter 3).

Overall, people tend to understand the relative size of different risks, but can struggle when judging absolute risk levels. People have some insight into how much they know, but can suffer from overconfidence or underconfidence. Risk perceptions are often reasonable, but can be so wrong as to produce poor choices. These faulty risk perceptions tend to reflect not stupidity, but ignorance about facts that people might learn with proper risk communications, the topic of Chapter 6.

Chapter 6
Risk communication

We need information in order to make sound risk decisions. Sometimes it seems to come at us from all quarters. The news media report plane crashes, oil spills, pesticides, water pollution, sports concussions, climate change, floods, droughts, mine collapses, rapes, gun violence, wars, terror, deflation, and hyperinflation. Politicians and merchants highlight risks that we should fear and that they can fix. Health and safety experts describe risks that they want us to fix, by changing how we eat, sleep, drive, exercise, or have sex. These messages reach us in the air, online, in magazines, and on shopping bags. They are embedded in insurance contracts, package labels, and film plots. They arise in conversations with friends, family, doctors, and car mechanics. There are one-way communications, targeting us with messages, and two-way consultations, seeking our input, such as public meetings, deliberative polls, or national dialogues, like those held in Sweden on nuclear power and in Britain on genetically modified crops.

Communications about risks involve issues central to our existence as individuals, societies, and beings in the natural world. When they succeed, we live better lives, making sounder decisions in our own lives and participating more fully in public policy-making. Like other communications, those about risk embody the social contract between the individuals involved. One ideal for that social contract is respectful, cooperative two-way communication, recognizing individuals' rights to be heard and to receive needed information about risks.

Over the past half century, vocal movements have advocated just such a social contract, asserting individuals' right to participate in risk decisions affecting their welfare. Patient advocates have pressed for shared decision-making, hospital performance evaluations, and medical record privacy. Environmental advocates have demanded advisory panels, green labelling, and independent audits. Each decision tests those rights, reflecting and shaping the balance of power in society. As a result, participants naturally ask whether the associated communication process has provided the information that they need. Of course, those who control that information may have other goals in mind, such as getting people to buy their products, save more, eat better, or accept pollution. Whatever their goals, though, they risk the public's wrath if they fail to meet their expectations.

The chapter begins with examples showing some of the costs and causes of poor risk communications. It then considers what it takes to create communications that serve the public's needs, in terms of both content (facilitating good decisions) and process (enhancing the public's role in risk decisions).

Some unhappy risk communications

Hurricane Katrina marked a tragic turning point in many lives and the fortunes of the Bush administration. Flawed communications, before, during, and after the hurricane, played a big role in the tragedy. However, aside from their drama and magnitude, these failures were nothing special. Most days, one can open the newspaper and find stories about poor risk communications threatening lives and reputations.

Lives and reputations at risk: a case study

The Bush administration's handling of Hurricane Katrina was a public health communication failure that left many people without the information that they needed to protect themselves. For example, some residents were misled by claims regarding the integrity of the levees protecting New Orleans; some understood the risks but were unable to act on them (such as disabled people needing transportation); some lacked assurances, such as whether they would receive the welfare cheques that they needed to survive financially, should they evacuate; some lacked information about loved ones, without whom they would not leave.

Katrina was also a public affairs communication failure, undermining faith in the administration. Citizens who needed practical advice heard self-centred messages, most memorably 'Brownie, you're doing a heck of a job' – President Bush's plaudits for his director of emergency services. Even though the administration maintained that state and local authorities, rather than Michael Brown, were responsible for the chaotic emergency response, it suffered in the court of public opinion, especially after promoting its ability to protect Americans following the 9/11 attacks.

All organizations need public affairs communications making the case for their policies. However, without fulfilling their public health responsibilities, organizations that manage risks have no legitimate case to make. In politics, public affairs can sometimes carry the day, by selling a favoured spin on events. With risks, facts matter and cheery words in a grim situation add insult to injury.

Having so many people in harm's way reflects an even more fundamental communication failure played out over many presidencies. New Orleans residents and officials had not grasped the peril they faced. As a result, by the time Katrina hit, there was a limit to what anyone could do or say.

While writing this book, some US examples included:

- During the run-up to the threatened H1N1 (swine flu) pandemic, public health officials were criticized by some people for not having enough vaccine and by others for forcing them to get vaccinated.
- A national task force recommended less mammography screening for women in their 40s, then was surprised by the hostile public reaction, despite a nearly identical controversy 12 years earlier.
- Consumers protested an ambitious programme for installing 'smart' electricity meters in homes, fearing an invasion of their privacy and undisclosed health risks.
- A blue-ribbon panel concluded that the Department of Homeland Security's colour-coded terror warning system 'lack [ed] public confidence', despite seven years of use.
- Another blue-ribbon panel, meant to guide a nuclear power 'renaissance', was criticized for holding public meetings that only well-heeled advocates could access.

In each case, one can ask whether those with the information did not care enough to inform their public or failed to deliver on good intentions. Whatever the reasons, when they stumbled, their opponents gladly amplified their failures. The Bush administration's critics cited Katrina as demonstrating its indifference to people in the hurricane's path. The Obama administration's critics cited the mammography screening guidelines as demonstrating its plans to ration healthcare, including alleged 'death panels' that would decide when people were too infirm to receive care. Some financial analysts estimate that 70% of many firms' market value lies in intangible assets, such as goodwill and reputation. Poor communication threatens that value by undermining trust, making firms seem unwilling or unable to provide needed information. Poor risk communications can similarly erode political capital.

Some risk communication problems reflect general problems, identified by behavioural research. For example, people overestimate the extent to which their beliefs are common knowledge and, as a result, leave too much unsaid. They overestimate how well they have conveyed their intent and, as a result, exaggerate how well others can read between their lines. People also overestimate how well others perceive the situational pressures on them and, as a result, neglect to explain important reasons for their actions. These biases make it 'only human' for risk communicators to believe mistakenly that they have fulfilled their duty to inform (e.g. about the risks and benefits of the H1N1 vaccine or of mammography).

Risk communications also face some distinctive challenges. In terms of their content, they require identifying the few most relevant facts in masses of technical information, then making them comprehensible to lay people. In terms of their process, risk communications must bridge gaps between experts and lay decision-makers, who often have very different values, social status, and life experiences. Risk communications may involve 'contested science', with partisans choosing convenient facts and manufacturing controversy, in order to forestall action. With topics like climate change, genetically modified crops, and vaccines, it can seem as though the warring parties draw on separate sciences.

Given the chance to interact directly with lay people, experts often learn which facts matter and how to convey them. Lacking such opportunities, though, experts are left guessing at what lay people need to know, already know, and make of their messages. Unless the experts guess right, they will lose that broader audience, without knowing why their friends and family can understand them, but not the general public. The frustration of these seemingly inexplicable failures must contribute to the disrespect that many experts have for the lay public. No one likes to be misunderstood, especially when they cannot figure out why.

The next section examines five examples of risk communications, in terms of how well they fulfil the duty to inform, in both their technical execution and the social contract that they express.

More and less right by design

Nutrition fact boxes

These ubiquitous, mundane displays might be the world's most widely distributed risk communications, available at the point of purchase for most packaged foods. In terms of their content, there is much to like. They provide information about both risks (sodium, transfats) and benefits (protein, vitamins, fibre), in explicit quantitative terms (grams, serving), sometimes with useful context (% of Recommended Daily Allowance), accompanied by regulatory agencies' guarantees of accuracy. Their standard format means that consumers who master one label then know how to use others.

However, achieving that mastery is not easy. Consumers must learn whether each recommended value is an upper limit (fat, sodium), a lower limit (D, B_{12}), or both (iron, for men and for women). They must determine how much each item matters to their personal health. They must decode unintuitive units (15g of mango chutney? 13% of recommended daily protein?). They must assess how far to trust the science underlying nutritional claims. For example, some scientists believe that when people consume more cholesterol, their bodies produce less; some nutritionists question how well the body absorbs vitamin and mineral additives. If knowing about those uncertainties would change consumers' decisions, then the labels have not adequately informed them.

However, adding information about scientific uncertainty presents a design challenge, in so far as it would make the labels more cluttered and less inviting. Similarly, adding information about allergens (soy, peanuts) would help people with those allergies, but make the labels less useful to everyone else, by making it harder to find the information that they need. The labels themselves face the challenge of cutting through the clutter of shopping environments and the strong habits that guide food buying and eating. So it should not be surprising that displaying nutrition information in restaurants has little effect on diners' behaviour, unless proprietors also actively promote healthier meals.

Nonetheless, manufacturers often resist informational labels, especially ones that reveal weaknesses in their products. Indeed, by some accounts, a main impact of nutrition labelling has been encouraging manufacturers to reformulate products so that they will not look bad on the labels. Thus, each item in the nutrition fact box reflects the outcome of a political process, in which consumers successfully asserted their right to know about some aspect of their food, such as its sodium or transfat content. Whether consumers gain full value from those victories depends on prosaic aspects of label design. American consumers have not won the right to know whether cattle have been tested for bovine spongiform encephalopathy (BSE, or 'mad cow disease'), partly because some meat producers have successfully argued that it would lead consumers to exaggerate the risk, based on their interpretation of the British experience.

Drug fact boxes
Figure 16 adapts the experience with nutrition fact boxes to communications about prescription drugs. It, too, lists both benefits ('Did Lunesta help?') and risks ('What are Lunesta's side effects?'), in the quantitative terms that people need (and not just vague statements such as 'Lunesta somewhat helped some people and somewhat bothered others'). Its units should be clear (minutes to fall asleep). The box compares two options, the

Drug Facts Box LUNESTA (ESZOPICLONE) for Insomnia in Adults

What is the purpose of this box?	To explain the benefits and side effects of Lunesta to help you decide whether or not you want to take this drug.
What is this drug for?	To reduce the symptoms of insomnia – trouble falling or staying asleep – experienced for at least one month.
Who might consider taking it?	Adults age 18 and older with insomnia.
What should I be aware of?	The drug may cause abnormal behaviors like sleepy driving and personality changes (like uncharacteristic aggressiveness).
What other choices are there?	Reduce caffeine intake (especially at night), increase exercise, establish regular bedtime, avoid daytime naps or consider other prescription (or over-the-counter) medications.

STUDY FINDINGS: LUNESTA VERSUS PLACEBO

788 adults with at least 1 month of insomnia—sleeping less than 6.5 hours per night or taking more than 30 minutes to fall asleep—were given LUNESTA or PLACEBO nightly for 6 months. Here's what happened:

	PLACEBO (No drug) 195 people	LUNESTA (3 mg each night) 593 people
What difference did LUNESTA make?		
Did LUNESTA help?		
People fell asleep 15 minutes faster	45 minutes to fall asleep	30 minutes to fall asleep
People slept 37 minutes longer	5 hours 45 minutes	6 hours 22 minutes
What are LUNESTA'S side effects?		
Serious side effects		
No difference between LUNESTA and placebo	None reported to date	
Symptom side effects		
More people had unpleasant taste in their mouth (additional 20% due to drug)	6%	26%
More had dizziness (additional 7% due to drug)	3%	10%
More had drowsiness (additional 6% due to drug)	3%	9%
More had dry mouth (additional 5% due to drug)	2%	7%
More had nausea (additional 5% due to drug)	6%	11%

Limitations Neither this trial nor the 2 smaller trials considered by FDA have shown that Lunesta helps people feel more rested or function better.
How long has the drug been in use? LUNESTA *was approved by FDA in 2005 based on studies involving about 1,200 people.* As with all new drugs, rare but serious drug side effects may emerge after the drug is on the market—when more people have used the drug.

Risk communication

16. A sample drug fact box

drug and placebo (a sugar pill), rather than describing just the drug. It does the maths of comparing the two options, by computing absolute differences in expected effects. It does not make the mistake of calculating relative risks (4.3 times as many cases of bad mouth taste), which mean little without knowing absolute risk levels. Doubling a risk could mean going from 0.01% to 0.02% or from 10% to 20%, with very different implications.

The box offers additional decision options under 'what other choices are there?' Although it gives no statistics for these options, reminding users about such common alternative 'treatments' might tell them enough to decide whether to try them before trying the drug. The box also says how good its evidence is, albeit in terms that require enough technical knowledge to sense what can be learned from a clinical trial of 788 healthy adults and users' experience since 2005.

Formal analyses of consumers' information needs were used to select the box's contents, by identifying the few facts that mattered most in users' risk decisions. Risk perception research guided the design. In field tests, most people in a representative sample of Americans could extract enough information from such boxes to identify the better option. Almost all of them wanted to have such boxes, in sharp contrast with patients' dislike of the dense 'consumer medication information' currently distributed with prescription drugs. The persistence of those poor communications reflects some combination of not wanting to serve users' needs (politics) and not knowing how to serve them (design).

Even the best general communication will not work for everyone. The text box describes one strategy for helping people who cannot access needed information by themselves, by connecting them with people who can.

Vaccines

Drug fact boxes seek to inform independent choices, allowing that a given drug might be right for some people and not for others. The information sheets that people receive with vaccines typically are designed with one choice in mind: get vaccinated. However, they

Community and communication

One test of a society is how well it ensures that its weakest members receive needed information. David Moxley, a social work professor working with older, homeless African-American women in Detroit, observed that many women in his programme could grasp the contents of a drug fact box (Figure 16), but would have trouble concentrating on it, given the turmoil in their lives. He believed that they could follow the information, though, if someone walked them through it, in a protected setting. He envisioned a well-trained paraprofessional preparing clients for a doctor's appointment with questions like: 'Could you show me your medications? According to the drug fact box, this one is for arthritis. Do you have that? It's taken twice a day. Can you do that? Are you ever dizzy, a side effect on the list? Let's write all this down, for you to show the doctor.'

Moxley's proposal uses community resources to extend the drug fact box's usefulness, by connecting people with others who can help them. A society might reasonably strive to have no member more than two degrees of separation from a competent interpreter of risk information. Social media might fill some of these roles, if they can place effective interpreters between authoritative information and those who need advice.

reflect a *non-persuasive* communication philosophy, trusting the facts to speak for themselves. As a result, they describe both benefits and risks, often in quantitative terms (as in the excerpt in the text box below). Nonetheless, vaccine communications are often challenged, as in the controversy over a claimed link between the measles-mumps-rubella vaccine (MMR) and autism, a charge that outlived having one of its primary advocates publicly discredited.

What are the risks from yellow fever vaccine?

A vaccine, like any medicine, is capable of causing serious problems, such as severe allergic reactions. The risk of a vaccine causing serious harm, or death, is extremely small.

Reactions are less likely to occur after a booster dose of yellow fever vaccine than after the first dose.

Mild problems:

 A. soreness, redness, or swelling where the shot was given
 B. fever
 C. aches

If these problems occur, they usually begin soon after the shot and last for 5–10 days. In studies, they occurred in as many as 25% of vaccine recipients.

Severe problems (estimates based on passive reporting):

 D. Life-threatening allergic reaction (approximately 1 reported per 131,000 doses)
 E. Severe nervous system reactions (approximately 1 reported per 150,000–250,000 doses)

Source: http://www.cdc.gov/vaccines/Pubs/vis/default.htm#yf

Vaccine communications often succeed in conveying their content, but not in creating the trust needed for its acceptance. Sceptics often question estimates of side-effect risks based on doctors' reports. Sceptics worry that such 'passive surveillance' underestimates the risks because physicians miss some problems and deliberately ignore others, in order to avoid the hassle of reporting. Some sceptics trust individual vaccines, but worry about children receiving many shots at once. Vaccine advocates have responses to these fears. However, those responses are not in the information sheets. People who rely on them have no way to know what vaccine advocates have to say – or even that they have relevant evidence.

In contrast, sceptics' risk communications explicitly address these fears. They also use everyday language, rather than technical terms. As a result, their messages are easily found on web searches. Those messages often tell vivid stories of health tragedies attributed to vaccines, in language that leaves lingering emotional effects, even if their specific claims have been disproven or forgotten. Public health communications may not be allowed to tell dramatic stories of vaccine successes, limiting their ability to defend vaccines in the rough-and-tumble of public controversy.

In preparation for the 2009/2010 H1N1 (swine flu) vaccine campaign, US officials bolstered their surveillance system, with the goal of producing evidence good enough for credible communications about side effects. Even though the vaccination campaign began in controversy (see above), it passed quietly. Fortunately, both the vaccine and the flu proved benign. However, had there been problems, having better evidence on vaccine side effects should have helped public health officials to provide the information that people needed for personal decisions, as well as to evaluate the decisions that officials make (such as whether to close schools after students fall ill). Thus, the earlier controversies led to changes in risk science, creating the evidence needed to support better risk communications.

Preventing sexual assault

Vaccine decisions involve two clear options (get the shot or not), with two clear outcomes (get sick from the disease or the shot). Some decisions are much more complex, such as those facing women trying to reduce their risk of sexual assault. Women need communications that help them to deal with many different situations and with many possible options for dealing with ambient risks (changing travel patterns, learning martial arts), threatening situations (leaving an uncomfortable party, challenging inappropriate behaviour), and actual assaults (resisting physically, screaming 'fire'). Women may wish to weigh the uncertain effects of these choices on many valued outcomes (completed assaults, other physical injuries, psychological harm, problems in the legal system, reduced personal freedom). They face uncertainties so great that, even after the fact, women may not know what difference their choices made. Would a suspicious man have stopped anyway? Was he malicious or just dense?

It is not hard to communicate the effectiveness of protective measures if the relevant evidence exists. However, although there is much research on how to counsel rape victims and on how society may stigmatise them, there is little research on the effectiveness of self-defence measures. Without such evidence, there is just opinion, which leads to communications that make unsupported claims about what decisions women should make. Some of these communications are explicit ('fight back', 'get an escort', 'dress modestly'). Others are embedded in social institutions (whether police have special rape units, how courts treat victims). Often, the advice is contradictory (do/do not resist physically). One reason for contradictory advice is that experts see different sets of incomplete evidence. Thus, police tend to see women for whom physical resistance has failed, then recommend against it. Workers at rape crisis centres help women with different experiences, then reach different conclusions. A second reason for contradictory advice is that experts may impute their own values to others. As a result, experts who focus on physical safety will provide different advice than experts who also consider psychological effects.

Similar problems may account for the failure of the self-defence courses taken by women students at many US colleges. Although these courses may increase self-confidence, they do not seem to reduce sexual assault risks. Their apparent flaw is focusing on decisions about strangers, rather than the male students who create most of female students' problems, in situations where women may want to balance protecting themselves with building relationships. Here, too, research has not produced the evidence that would support stronger advice.

Risk communications do people no service, if they increase their confidence without increasing their ability to make sound choices. They make matters worse if they make situations seem more manageable than they actually are. Contradictory advice means that, if things go badly, whatever a woman does, some 'experts' advised otherwise. Such advice is flawed, as is the society that has failed to produce the evidence, and provide the safety, that women need.

Intelligence analyses

Whereas many risk communications address broad audiences, intelligence analyses often are conducted for a single decision-maker. In his essay 'Words of Estimative Probability', veteran analyst Sherman Kent argued that vague quantifiers undermine the value of many analyses. As an example, he used the phrase 'a serious possibility', drawn from an authoritative US analysis of the chances of the USSR invading Yugoslavia in the early 1950s. When asked what probability that phrase implied, analysts gave values from 20% to 80%, indicating very different risks and implying very different US policies.

Kent argued that national security risk communications had to state clearly both analysts' conclusions and their confidence in them. 'Let the judgement be unmistakable and let it be unmistakably ours.' In the Yugoslavia case, he argued that the conclusions had to be weak because the Soviet Union had not yet made its decision and might even be waiting for President Eisenhower to act. Kent observed that analysts prefer to get numeric predictions, but to give verbal ones – just like non-experts (Chapter 5).

Communicating uncertainty in intelligence analysis: an explanation of estimative language

We use phrases such as *we judge*, *we assess*, and *we estimate* – and probabilistic terms such as *probably* and *likely* – to convey analytical assessments and judgments. Such statements are not facts, proof, or knowledge...intended to imply that we have 'proof' that shows something to be a fact or that definitely links two items or issues.

Estimates of likelihood

Because analytical judgments are not certain, we use probabilistic language to reflect the [Intelligence] Community's estimates of the likelihood of developments or events. Terms such as *probably*, *likely*, *very likely*, or *almost certain* indicate a greater than even chance. The terms *unlikely* and *remote* indicate a less than even chance that an event will occur; they do not imply that an event will not occur. Terms such as *might* or *may* reflect situations in which we are unable to assess the likelihood, generally because relevant information is unavailable, sketchy, or fragmented. Terms such as *we cannot dismiss*, *we cannot rule out*, or *we cannot discount* reflect an unlikely, improbable, or remote event whose consequences are such that it warrants mentioning.

Confidence in assessments

Our assessments and estimates are supported by information that varies in scope, quality and sourcing. Consequently,

F. *High confidence* generally indicates that our judgments are based on high-quality information and/or that the nature of the issue makes it possible to render a solid judgment. A 'high-confidence' judgment is not a fact or a certainty, however, and such judgments still carry a risk of being wrong.

Responding to allegations of oversold intelligence before the Iraq War, the US Office of the Director of National Intelligence revised its risk communication procedures to address Kent's concerns. The text box shows the resulting guidance on how to express the likelihood of an event and the confidence placed in predictions. It is an empirical question whether this elaborate system of verbal quantifiers communicates any better than the 'serious possibility' that vexed Kent. If not, then policy-makers may put too much confidence in analyses that are not being deliberately oversold. Of course, policy-makers can still go wrong, if they correctly interpret forecasts that are themselves overconfident, as found by Philip Tetlock in his studies of political analysts (Chapter 3).

Whereas policy-makers can sometimes demand that analysts make their forecasts more explicit, most people lack that opportunity. In the UK, intelligence analyses are translated into five 'terror threat' levels: *low* (an attack is unlikely), *moderate* (an attack is possible, but not likely), *substantial* (an attack is a strong possibility), *severe* (an attack is highly likely), and *critical* (an attack is expected imminently). Those terms may say enough for officials who have contingency plans for each alert level, but too little for parents

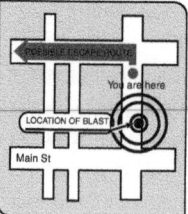

1. Take cover immediately, below ground if possible, though any shield or shelter will help protect you from the immediate effects of the blast and the pressure wave.

2. Consider if you can get out of the area;

3. Or if it would be better to go inside a building and follow your plan to 'shelter-in-place'.

http://www.ready.gov/america/_downloads/nuclear.pdf

Disclaimer

We are not responsible if information that we make available on this site is not accurate, complete or current. The materials on this site are provided for general information only, and any reliance upon the material found on this site will be at your own risk. We reserve the right to modify the contents of the site at any time, but we have no obligation to update any information on this site. You agree that it is your responsibility to monitor changes to the site.

http://www.ready.gov/america/other/notices.html

17. Two screen shots from www.ready.gov, maintained by the US Department of Homeland Security. The top figure has instructions for responding to a nuclear explosion. Panel 1 assumes the existence of fall-out shelters and signs, not used in the US since the Cold War. Panel 2 implies that people can outrun a blast. Panel 3 uses wording ('or would it be better') that shifts decision-making responsibility to lay people unlikely to know enough to choose well. The bottom panel throws the top one (and everything else at the site) into question

wondering whether to send their kids to school. In this case, ambiguity may surround both the likelihood and the event being predicted (what exactly does 'attack' mean?). The US National Weather Service once considered eliminating probability-of-precipitation forecasts, based on seeming public confusion about their meaning. However, the problem turned out to be with the event, not the number. That is, did a '60% chance of rain' mean 'rain 60% of the time', 'rain over 60% of the area', or '60% chance of measurable rain'? (It is the last.)

The top panel in Figure 17 shows how poor execution can undermine an attractively executed communication of intelligence information. The bottom panel, from the same site, shows how an institution can undermine its public's trust by not honouring its social contract and standing by its word.

Do risk communications leave recipients adequately informed?

From a decision-making perspective, people are adequately informed when knowing more would not affect their choices. That test allows assessing whether risk communications have served the practical purpose of letting people make effective risk decisions. The test is somewhat different when applied to the three elements of any decision: facts, values, and options.

People are adequately informed about the facts of a decision when there are no additional facts that would change their choices. Bioethicist Jon Merz applied this value-of-information test to characterize informed consent for medical procedures. As an example, he used carotid endarterechtomy, a surgery that scrapes plaque from the artery leading to the brain. If successful, it reduces the risk of stroke and death. However, many things can go wrong, ranging from broken teeth to death. Merz concluded, however, that only three of those many risks were probable and severe enough to matter much: death, stroke, and facial paralysis. He argued that, while doctors should hide nothing, communicating these three risks does most of their job.

People are adequately informed about the values raised by a decision when they have considered all perspectives that might change their choices. Thus, they should never feel the remorse of 'It never occurred to me to think about what it would mean to live with that choice' or 'Had I looked beyond the default value, I'm sure that I would invested differently (or become an organ donor)'. Seeing all relevant perspectives need not mean knowing which one to adopt. Risk decisions can pose cruel trade-offs, like those facing parents of extremely premature infants (Chapter 1) and children of very sick parents. Recognizing that one is of two minds can be an important insight, locating the difficulty in the decision, not the decision-maker. It suggests looking for moral guidance, not for facts that will somehow reveal what to do. It shows the need for procedures that help people with difficult value questions, such as living wills and medical guidelines.

People are adequately informed about a decision's options when they know which options are readily available, such as those on the drug fact box, and which could be created, such as healthier lifestyles. Knowing about possible options means having an accurate mental model of how risks are created and controlled. There are 'literacy' tests for many domains (biology, toxicology, health, finance), assessing whether people have the active mastery needed to shape their environment.

Determining whether people are adequately informed assumes that the goal of risk communication is enabling informed decision-making. Other goals are possible. Some communications are designed to fail. That can be obvious, as when risk information is buried in jargon, dense text, or unreadable capital letters. Or it can be hidden, as with ambiguous terms like 'natural', 'popular', and 'safe'. Other communications try to manipulate people 'for their own good'. They include social marketing of healthy behaviours radon testing, regular flossing, safe sex), defaults encouraging good choices (sometimes called 'libertarian paternalism'), and financial incentives (subsidies for healthy foods, lower insurance premiums for non-smokers).

Whatever their goal, risk communicators need evidence to know how well they are doing. Without it, they may just follow 'best practices' that are terrible, misled by the flawed intuitions that cause people to exaggerate how well they are communicating. For example, many programmes try to reduce sexually transmitted infections, and these programmes must seem effective to those implementing them. However, a 2010 US review found only 4 programmes in the preceding 20 years that had succeeded. Ineffective communications not only waste the resources invested in them, but undermine faith in those who are positioned to provide needed information.

Participatory risk communication and management

The first meeting of the international Society for Risk Analysis, in 1981, was dedicated to 'The Analysis of Risks: Real versus Perceived'. Although that theme recognized the importance of communication, its formulation treated experts' judgements as facts and lay beliefs as suspect. Since then, pressure for greater public engagement in risk decisions has forced the technical community to grapple with how to involve the public in its work. Figure 18 shows one approach to improving communication without sacrificing scientific accuracy. It seeks to honour the social contract of democratic societies, despite large disparities in technical knowledge, by making the public integral to risk management. Although written for governments and corporations, it could apply, in principle, to doctors, financial planners, or even parents.

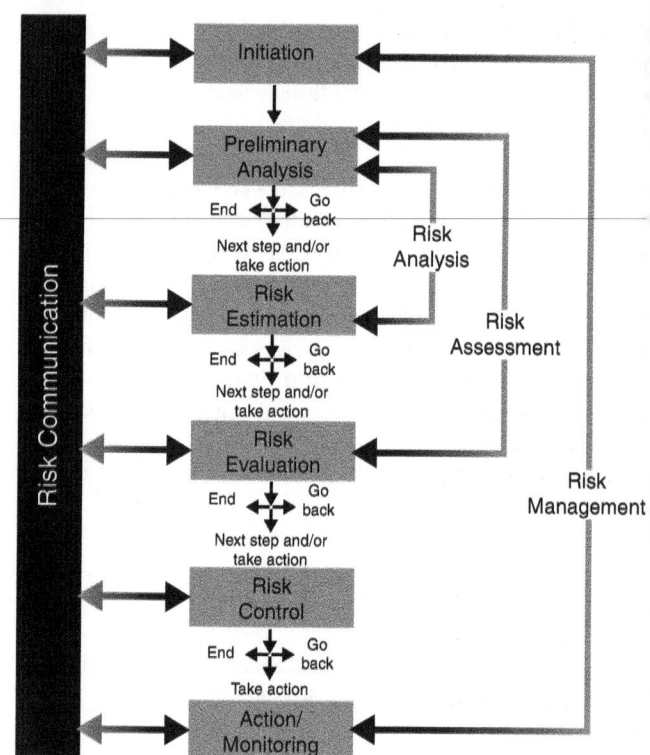

18. Recommended procedure for managing risks

Its centrepiece is a fairly conventional depiction of risk management, going from Initiation to Action/Monitoring. It is distinguished only by the four-way arrows between stages, requiring self-criticism that could lead to repeating a stage or even to abandoning the process (End). It offers, however, a distinctive view of public involvement, with double-headed arrows connecting the Risk Communication bar to each stage of risk management. Thus, rather than waiting for the experts to sort things out, then communicate their conclusions (sometimes called 'Decide-

Announce-Defend'), the public is involved throughout. From a project's very Initiation, the public is entitled to know what is happening and provide input to the process.

What this process means depends on the risks. With drug and nutrition labels, the process requires behavioural research, surveying the public to learn what information people need, then testing draft messages, to see how well they work. With vaccines, there may need to be special attention to the Monitoring stage, addressing public concerns about the quality of post-licensing surveillance. With sexual assault prevention, women should be involved throughout the process, creating a safer environment, informed by better evidence.

Although behavioural research can assess what the public wants and understands, it keeps the public at arm's length from risk management. Direct participation can take many forms. One extreme entails conflict, with perhaps more heat than light. The other extreme entails respectful consultations, with experts acting as the public's servants, producing facts and analyses that facilitate public engagement. The risk-ranking exercises of Chapter 2 follow this strategy. An early example of such an 'analytical-deliberative' approach was Sweden's national discussion on nuclear power, involving 80,000 people, in the late 1970s. Some observers faulted the process for leaving many participants more uncertain than when they started. Other observers, though, thought that increased uncertainty was a sign of increased understanding, realizing how complex the issues are. Supporting the latter position, the national referendum that followed these deliberations endorsed a compromise solution (keep the existing plants, build no new ones) lasting many years.

Today, many environmental impact studies include some kind of 'stakeholder involvement'. The goal of such consultations need not be consensus. A respectful airing of the issues can lead to fewer but better conflicts, by focusing the parties on legitimate disagreements.

Conclusion: from analysis to informed choice

Risk communications affect both individuals' ability to make sound choices and their place in society. Communications can be judged in terms of both the social contract that they express and their technical execution. Judgements of the social contract ask whether the communication process assumes that the public has a right to know and to be heard, involves it in all stages of risk management, and creates the evidence needed to inform choices. Judgements of technical execution ask whether the communication process clearly conveys risks and benefits, elucidates value issues, acknowledges the limits to expert knowledge, reaches the relevant publics, and subjects itself to empirical evaluation.

The costs of poor risk communication can be high. For the public, they include needlessly poor decisions and denial of the right to know and participate. For the authorities, the costs include wasted effort, lost reputations, and shame over failing to protect the public. For both, they erode the commons of goodwill and trust that any society needs. If the quality of their decision-making is underestimated, then lay people may be denied deserved freedom of choice. If it is overestimated, then they may be denied needed protections. Overall, experience suggests reason for guarded optimism regarding the value of well-designed communications. However it does not happen by accident. Risk communications are part of the broader fabric within which societies respond to risk and danger, the topic of the next and concluding chapter.

Chapter 7
Risk, culture, and society

In her classic book *Purity and Danger*, the anthropologist Mary Douglas argued that societies define themselves by how they define and manage dangers. Her account followed the lead of her mentor, Edward Evans-Pritchard. Living with the Azande of north-central Africa during the late 1920s, Evans-Pritchard observed that they invoked witchcraft as causing risks as diverse as building collapses, adultery, theft, sickness, and crop failure. They relied on fallible oracles to divine the workings of witchcraft, which was held to issue from a substance in the belly. The oracles intuited the effects of witchcraft through ritualized methods such as observing the fate of a chicken given small doses of poison when probing an accidental death.

As exotic as the Zande beliefs were, Evans-Pritchard refused to treat them as primitive. He argued instead that, although witchcraft could not predict future risks, it could still affect them. By interpreting misfortunes as sanctions for unsocial behaviours (marital infidelity, violence, theft), witchcraft enforced social norms. At the time, Evans-Pritchard's work was controversial because it did not privilege modern views of causation and the physical world. However, by showing witchcraft's role in society's practical reasoning and schemes for social accountability, he cast the Azande as a kind of 'risk society' (a term coined later by sociologist Ulrich Beck), organized around its management of dangers.

Extending this perspective to modern societies, Douglas depicted the applied sciences that deal with risks as assuming the role of witchcraft, when they interpret social rules for dealing with danger and pollution. According to Douglas, societies reveal their deepest values in the priorities they set among physical and symbolic risks. In her own society, she observed groups preoccupied with risks identified by their sources (chemicals, electromagnetic fields), pathways (water, air, soil, infected people), exposures (to people, animals, art works), and consequences (sickness, death, financial collapse). These concerns shape how members of these groups define, study, value, perceive, and communicate about risks. Douglas also observed, especially in her collaboration with political scientist Aaron Wildavsky, how societies fragment when their constituent groups (corporations, environmentalists, ethnic minorities, religious groups) see dangers too differently.

The psychologist and philosopher William James characterized pollution and danger as like dirt, 'matter out of place'. In that light, any definition of risk implies a sense of order, linking causes and effects, before something is deemed dangerous. Science challenges traditional notions of danger by revealing new kinds of order (climate, genetics) and disorder (trace contaminants, cosmic radiation). Each risk has its own cadre of experts, often coming from multiple disciplines, each with its 'fire hose' of potentially relevant uncertain facts. Risk analysis brings order to the flood of facts by characterizing diverse risks in common terms.

Although vastly more sophisticated than oracles, risk analysts face similar challenges of social legitimacy. Risk analysis alone does not provide the stable rules that a society needs for allotting blame and responsibility. That requires the kind of social accounting that Evans-Pritchard observed, whose modern equivalent works through regulations, politics, the courts, the media, and other institutions. Although those institutions may endorse analytical decision-making methods, they still need society's acceptance. That may come because people like the methods or like the results that the methods produce. Thus, some people support cost–benefit analysis because of the comfort that its orderly thinking brings; others because it favours the easily monetized outcomes that they value. Some people value analysts' independence; others value analysts' subservience to those who can pay for their services. Some people value analysts' access to the latest science; others resent having to take analysts' results on faith, not knowing what social controls keep them honest. Some people abide by analysts' results; some get their own analysts when they dislike the conclusions.

In these ways, analysts, like oracles, play roles that their society needs. How they play those roles further reflects their society's values, seen most clearly in battles over the terms of their work. For example, partisans in the tobacco wars have fought hard over whether analyses of its risks should include just inhaled tar and nicotine or also second-hand smoke, over whether its sources are just cigarettes or also the advertisements promoting them, over which options to analyse (heavy taxes? outright prohibition? stigmatization of users?), and over whether tobacco is a drug. Environmental justice advocates work to ensure that analyses capture the distribution of risks across race and class, so as to document when noxious facilities or transportation corridors are disproportionately sited near low-income neighbourhoods. The intensity of these definitional disputes reflects what Mary Douglas called battles of 'the system against itself'.

Such struggles over risk definitions reflect how slowly, and sometimes tragically, societies develop rules for newly recognized dangers. For example, when HIV/AIDS emerged as a danger, old rules impeded the creation of needed new ones. Most blood banks initially refused to require donor screening, fearing the loss of needed blood (and revenue). Bathhouses resisted risk communications promoting 'safe sex', fearing lost business. The Reagan administration delayed public discussion of HIV/AIDS, fearing the wrath of supporters opposed to homosexuality. Some African countries avoided the problem altogether, fearing impossible demands on their impoverished health systems. Even 30 years on, tangled HIV/AIDS decisions persist, such as whether pharmaceutical companies should assert patent rights for their products and whether abstinence programmes constitute neo-colonialism.

When new dangers emerge, society must learn their causes and controls, weigh their demands, and give meaning to the choices that follow. The study of risk offers systematic, imperfect approaches to these perennial questions, grounded in probability and decision theory. These methods have their own intertwined intellectual and social histories.

From probability to statistics to uncertainty

Although probability theory was originally devised in the 17th century to analyse games of chance, observers soon realized that it could be extended to other chance-like events, such as predicting jury verdicts. The growth of bureaucratic European states in the 19th century spurred extensions to analysing systematically collected statistical data. These early applications often focused on people seen as social risks (orphans, criminals, the sick, the poor), defining them in the process – 'making up people', in historian Ian Hacking's phrase. The invention of mortality tables led to calculating annuity rates for making payments over individuals' expected remaining lifetime, providing a first economic expression of the value of human life.

By the early 20th century, statistical methods allowed not just describing patterns, but also assessing their stability, answering questions such as whether increased disease or unemployment rates were random fluctuations or worrisome changes – and, if so, what might be their causes. Statistical methods for studying actual events evolved into probabilistic risk analyses of potential events, such as how major environmental stressors (drought, invasive species) might affect a country's financial stability, public health, or foreign policy. Some analyses combine theory and evidence to predict hypothetical risks, such as the reliability of novel technologies or the impacts of geoengineering.

Each component of these complex models can raise value-laden questions and controversies. For example, even seemingly simple national censuses have been attacked as tools of social control or invasions of privacy, while provoking disputes over how to define terms such as 'race' and 'employed'. The normal probability distribution, captured in the familiar bell-shaped curve, has been attacked for characterizing people by their deviance from a norm. Risk research has shown that value judgements are inevitable, when deciding which outcomes to measure and how to measure them (Chapter 2). If analyses of mortality risks consider age at time of death, then they favour policies focused on deaths among the young; if they treat all deaths as equal, then they do not. If water quality analyses use smaller observation periods and ecological scales, then they increase the chances of observing troubling anomalies and triggering protective policies. If the official residences of American inmates are defined as their prisons, then those locales, typically in conservative rural areas, receive more resources, such as federal grants and legislative seats; the opposite happens if their official residences are the liberal urban areas where most live when not incarcerated. In these ways, seemingly mundane procedures can embody potent value judgements.

Extending risk analysis from repeated events, like hands of cards, to hypothetical events, like geoengineering, increases the need for scientific judgement. For example, ecologists often have large data sets and sophisticated theories for understanding current conditions. However, when looking into uncertain futures, as when predicting the rate of species extinction (decades? centuries?), they must make judgements about questions such as: How should we treat 'Methuselah species', still living, but no longer viable? How will historically stable patterns change in a warmer, dryer world, with expanded global trade (transporting invasive species and diseases)? If coral reefs disappear from acidic oceans, what new ecological regimes will replace them?

Analogous judgements are needed when analysing purely human risks, like terror. Do 'terrorists' include passive supporters of the cause? What distinguishes terrorists from freedom fighters? How far can historical records be trusted? How will terrorists' identities, targets, and capabilities change over time? Some terror risks can be modeled quantitatively, as with the dispersion models that predict the spread of radioactive material from a 'dirty bomb', using estimates of wind patterns, bomb size, explosive strength, and dose-response models of health effects. Yet even these models depend on judgements, such as which targets terrorists prefer and how they recruit agents.

Thus, the modern study of risk began with the countable (gambles, insurance, social problems) and progressed to the novel (species extinction, terror). When science extends itself to new dangers, society depends on it to share that knowledge, including a candid assessment of its limits. For example, industrial risk analyses (nuclear power plants, cement kilns, liquid natural gas terminals) often focus on site-specific problems (maintenance, earthquake vulnerability), while neglecting recurrent ones (design flaws, lax inspection). Unless analysts reflect on such limits, others cannot know how far to trust their work.

Analysts often express their knowledge as subjective probabilities, statements of belief that aspire to logical consistency. However imperfect, such judgements can provide useful summaries of complex, uncertain, heterogeneous knowledge, if they are expressed in clear and consistent numeric terms. Probability has therefore become essential to the *lingua franca* of technical communities and part of their communications with the lay public, increasingly accustomed to hearing and using probabilities in contexts as diverse as weather forecasts, sports bets, and economic predictions.

Causes

Formal risk models naturally emphasize readily quantified factors, such as physical processes (throw-weights of ballistic missiles, dispersion plumes of groundwater contaminants) and computable biological ones (dose-response relationships, disease transmission rates). Conversely, they largely neglect human determinants of risk levels, such as worker training and compliance with medical regimens.

As a result, the study of the social factors affecting risks has typically taken a piecemeal view, rather than an integrative analytical one. For example, social scientists have dissected how advertising promotes smoking, through images like the Marlboro man and the Virginia Slims woman. They have linked these observations with general processes, like the tendency to forget where we hear things, so that mere repetition makes advertising claims seem credible. As with natural science phenomena, some social processes have been modelled quantitatively, such as the diffusion of innovations, which can include both new technologies and deviant behaviours. These models, too, require a heavy dose of expert judgement.

Some risk factors are mostly social. Biology produces about 105 male births for every 100 females. In many Western countries, that ratio shrinks, then flips as people age. However, in parts of northern Africa, adverse living conditions reverse that pattern. Seeing such disparities in Asia, economist Amartya Sen estimated that discrimination had caused the premature deaths of 100 million 'missing' women in the 1980s. In China, women's life expectancy increased with economic improvements in the late 1970s. However, female infant mortality increased from 38 to 67 per thousand between 1978 and 1984, with the one-child-per-family policy begun in 1979 – which the Chinese government has since relaxed for families with first-born daughters. On the other hand, the poor Indian state of Kerala and many countries in sub-Saharan Africa have biologically expected gender ratios.

Social and biological factors are also intertwined in the tuberculosis endemic to dense shantytowns. Although the immediate risk factor is cramped quarters, its effects are amplified by predisposing risk factors that suppress disease resistance. Those risk factors include malnutrition, chronic diseases, and poor sanitation. Their impacts are amplified, in turn, by the political inequality that diverts resources from the poor. According to physician and humanitarian Paul Farmer, 'inequality itself constitutes our modern plague'.

Including social factors in risk analyses increases the chances of addressing them. It also reduces the temptation to blame victims for their fate – by showing the forces working against them, such as the economic and social pressures that lead some women to become sex workers, exposing themselves to HIV-infected clients. However they are formulated, risk analyses should treat all deaths, illnesses, and reduced wellbeing respectfully and without moralization, open to evaluating any possible cause.

Symbolic dangers

Among the most powerful social risk factors are the images that assign blame for fearsome dangers. We now know that bacteria carried by fleas and rats most likely caused the 14th-century Black Death. But at the time, desperate people readily blamed marginal groups, such as Jews, beggars, and lepers. Those stigmatizing beliefs not only protected their own sense of worth, but also legitimated expelling the indigent from crowded towns and confiscating property belonging to the wealthy. For centuries, individuals were identified as witches when their beliefs contradicted those of church authorities.

Once the shadow of stigma falls, it can be hard to erase. Early in the AIDS epidemic, people who disliked or feared homosexuals, drug addicts, or haemophiliacs blamed them for taking risks that they could not have recognized and isolated them beyond any conceivable effect on disease transmission. In South Asia, despite anti-discrimination laws, many people still consider Dalits (untouchables) impure by birth, censuring them if their polluting shadows fall on Brahmins. Restricting Dalits' employment to tasks like excrement collection reinforces that stigma, as did historic limits on permissible Jewish professions (money lending, peddling). In many Western countries, until recently, people avoided discussing cancer, even when they did not shun its victims.

Such stigma can be immune to evidence. Before penicillin became widely available after World War II, medical treatments for venereal diseases were very limited. Although behavioural methods of disease prevention (condom use, education) were available, a powerful 'social hygiene' movement opposed them on moral grounds. Members of this movement especially objected to programmes that served prostitutes or allegedly 'promiscuous' African-Americans. Their opposition was eventually broken, not by evidence of condoms' efficacy, but by a countervailing moral concern: protecting American GIs from being infected by women, mostly European prostitutes from less stigmatized groups. The stigma of AIDS also diminished as awareness increased of 'innocent victims' who had contracted HIV through blood transfusions, like tennis star Arthur Ashe. Stigma still underlies opposition to needle-exchange programmes for injection drug users, despite the evidence that they reduce HIV transmission.

Symbolic imagery can also do good. Public health campaigns that stigmatize smoking compete with advertising campaigns that glamorize it. In the US, a canonical symbol of danger was the 'poster child' polio victim, in braces or a wheelchair. Children in the national vaccine trial were honoured as 'polio pioneers', heroes in conquering the epidemic. On the other hand, Franklin Delano

19. Works Progress Administration poster from the 1930s, deliberately attacking the syphilis 'shame' encouraged by 'hygiene' groups

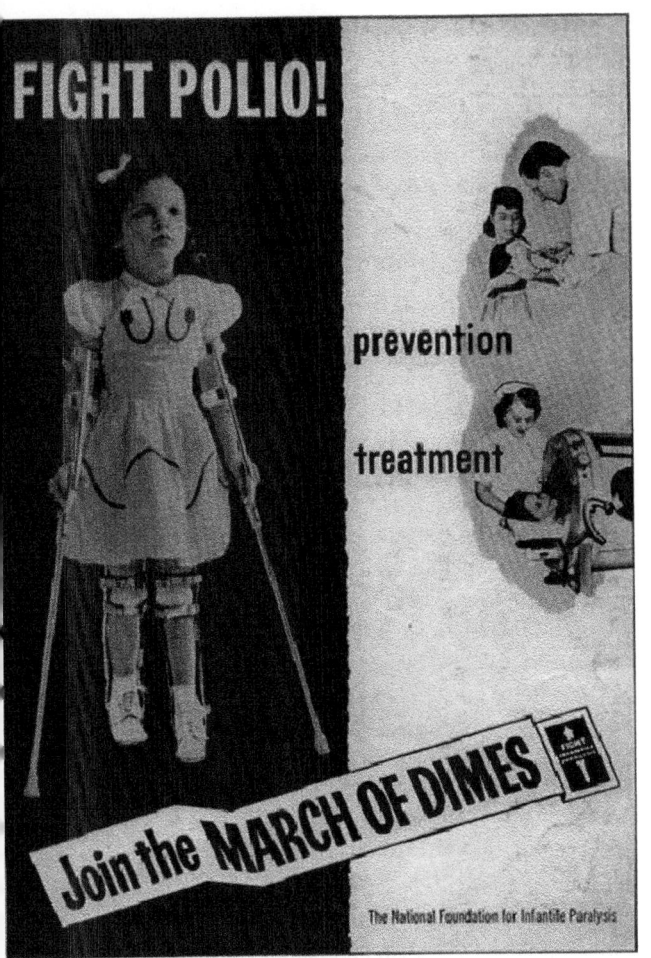

FIGHT POLIO!

prevention

treatment

Join the **MARCH OF DIMES**

The National Foundation for Infantile Paralysis

20. Many polio images from the 1950s featured crippled children and the expensive iron lung machines needed for victims

Roosevelt avoided being seen in a wheelchair, despite strongly supporting polio research, in order to protect his image as a strong leader. Stigmatizing smoking has inadvertently reduced support for lung cancer research, by holding victims responsible for their fate, even though many have never smoked. Some people dread vaccines that protect against diseases that were once dreaded.

Values and the framing of choice

If individuals want to think, rather than emote, their way through risk decisions, they often have their work cut out for them. The science and society that make risk analysis possible can also frustrate that process. Many risks involve such complex technological and social processes that no one understands them fully. Individuals enmeshed in risk decisions may feel as bewildered as their ancestors, trying to sort out the claims of competing oracles. When the stakes are high, powerful forces may manufacture uncertainty, hoping to confuse lay decision-makers and forestall actions that reduce risks. In order to understand risks, people need mental models of the factors affecting each valued outcome.

People who know the facts still may not fully understand what they mean, as they struggle to imagine possible futures. The feeling that one should be able to make a risk decision can add insult to injury, when it creates difficult value trade-offs. For example, if people are passionate about teen abstinence, should they oppose programmes that reduce unplanned teen pregnancy by teaching safe sex? If they are passionate about relieving end-of-life suffering, should they fight programmes that include assisted suicide? If they value military readiness, should they suppress their opposition to homosexual soldiers? If they hate taxes, should they accept a carbon tax to reduce dreaded effects of climate change? If they really want something now, how should they weigh the interests of their future selves? Traditional societies resolve such issues for their members; modern ones force each person to be a moral arbiter.

Applied to the fact side of risk decisions, analysis can make life easier, by summarizing the facts most worth knowing. Applied to the value side of risk decisions, analysis can make life harder, by bringing difficult trade-offs into sharp relief, showing just how hard many risk decisions really are. Because it is neutral about which outcomes matter and how to weigh them, decision analysis forces people to identify and reconcile their own sometimes conflicting values.

Economics provides one way to escape such freedom, by translating all outcomes into their monetary equivalent. But, that succour comes at a price: implicitly favouring outcomes with ready price tags. So, although there are methods for monetizing outcomes without markets (honour, endangered species), these estimates are inherently weaker than direct measures, such as jobs and revenues. Moreover, monetization implicitly endorses the principle that 'money matters – more than anything else'. It often means accepting the analytical convention of comparing total risks and benefits, ignoring who gets them. Thus, analysts, like oracles, provide an incomplete picture of danger.

Not knowing how to judge the quality of analyses or their implicit social values leads some people to abandon analytical decision rules in favour of precautionary principles, which require avoiding actions that might pose catastrophic risks – even if little is known about such worst-case scenarios or actions intended to avoid them. Originally advanced in Sweden and Germany, precautionary principles have been advocated for risks as adverse as acid rain, nuclear power, genetically modified crops, climate change, and marine pollution. One variant is former Vice-President Cheney's 'one-percent principle', which treats any catastrophic terror threat as unacceptable. Applied to possible weapons of mass destruction, this precautionary rationale was used to justify the US invasion of Iraq.

Like sacred values that preclude some trade-offs, precautionary principles provide a way to interpret complex issues, one that expresses deep aversion to poorly understood risks. Risk analysis provides such a perspective for people comfortable with an instrumental approach that breaks decisions into manageable parts. Each framework suits those comfortable with its strengths and weaknesses.

Risk and the good life

Risk decisions do not occur in isolation, but in the context of a society's shared and conflicting norms and practices. Individuals' risk decisions serve to define them in relation to their society. They may express solidarity with the socially shared values at stake, which might include the sanctity of life, nature, equality, progress, or freedom. Getting these values right is essential to living with oneself and with others.

A society's essential values include not only risks to avoid, but also positive goals to achieve, such as nurturing the young, continuing cultural traditions, sharing freedoms, and finding meaningful labour and personal expression. Taking the best gambles for achieving 'the good life', to use Aristotle's term, requires seeing risk decisions in the context of personal, community, and societal values. The word 'risk' derives from the early Italian *risicare*, meaning 'to dare' or act in the face of uncertainty. Risk analysis is an intellectual tool for achieving wellbeing by reducing dangers and limiting the role of chance.

If 'dirt is matter out of place', then risks can be so deeply embedded in our perceptions and lives that we are barely aware of them. The study of risk increases that awareness, by helping us to reflect on how risk decisions are framed, how risks are defined, how our beliefs reveal the world, and how to discover our priorities. As characterized by scholars like Ulrich Beck and Anthony Giddens, such reflection is a distinctive property of modern societies' approach to risk – unlike the Azande, dry farmers in ancient Mesopotamia, or any other society limited to its oracles' divinations, without critical examination of the forces shaping them and their members' responses.

In order to serve their society, analysts must reflect on the limits to their practice. One such limit is the reductionist spirit of many risk analyses, treating pieces of problems in isolation, while neglecting their broader context. For example, the study of ecosystems is incomplete if it overlooks their role in human health, culture, and wellbeing – as seen in what children lose when isolated from nature (by crime, traffic, or computer games). The study of education is incomplete if it considers only its contributions to earning power, while overlooking its role in developing character, intellect, and social cohesion. Successful risk analysis provides a meeting ground for scientists from the diverse disciplines needed to provide a full picture. Those meetings advance the disciplines as well, by helping them to reflect on their natural blinders.

Risk analysis provides a disciplined form of practical reasoning, using scientific tools to understand dangers and to inform decisions about them. Its tools are now an intrinsic part of lives that rely on modern technologies and a global commons. It provides a perspective for assessing how well individuals and societies deal with risks. Can they understand the risks? Can they reconcile the conflicting values at stake? Can they get the information that they need? Can they communicate their views and desires? Can they engage their emotions properly? Do they realize their dependence on one another and the commons?

Answering those questions can reveal poor decision-making or poor analysis. Sometimes, analysts, like oracles, exaggerate how much they know, ignore valued outcomes, or fail to reveal (or realize) the values embedded in their definitions of risk and benefit. Thus, the value of analysis depends on how well its limits are understood. This book has taken a quick tour of the ideas essential to having a critical perspective on this uniquely modern enterprise. Risk definitions reflect norms about how the world is and should be. Knowing that, risk analyses help people to handle dangers and live the good life as they see it.

Further reading

Chapter 1: Risk decisions

Books describing diverse risk decisions, drawing on core concepts from decision analysis, probability, and statistics to summarize knowledge drawn from many sciences.

P. Bernstein, *Against the Gods: The Remarkable Story of Risk* (New York: John Wiley, 1998). A readable, candid history of risk in insurance, finance, and investment, starting with the invention of mathematical probability in the 17th century.

R. T. Clemen and T. Reilly, *Making Hard Decisions with Decision Suite Tools* (Belmont, CA: Wadsworth, 2010). A comprehensive practical introduction emphasising decision trees, influence diagrams, and computer implementations.

T. Glickman and M. Gough (eds.), *Readings in Risk* (Washington, DC: Resources for the Future, 1990). A useful collection of scientific articles, focusing on health risks.

J. Hacker, *The Great Risk Shift* (New York: Oxford University Press, 2006). An examination of changes in risks to households' finances and wellbeing as a result of policy and political choices.

J. S. Hammond, R. L. Keeney, and H. Raiffa, *Smart Choices: A Practical Guide to Making Better Decisions* (Boston, MA: Harvard Business School, 1999). A how-to guide written by noted scholars.

R. Keeney, *Value-Focused Thinking* (Cambridge, MA: Harvard University Press, 1992). A guide to the challenges raised by multiple and competing values, ranging beyond traditional economic conceptions of value.

R. Posner, *Catastrophe: Risk and Response* (New York: Oxford University Press, 2005). A noted jurist's interpretation of the risk decisions facing individuals and society.

V. Smil, *Global Catastrophes and Trends: The Next Fifty Years* (Cambridge, MA: MIT Press, 2008). A vigorous examination of global risks, including climate change, pandemics, and terrorism, emphasizing long-term perspectives and deep uncertainties.

D. von Winterfeldt and W. Edwards, *Decision Analysis and Behavioral Research* (New York: Cambridge University Press, 1986). An excellent introduction to decision science, integrating analytical and behavioural research.

S. Watson and D. Buede, *Decision Synthesis: The Principles and Practice of Decision Analysis* (Cambridge: Cambridge University Press, 1987). A guide to decision and risk analysis as intellectual technology and an applied 'craft'.

Chapter 2: Defining risk

How risk is defined from multiple perspectives and how those definitions are incorporated in public policies.

R. Bullard, *Dumping in Dixie: Race, Class, and Environmental Quality*, 3rd edn. (Boulder, CO: Westview Press, 2000). A seminal treatment of how definitions of risk and benefit can accommodate (or ignore) relative effects on the poor and disenfranchised.

G. Daly (ed.), *Nature's Services: Societal Dependence on Natural Ecosystems* (Washington, DC: Island Press, 2007). Assessing the economic value and replacement costs of ecological processes.

B. Fischhoff et al., *Acceptable Risk* (New York: Cambridge University Press, 1981; Peking University Press, 2009 [in Chinese]). Analytical and behavioural methods for addressing health, safety and environmental risks.

S. Funtowicz and J. Ravetz, *Uncertainty and Quality in Science for Policy* (Dordrecht: Kluwer, 1990). An introduction to 'post-normal' science for risks of great scientific uncertainty and high social stakes.

S. Jasanoff, *The Fifth Branch: Science Advisers as Policymakers* (Cambridge, MA: Harvard University Press, 1990). Examines the role of applied science in risk debates and regulation, including how scientific practices can impose value-laden definitions.

S. Krimsky and D. Golding (eds.), *Social Theories of Risk* (Westport, CT: Praeger, 1992). Essays on roles for political and social analysis of risk debates and decisions.

National Research Council, *Understanding Risk: Informing Decisions in a Democratic Society* (Washington, DC: National Academy Press, 1996). Integrates risk analysis with institutional and political requirements of public policy, debate, and choice.

J. Sachs, *Common Wealth: Economics for a Crowded Planet* (New York: The Penguin Press, 2008). Global economics of population, resource depletion, development and climate change.

A. Sen, *Ethics and Economics* (Oxford: Blackwell, 1987). Essays on the assumptions embedded in economic analyses.

R. Wilson and E. A. C. Crouch, *Benefit-Cost Analysis*, 2nd edn. (Cambridge, MA: Harvard Center for Risk Analysis, 2004). Introduction to risk concepts, emphasising the importance of definitions in establishing the terms of analyses.

Chapter 3: Analysing risk

A sample of risk analysis methods and applications.

K. Foster and P. Huber, *Judging Science: Scientific Knowledge and the Federal Courts* (Cambridge, MA: MIT Press, 1997). An analysis of scientific evidence in risk controversies as they have evolved through the law, regulation, and court cases.

D. M. Kammen and D. M. Hassenzahl, *Should We Risk It? Exploring Environmental, Health, and Technological Problem Solving* (Princeton, NJ: Princeton University Press, 2001). A comprehensive text assuming some background in natural science, engineering, or statistics.

M. Monmonier, *Cartographies of Danger: Mapping Hazards in America* (Chicago, IL: University of Chicago Press, 1997). A geographical perspective on technologies, natural hazards, populations, and human health risks.

M. G. Morgan and M. Henrion, *Uncertainty: A Guide to Dealing with Uncertainty in Quantitative Risk and Policy Analysis* (New York: Cambridge University Press, 1990). An introduction to risk and uncertainty, emphasizing the role of expert judgement, focused on engineering examples.

A. O'Hagan, C. E. Buck, A. Daneshkhah, J. E. Eiser et al., *Uncertain Judgements: Eliciting Expert Probabilities* (Chichester: Wiley, 2006). A summary of theory and practice on eliciting experts' judgements.

C. Perrow, *Normal Accidents: Living with High-Risk Technologies*, revised edn. (Princeton: Princeton University Press, 1999). An introduction to the author's concept of 'normal accidents', arising from the very complexity of technologies and their management, with many examples.

J. Reason, *Human Error* (New York: Cambridge University Press, 1990). A summary of the sources of human error in behaviour, including organizational forces beyond individuals' control.

N. Roubini and S. Mihm, *Crisis Economics: A Crash Course in the Future of Finance* (New York: The Penguin Press, 2010). One of many excellent accounts of the financial crisis of 2008.

G. Suter (ed.), *Ecological Risk Assessment*, 2nd edn. (Boca Raton, FL: CRC Press, 2006). A comprehensive text emphasizing methods used for human health while accommodating ecological complexity.

A. Wildavsky, *But is it True? A Citizen's Guide to Environmental Health and Safety Issues* (Cambridge, MA: Harvard University Press, 1995). A critical approach to public policies and views for many technology and health risks.

Chapter 4: Making risk decisions

A sample of popular and scientific accounts of how risk decisions should be and are made.

J. Baron, *Thinking and Deciding*, 4th edn. (New York: Cambridge University Press, 2007). A comprehensive survey of decision-making research.

R. Frank, *Passions within Reason* (New York: W. W. Norton, 1988). A challenging examination of how emotions can support or undermine decision-making.

G. Gigerenzer, P. Todd, and the ABC Group, *Simple Heuristics That Make Us Smart* (New York: Oxford University Press, 1999). A summary of studies into the practical value of heuristics.

D. T. Gilbert, *Stumbling on Happiness* (New York: Knopf, 2006). An engaging summary of research into how well people know what makes them happy.

R. Hastie and R. M. Dawes, *Rational Choice in an Uncertain World: The Psychology of Judgment and Decision Making* (Thousand Oaks, CA: Sage, 2010). An authoritative, accessible text integrating analytical and behavioural research, with many applications.

S. Iyengar, *The Art of Choosing* (New York: Twelve, 2010). A personal essay integrating many research results, focused on unrecognized influences on choice.

D. Kahneman and A. Tversky (eds.), *Choices, Values, and Frames* (New York: Cambridge University Press, 2000). A collection of foundational papers at the interface of psychology and economics.

S. Plous, *The Psychology of Judgment and Decision Making* (New York: McGraw-Hill, 1993). An introductory text, including cognitive and social psychology.

B. Schwartz, *The Paradox of Choice: Why More is Less* (New York: HarperCollins, 2004). Research on the difficulties posed by having too many choices.

R. Thaler, *The Winner's Curse: Paradoxes and Anomalies of Economic Life* (Princeton, NJ: Princeton University Press, 1992). An accessible introduction to behavioural finance and the psychology of choice.

Chapter 5: Risk perception

Popular and scientific accounts of how people deal with risks.

D. Ariely, *Predictably Irrational* (New York: HarperCollins, 2009). A lively account of the limits to human judgement which compassionately accentuates the negative.

K. Foster, D. Bernstein, and P. Huber (eds.), *Phantom Risk: Scientific Inference and the Law* (Cambridge, MA: MIT Press, 1993). A pointed analysis of prominent risks that once raised great concern but were later judged to be much less significant than first thought.

G. Gigerenzer, *Calculated Risks: How to Know When Numbers Deceive You* (New York: Simon and Schuster, 2002). An account of the barriers to calculating and communicating risk estimates.

T. Gilovich, D. Griffin, and D. Kahneman (eds.), *Heuristics and Biases: The Psychology of Intuitive Judgment* (New York: Cambridge University Press, 2002). A collection of important essays about thinking under conditions of uncertainty.

D. Kahneman, P. Slovic, and A. Tversky (eds.), *Judgment Under Uncertainty: Heuristics and Biases* (New York: Cambridge University Press, 1982). A classic collection of research into choice, uncertainty, and human psychology.

N. F. Pidgeon, R. Kasperson, and P. Slovic (eds.), *The Social Amplification of Risk* (New York: Cambridge University Press, 2004). A collection of case studies of how risk messages and perceptions can ripple through societies.

P. Slovic (ed.), *The Perception of Risk* (Sterling, VA: Earthscan, 2000). A collection of prominent studies of risk perception.

K. Stanovich, *Rationality and the Reflective Mind* (New York: Oxford University Press, 2011). An essay considering decision-making as an aspect of intelligence, including controversies over how rational people are.

N. Maclean, *Young Men and Fire* (Chicago, IL: University of Chicago Press, 1992). Penetrating study of life-and-death decisions by 'smokejumpers' caught in a remote forest fire in 1949 Montana.

Chapter 6: Risk communication

Historical and experimental studies of how risk information is shared with the public.

J. S. Armstrong, *Persuasive Advertising: Evidence-Based Principles* (New York: Macmillan Palgrave, 2010). A comprehensive review of what does and does not work.

R. M. Faden and T. L. Beauchamp, *A History and Theory of Informed Consent* (New York: Oxford University Press, 1976). A seminal analysis of how the right to informed consent arose and was defined.

H. Kunreuther et al., *Disaster Insurance Protection: Public Policy Lessons* (New York: Wiley Interscience, 1978). Landmark study of risk decisions confounded by poor risk communication.

J. Kinsella, *Covering the Plague: AIDS and the American Media* (New Brunswick, NJ: Rutgers University Press 1989). A detailed history of AIDS coverage during the epidemic's emergence.

S. Krimsky and A. Plough, *Environmental Hazards: Communicating Risks as a Social Process* (Dover, MA: Auburn, 1988). Detailed analyses of risk controversies as they evolved in the public arena.

W. Leiss and W. Powell, *Mad Cows and Mother's Milk*, 2nd edn. (Montreal: McGill University Press, 2004). Case studies of the confusion that can fill the void created when officials fail to communicate clearly.

M. G. Morgan et al., *Risk Communication: A Mental Models Approach* (New York: Cambridge University Press, 2002). A systematic approach to identifying and organizing risk science and converting it into useful risk communications.

National Research Council, *Improving Risk Communication* (Washington, DC: National Academy Press, 1989). A wide-ranging report on research, policy, and practice.

R. Thaler and C. Sunstein, *Nudge: Improving Decisions about Health, Wealth and Happiness* (New Haven, CT: Yale University Press, 2009). An engaging essay on factors shaping risk choices and how they could be channelled to improve social welfare.

S. Woloshin, L. M. Schwartz, and H. G. Welch, *Know Your Chances: Understanding Health Statistics* (Berkeley, CA: University of California Press, 2008). A lay guide to interpreting health information.

Chapter 7: Risk, culture, and society

A few of the many broad-ranging social and historical approaches to danger and uncertainty as major dimensions of contemporary risk decisions.

U. Beck, *Risk Society: Toward a New Modernity* (New York: Sage, 1992). An influential analysis of the modern 'risk society', with its preoccupation with the uncertainty and dangers that technologies create.

L. Daston, *Classical Probability in the Enlightenment* (Princeton, NJ: Princeton University Press, 1988). The remarkable historical origins of converting uncertain reason into a mathematical calculus of probabilities and 'expectation'.

D. DeLillo, *White Noise* (New York: Viking, 1985). A biting satirical novel on contemporary attitudes towards uncertainty and danger in consumer society.

M. Douglas, *Edward Evans-Pritchard* (New York: Viking, 1980). A short introduction to the social anthropologist and his ideas about danger and knowledge.

M. Douglas, *Purity and Danger: An Analysis of the Concepts of Pollution and Taboo* (New York: Penguin, 1966). A classic analysis of danger and pollution written before the advent of 'risk', building on Evans-Pritchard's insights on social accountability and cultural knowledge.

P. Farmer, *Infections and Inequalities: The Modern Plagues* (Berkeley, CA: University of California Press, 1999). An analysis of disease and poverty as combined problems of biology, public health, and political oppression.

A. Giddens, *The Consequences of Modernity* (Stanford: Stanford University Press, 1990). An important statement of how risk transforms society.

I. Hacking, *The Emergence of Probability* (New York: Cambridge University Press, 1975) and *The Taming of Chance* (New York: Cambridge University Press, 1990). Histories of how probability and statistics became central to modern conceptions of uncertainty.

M. Nussbaum, *The Fragility of Goodness: Luck and Ethics in Greek Tragedy and Philosophy* (New York: Cambridge University Press, 1986). An essay on conceptions of practical reason, uncertainty, and value in the ancient world.

C. Ó Gráda, *Famine: A Short History* (Princeton, NJ: Princeton University Press, 2009). A comparative study of the causes and consequences of famines, in history to the present day.

Index

Risk

Expand your collection of
VERY SHORT INTRODUCTIONS

ADVERTISING
A Very Short Introduction
Winston Fletcher

The book contains a short history of advertising and an explanation of how the industry works, and how each of the parties (the advertisers, the media, and the agencies) are involved. It considers the extensive spectrum of advertisers and their individual needs. It also looks at the financial side of advertising and asks how advertisers know if they have been successful, or whether the money they have spent has in fact been wasted. Fletcher concludes with a discussion about the controversial and unacceptable areas of advertising such as advertising products to children and advertising products such as cigarettes and alcohol. He also discusses the benefits of advertising and what the future may hold for the industry.

www.oup.com/vsi

LEADERSHIP
A Very Short Introduction
Keith Grint

In this *Very Short Introduction* Keith Grint prompts the reader to rethink their understanding of what leadership is. He examines the way leadership has evolved from its earliest manifestations in ancient societies, highlighting the beginnings of leadership writings through Plato, Sun Tzu, Machiavelli and others, to consider the role of the social, economic, and political context undermining particular modes of leadership. Exploring the idea that leaders cannot exist without followers, and recognising that we all have diverse experiences and assumptions of leadership, Grint looks at the practice of management, its history, future, and influence on all aspects of society.

www.oup.com/vsi

ONLINE CATALOGUE
A Very Short Introduction

Our online catalogue is designed to make it easy to find your ideal Very Short Introduction. View the entire collection by subject area, watch author videos, read sample chapters, and download reading guides.

http://fds.oup.com/www.oup.co.uk/general/vsi/index.html

SOCIAL MEDIA
Very Short Introduction

Join our community

www.oup.com/vsi

- Join us online at the official Very Short Introductions **Facebook** page.
- Access the thoughts and musings of our authors with our online **blog**.
- Sign up for our monthly **e-newsletter** to receive information on all new titles publishing that month.
- Browse the full range of Very Short Introductions online.
- Read **extracts** from the Introductions for free.
- Visit our library of **Reading Guides**. These guides, written by our expert authors will help you to question again, why you think what you think.
- If you are a teacher or lecturer you can order inspection copies quickly and simply via our website.